Flying Carpet

The SOUL of an Airplane

Praise for Flying Carpet: The SOUL of an Airplane

"Buckle in with Greg Brown and head off to chase a solar eclipse or wrestle with ice on your wings or try to outwit troublesome mountain waves. Each chapter of *Flying Carpet* is a new ticket to extraordinary adventures that transform a pilot from novice to journeyman and, eventually, skilled aviator.

"More than just flying stories, this is the tale of a person who evolves to think with the mind of a pilot, question with the curiosity of a philosopher, and see with the eyes of a poet. Pilots will be entertained and wiser for having read it. Non-pilots will thrill to sharing the wings of a skilled aviator. I'm hooked!"

— Rod Machado, aviation author, flight instructor, speaker and official flight instructor for Microsoft's Flight Simulator

"A well-written, entertaining and humorous look into our own human nature—and cool flying stories too!"

— Joe Geare, longtime pilot

"Thankfully, we have great storytellers like Greg Brown who conveys his love of flying while sharing valuable insights that come only with experience. Great books about flying are timeless. Talented writers, like Greg Brown, are priceless."

— Laurel Lippert, Editor-at-Large,
Pilot Getaways magazine

Flying Carpet
The SOUL of an Airplane

Greg Brown

Foreword by Stephen Coonts

Aviation Supplies & Academics, Inc.
Newcastle, Washington

Greg Brown's love of flying is apparent to anyone who reads his "Flying Carpet" column in *AOPA Flight Training*, or his stories in *AOPA Pilot* and other magazines. A pilot since 1972, Greg was 2000 National Flight Instructor of the Year, winner of the 1999 NATA Excellence in Pilot Training award, and the first NAFI Master Flight Instructor. He holds an airline transport pilot certificate with Boeing 737 type rating, and flight instructor certificate with all fixed-wing aircraft ratings. Other books by Greg include *The Turbine Pilot's Flight Manual*, *The Savvy Flight Instructor*, *You Can Fly!*, and *Job Hunting for Pilots*.

Cover Photo by David Zickl.

© 2003–2007 Gregory N. Brown
Foreword © 2003–2007 Stephen Coonts
Copyrights to all photographs in this book are held by the respective photographers.

Published 2007 by
Aviation Supplies & Academics, Inc.
7005 132nd Place SE
Newcastle, WA 98059
email: asa@asa2fly.com
website: www.asa2fly.com

First edition, 2003. Third printing in softcover 2007.

Printed in the United States of America

2010 2009 2008 2007   10 9 8 7 6 5 4 3

ASA-FLY-CARPET
ISBN 1-56027-622-3
     978-1-56027-622-7

Library of Congress Cataloging-in-Publication Data:
Brown, Gregory N. (Gregory Neal), 1953-
  Flying carpet: the soul of an airplane / Gregory N. Brown.—1st ed.
  p. cm.
  1. Private flying—Anecdotes. 2. Private planes—Anecdotes. 3. Air pilots—United States—Anecdotes. 4. Brown, Gregory N. (Gregory Neal), 1953—Anecdotes. I. Title.
  TL721.4.B76 2003
  629.13'092—dc21

"The engine is the heart of an aeroplane, but the pilot is its soul"

—Sir Walter Raleigh,
The War in the Air, 1922

Dedication

This book is dedicated to Penny Porter, who taught me that the biggest part of personal adventure is facing what comes from within, and to my family, Jean, Hannis, and Austin, who have not only joined me on my flying adventures, but inspired so many of them.

Table of Contents

Acknowledgments

I owe deep appreciation to the many colorful characters who have enriched my skies, including those who make appearances in this book and the many others who do not. The stories told here are based primarily on personal memory and accounts related to me by others; my apologies for any inaccuracies that might have introduced themselves as a result. Names have been changed where appropriate.

Many stories in this book originally appeared in whole or in part in other publications, including *AOPA Flight Training* and *Pilot* magazines (published by Aircraft Owners and Pilots Association), *NAFI Mentor* magazine (National Association of Flight Instructors), and my book, *The Savvy Flight Instructor* (ASA, 1998). Thanks to editors Tom Haines, Elizabeth Tennyson, Michael Collins, Scott Spangler, and Pat Luebke for so generously allowing me to follow my muse in magazine writing, which led up to this work.

I am particularly grateful to the talented professional writers who reviewed my final manuscript: Heather Baldwin, Kaye Craig, and Laurel Lippert, and to my editor, Nancy Albright. Others who shared wisdom and encouragement during development include Penny Porter, Jane Zaring, Nina Bell Allen, Sara Miller, Ray Newton, Jim Woods, Vern Martin, Jacopo Lenzi, Jackie Spanitz, Jennie Trerise, Mark Holt, Mark Davis, Cyndy Brown, George Larson of *Smithsonian Air & Space* magazine, Jo Graff, Tom Lindvall, Andy Collins, Doug Stewart, Doug Smith, and many more. Nancy Otte, teacher of the hearing-impaired, reviewed "Talking Spirits" for appropriateness, and Daniel Gibson, editor of *Native Peoples* magazine, offered guidance on appropriate terminology for stories involving Native Americans. Special thanks to Stephen Coonts for graciously writing the Foreword, and to Rod Machado, who through words and pen inspires others to the rich breadth of flying beyond handling the controls.

Kudos to photographer David Zickl for the marvelous cover photo, and to Arv Schultz of *America's Flyways* magazine for loaning the 1940 WACO YPF-7 biplane depicted in it. Thanks also, to the other fine photographers who contributed images to this work, including Arnie Dworkis, Adriel Heisey (and Miss Navajo Nation, Sharon Watson), George Kounis of *Pilot Getaways* magazine, Chris Sis, and Tom Till. All other contemporary photos were shot by the author. Thanks to Jill Benton of AOPA for her assistance in scanning many of these images. Maps were created by the author in Adobe Illustrator, using Mountain High and USA Relief map source files from Digital Wisdom, Inc., and Premier USA map source files by Map Resources.

Foreword

Throughout history, people have dreamed of flight. Inspired by the birds, their musings are one of the great themes of literature. Before the dawn of the machine age, most of the flight dreams involved magic or a gift from the Gods to a favored hero. One of the most powerful stories from the pantheon of Greek mythology involved a legendary builder, Daedalus, who used his own wit and cunning to fashion two sets of wings from wood, wax, and feathers so that he and his son could escape imprisonment on the island of Crete.

According to the story, Daedalus' son, Icarus, disregarded his father's advice, as sons are wont to do, and flew too near the sun. The heat melted his wings, and he became aviation's first fatality. If Icarus and Daedalus were the first to attempt flight on homemade wings, they certainly weren't the last.

When he wasn't daubing paint on the Mona Lisa or The Last Supper, Leonardo da Vinci also dreamed of flight. He was a genius and his ideas were good. He sketched a rudimentary helicopter that had promise, yet he lacked a means of propulsion—an engine—so all we have are his drawings, meticulous works of art that reveal his glimpse hundreds of years into the future.

One of the popular poems in the 19th century, "Darius Green and His Flying Machine," by J. T. Towbridge, chronicled the attempt by a young country bumpkin to fly from his father's hayloft wearing a set of leather wings. The flight was short and vertical, but no blood was spilled. The popular poem struck people as satire because in the later part of that century a lot of people, many of them deadly serious, were trying to build machines that would fly. The art of the period captured the popular view of what these flying machines would eventually look like, ships that somehow sailed the sea of air. Visions of these machines appear in the works of Alfred Lord Tennyson, H. G. Wells, and James Matthew Barrie, to name just three. Alas, it would take more than pixie dust to get us aloft.

Balloons took advantage of the one physical fact folks were sure of, that hot air was lighter than cold; a balloon full of it would rise like smoke. Before the Wright brothers, no one really understood the physics that allowed a bird to fly. The Wrights' great scientific achievement was to document the amount of lift that various wing shapes produced. They used this knowledge to engineer their way off the ground. Unlike Michelangelo, they had access to gasoline—yet in 1903, engine technology was so primitive that they had to build their own.

Today you and I live in a golden age. When we dream of flight, like Daedalus, Leonardo, and the Wright brothers, we can leap from the shoulders of giants and actually do it. Small airports dot the nation, airports lined with airplanes that would have brought tears to the eyes of the ancients. Aviation gasoline is for sale at almost all these airports, every small town has a motel and a fast-food joint, and all those folks are delighted when you drop in. Best of all, in America personal aviation has yet to be regulated and taxed out of the reach of most middle-class wage earners, as it has been in Europe and most other developed countries. The opportunity to take flying lessons, get a license, and pilot a small plane anywhere in the country whenever the weather permits and the whim seizes you is perhaps our most delightful freedom. For many of us, it's one of the most precious.

General aviation—the personal airplane—didn't just happen. The man who inspired it all is Charles Lindbergh, who flew a plane about the size of a large Cessna from New York to Paris in 1927. Honestly, I believe that flight has inspired every person since who climbed into an airplane and waggled the controls and thought, *Oh, wow! Maybe I really could learn to fly this thing, and take it to the beach some weekend, or to visit my cousin, or to court my honey three counties over.*

One person in a small plane, the great open sky beckoning . . . that was the dream of the ancients. Today you—yes, *you*—can fly on personal wings, watch the sunset from the sky, fly the cloud halls of Valhalla, leap mountains in a single bound, soar with the hawks and eagles, go from here to there and back again, and take along your main squeeze and a kid or two—and you can do it all for not a lot of money. Amazingly, in America these days a personal airplane can be had for about the price of a second car. For this price, your winged chariot won't be new, of course. But with regular maintenance, it will fly just fine. And if you don't want to buy—hey, this is *America.* You can rent a plane by the hour.

In this book, Greg Brown shares the dream with you as he has lived it through the years. If he can't inspire you to join us in the sky, no one can. You're hopeless, without a smidgen of romance in your soul, and should probably stick to video poker and slot machines for recreation.

So come on, read Greg's tales, get inspired, and join us in mankind's greatest adventure.

Stephen Coonts

Introduction
The Lure of the Map

Magic! No sooner had the engine stopped when the whining of gyros from our flight instruments gave way to mystical drums and rhythmic chanting, crazily mixing images of flight with those of ancient and sacred ceremonies. Chills traveled our spines 'round the cockpit—we could scarcely have been more astonished had we arrived by flying carpet.

Adventurer Richard Halliburton would have appreciated our situation. After hitching around the world by freighter and camel in the 1920s, he became obsessed with visiting the remotest spot he could find on a map—Timbuktu, legendary mid-Sahara caravan stop.

The best way to get there, Halliburton decided, was by *The Flying Carpet,* a black-and-crimson Stearman biplane he bought for the purpose in 1931. In open cockpits, he and pilot Moye Stephens traveled the ancient world, captivating princesses and paupers alike with first airplane rides at exotic places like Baghdad, the Dead Sea, headhunter country in Borneo, and yes, Timbuktu.

It's tempting to look back at those times and think we missed the real adventure of flying. Well, we didn't. Flying was out of reach for all but the wealthiest people in Halliburton's day, so his audience could enjoy flying only vicariously through his writing.

Today's aviators live exploits Halliburton's readers could only dream of—piloting our own flying machines on our own adventures. But like Halliburton we're still drawn obsessively by the map. Each unseen mountain and city promises new aerial adventure. That's why for true aviators flying is so much more than just a career or avocation; rather it's a perverse blend of odyssey, religion, and addiction.

This particular day our own *Flying Carpet* had brought us to a place many would find as mystical and exotic as Timbuktu—Window Rock, Arizona, capital of the Navajo Nation. Here my wife and I had invited friends to explore the annual Navajo Nation Fair.

Our aerial journey had carried us from the sweltering Sonoran Desert near Phoenix, over cool mountains festooned with ponderosa pine, to the remote high-desert Navajo homeland, where wind-sculpted buttes and pinnacles culminate in Monument Valley to the north.

Beautiful and varied as the flight was, nothing could have prepared us for the sound of Native American drums filling our cockpit upon arrival, beckoning us to the fair's parade in progress only a quarter-mile away. There we were captivated by sights Halliburton would have appreciated. Lovely beaming Indian princesses passed on horseback, accompanied by their courts. Marching alongside were senior women of the tribe, wearing massive squash-blossom necklaces of silver and turquoise.

Mystical dancers flashed colorful feathers, prancing to rhythms everyone in the audience seemed to know but us. We strained to understand the parade announcer until realizing our difficulty comprehending wasn't the garbled sound system, but rather the unfamiliar Navajo language transmitted through it. Ninety minutes had carried us a whole world away from home.

Men in traditional dress walked the sidelines, distributing sweets. "Good morning . . . " was offered to young admirers with each piece of candy, and "Thank you for coming." The children laughed, squealed, and ran for goodies like kids at any parade. Only later did we realize that during the entire visit we never once heard a child fuss or cry.

Alongside Navajo cowboys marched high school bands, church groups, and country-western combos. Even the Window Rock detention center had its float. It was just enough like the parades of my own Midwestern hometown to make the contrasts all the more exotic.

This spectacle would have pushed thoughts of flying to the remotest corners of my mind, had it not been for rumbling dark clouds displacing brilliant blue sky from the northwest. Along with topographic maps, another type of chart preoccupies every aviator—the weather map. Although the ground beneath us hardly changes, every flight presents new challenges of commanding your ship through uncharted atmospheric waters. A swirling mass of unpredictable geography, the skies offer their own distinctive views and terrain that differ on each and every passage.

Modern-day princess, Miss Navajo Nation Sharon Watson soars over Window Rock in an ultralight aircraft. (Photo by Adriel Heisey.)

Obstacles, both visible and invisible, leap to confront pilots as they transition this aerial landscape. Between cumulative geography of earth and sky, the pilot's reality varies moment by moment from the warmth of a patchwork quilt on a sunny day—the work of friendly farm families below—to bottomless chasms between colossal thunderheads, towering with dangers hard as any rock.

By the time we walked to the fair and dined on "Navajo tacos" of frybread, beans, and vegetables, the wind was howling and our novice passengers were voicing concern: "Will we make it home tonight?"

"Let's not worry about that until time to leave," I said. If we limit our flying by what might happen on the return trip, too many great adventures pass us by. Better to make weather decisions one leg at a time, and accept the occasional night away from home as the price of adventure.

Wandering the Navajo Nation fairgrounds, we admired everything from giant squash to sheep-shearing to Native jewelry. We were en route to the Pow Wow dance competition when the thunderstorms fulfilled their threats. An hour-and-a-half downpour crowded us and herds of other fairgoers under shelter, with the smell of damp straw and murmur of soft talk.

Later we slogged with our passengers through mud back to the airport, just in time for another cloudburst. There we found the terminal building locked, its only telephone tantalizingly unreachable behind the secured front door.

Fat chance that these friends will fly with us again, I thought, discouraged. The four of us huddled cold and wet under an awning, knowing that the only two hotels in town were full. Fortunately a passing Navajo family offered a cell phone so I could get a weather briefing. Despite the apparent futility, I now found a bit of good news. Although our route home was blocked by a massive area of thunderstorms, the airport at Gallup, New Mexico, was accessible in better weather to the southeast. There we could at least find dinner and hotel rooms. Dripping, we made our way to the airplane and took off into gray skies.

Once airborne, however, a cheerful radio voice offered guidance around the weather toward home, via east and south.

"St. Johns, Arizona, is in the clear," said the air traffic controller. "It's out of your way, but flying in that direction just might get you to Phoenix." Knowing I could land safely at points along the way, I accepted his counsel.

The route to St. Johns was outside the boundaries of the weather; by the time we arrived there a convoluted corridor had opened to Phoenix. Flying tentatively from one potential landing site to another, we bounced like a pinball between silvery cumulus towers, while dark shafts of rain pummeled green mountains on either side of our wind-tossed craft.

Not until clearing skies offered the promise of home did I remember the two nervous passengers riding close behind me. "Are you two okay?" I asked, turning around.

"Are you kidding?" they replied in gleeful unison from the back seat. "This is incredible!" The rain and mud hadn't discouraged them, nor had the turbulent flight. We touched down in the orange glow of a Western sunset, and were home in time for dinner.

Richard Halliburton's flying carpet might have been more colorful than ours, but I doubt he had many better days of adventure than this one. His spirit rides along on every flight, relentlessly urging new exploration of the map.

Unfortunately, that inspiration goes beyond wonders of the Earth to dangers of the sky and the weather it contains. Halliburton disappeared in a 1939 storm, while attempting to sail a Chinese junk from Hong Kong to San Francisco. "Southerly gales, squalls, lee rail under water, wet bunks, hard tack, bully beef," read his last radio transmission, "wish you were here—instead of me!"

Not relishing such a heroic ending for myself or my family, I would, over years of flying, attempt to reconcile the treasures of one map with the hazards of the other. That would prove a daunting task. Flying is by nature episodic; therefore, many flights must pass before the scattered bits and pieces of an aviator's experience resolve into a comprehensible whole. Following the lure of the map would deliver a turbulent ride—but a rich one.

PEDIGREE OF A PILOT

Some Lessons
a Pilot Never Forgets

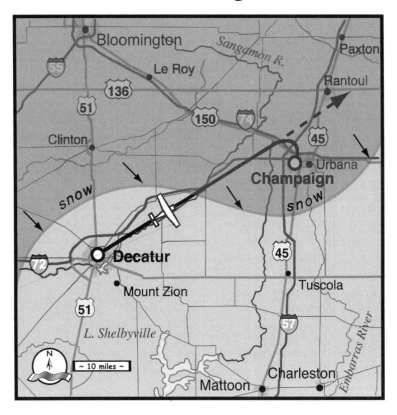

So this must be vertigo, I thought. Nausea circled my gut like the snowflakes orbiting my propeller. I peered out the windshield for landmarks, but snow obscured all but a tiny spot of ground beneath me, even at an altitude of only 1,000 feet. To make matters worse, the navigational radio had obviously failed—how could I possibly have drifted so far off course as it suggested, on a flight of only forty miles?

It was almost Christmas, and I was a young University of
Illinois student transporting precious parts for my Suzuki
X-6. One of the hottest small motorcycles of its day, the
X-6 was also notorious for its temperamental transmission.
Sure enough, after just a few rides to impress my new girlfriend, I'd been forced to disassemble it for overhaul. The
nearest dealer was in Decatur, so each discovery of another
worn-out component meant another eighty-mile round trip
to replace it. Today was a big day, because after months of
waiting, the major transmission parts had finally arrived. To
celebrate I decided to make the pickup by airplane.

"There's a storm system approaching from the northwest," said the weather briefer that morning prior to my
departure, "but we don't expect it here before suppertime."

"No problem," I said. "I'll be back by early afternoon." I
flew to Decatur under clear skies, hitched a ride to the
motorcycle dealership, and collected a bagful of gears and
shafts. Then I headed for the Decatur airport restaurant to
savor its infamous double-decker burger slathered with
peanut butter and Bermuda onions. On the way, however, I
noticed hazy clouds materializing. *Was that a snowflake?*

Forgetting food, I phoned flight service, only to learn
that the weather system was advancing far more quickly than
forecast.[1] "Get out right now and you'll be okay," said the
briefer. "The weather's approaching from the northwest.
Going east you should reach Champaign well ahead of it."

By the time I finished my preflight inspection of the
plane, the cloud ceiling was slate gray, and light snow was
falling. Quickly, I took to the air. As expected, the weather
rapidly improved. To my surprise, however, it soon began

---

[1] Flight service stations provide weather and operational information to
pilots, along with processing and monitoring flight plans.

deteriorating again. Not being trained for flight by cockpit instruments alone, I descended lower and lower to keep the ground in sight.

Now I was getting nervous. Turbulence increasingly unsettled me, and the nose of my airplane pointed at a crazy angle far different than the course I was tracking over the ground. This dramatic crab angle (named for the sidewise movement of the crustacean) indicated powerful winds trying to blow me off course. Worse yet, flight visibility was diminishing in snow, though for a short time better weather could be seen off my wing to the south.

Ominously, the words of my former flight instructor filled my head. "Never enter precipitation you can't see through to the other side," Bob had often warned me.

No pilot ever forgets that flight instructor who first delivers the secrets of flight. Usually primary instructors are remembered with reverence, and their faces reappear at appropriate times to chastise us about mistakes we are about to make. Unfortunately, those words are rarely heeded until afterward.

On recent flights, Bob's apparition had largely stopped admonishing me. I took that to mean that with four years of generally safe flying experience I had a pretty good handle on my limitations. But now here was that pesky Bob, whispering in my ear again. Brushing him off, I continued toward Champaign.

Knowing I couldn't be far from home, I tuned in the recorded weather. "Ceiling indefinite 1,500 feet," it said, "visibility four miles in snow." If the clouds descended below 1,000 feet above ground, or the visibility diminished below three miles, I would no longer be legal to land. How could this weather system be beating me to Champaign? *Ugh, that snow swirling around the propeller is making me dizzy.*

Looking at my single navigational instrument, I noticed the needle pegged to the right instead of centered where it should be. *That can't be accurate,* I thought, *I already have ten degrees wind correction.* Surely that frail sliver of metal was wrong, so I maintained my previously calculated heading.

By now the strengthening snowstorm offered just a tiny window to the ground, straight down and seemingly only inches in diameter. Through it passed nondescript bits of farm fields—no sign of the interstate highway or other familiar landmarks.

In an effort to remain calm, I visualized reassembling my motorcycle from components scattered across my apartment living room. Looking back at my new parts in the airplane's back seat proved to be a mistake, however; turning my head only accentuated the vertigo.

Champaign now reported indefinite 1,200 feet overcast and three miles visibility. *What if the airport goes below visual minimums?* Fighting panic, I refocused thoughts on my girlfriend, who'd shown such faith in me as a pilot. Jean was unlike most other girls I'd invited aloft—she viewed my flying as adventure, rather than aberration. It was almost Christmas, and this year for the first time she was to meet my parents. *What if I don't make it home?*

With that, my mind began running away from me, filling with horrific images of my cockpit spinning in whiteness toward the ground.

Not being trained in instrument flying, I'd received only rudimentary instruction in how to maintain control when unable to see out the window, and that had been years ago. All I knew at this point was that the outcome after losing control was predictably bad. *The graveyard spiral! How many other aviators had succumbed to it before me?*

Just then a fragment of a huge grain elevator crossed my shrinking peephole to the ground. Probably it saved my life. So distinctive was this landmark, that even glimpsing just a bit of it told me immediately and undeniably my exact location; expectations could no longer disguise reality. The nav radio was right after all—it always is in such situations—so I centered the needle to obtain the correct course, and turned southeast to follow it. Had I continued on my heading I would have passed north of town, seeing nothing but cornfields until . . . *until* . . .

With the city soon in sight to guide me, and the warm voice of a familiar tower controller for encouragement, I came upon the airport. Visibility was so poor I couldn't see the runway until flying over it; a turn back around was required to line up on final approach. It wasn't much of a landing, given my state of mind and that nauseating snow still circling the propeller. But I knew that I'd cheated fate, and should avoid testing it so aggressively in the future.

After staggering out the cabin door and tying down the airplane, I made my way to the flight service station then located on the field.

"Can I help you?" asked the briefer. "It's not a good day for flying—I can tell you that right up front."

"Actually, I'm here to close my flight plan," I replied. The man's cheery smile turned expressionless as he eyed the snow frosting my head and shoulders. It was not a look of surprise, but rather one of weariness from a man who over time had seen many fools cross his threshold.

After telling my story to the briefer, I learned what had gone wrong. It turned out that the bad weather had approached more from the north than the west; unwittingly I'd taken off into a scallop in the advancing leading edge. Although I thought I was flying into better conditions, Champaign's weather had come down only minutes after Decatur. The preflight briefing had yielded no clue to this, and given the favorable forecast for such a short flight, it hadn't crossed my mind to radio for an update.

There are always decisions made by pilots, in such situations, that determine whether there will be a crisis or not. All I really needed to do when the weather began deteriorating was to turn south, where safe haven waited in good visual conditions. But frankly, that never occurred to me, either. All I could think of was my closeness to home and getting there promptly.

From that day forward I've always made it a point to know before takeoff which way to turn for better weather, even when flying on instruments. After all, it doesn't take reaching the destination to make a flying mission successful —just landing somewhere safely. It was one of those lessons a pilot never forgets, assuming he lives to tell about them.

It was almost Christmas, and I might have missed it. I took that special girl home to meet my parents, and there she gave the first of many holiday gifts to win my heart—a complete set of metric box wrenches for my motorcycle.

Spring Break!

Spring break! To a college student those words conjure visions of bikinis and beaches and beer—exactly why most of my classmates had planned Florida road trips for vacation.

But I was a pilot, craving adventure in exotic places only an airplane could take me. Heck, anyone can drive to Florida. My roommate, Al, and I thought that was passé.

Getting the "Flying Illini" Cessna 172 for spring break wasn't going to be easy, however. The little four-seat Sky-hawk was the most popular of the club's planes and would be delegated by sealed bidding to the pilot proposing the most flight hours over vacation. With several hundred members vying for only three airplanes, competition would be tough. Al and I pored over my charts, seeking destinations far enough away to snatch the plane from other spring-breakers, but close enough so we wouldn't go broke completing the adventure.

Our dream goal materialized amusingly close to everyone else's Florida destination, yet at the same time excitingly far away—the Bahamas. We won the bid, and filled with visions of flying to an exotic island country, invited our neighbor Howard to join us and share expenses. Howard qualified for this mission because he could ride a motorcycle "wheelie" farther than anyone else outside a county fair. He seemed like the only other guy nutty enough to blow his summer earnings on such an expedition. He readily accepted.

A 175-hour private pilot at the time, my recent flight experience consisted mostly of those motorcycle-parts trips to nearby Decatur. I had a few cross-country excursions to Chicago and southern Wisconsin under my belt, but this trip would exceed 1,200 miles each way. That would be a long haul in our little Cessna, cruising at maybe 110 miles per hour. Clearly, preparation would be required to safely complete our mission.

I ordered Bahamas travel information, and then began researching the most thought-provoking leg of our trip—flying seventy miles of open ocean between the Florida coast and Grand Bahama Island. There's nothing like studying flotation devices and ditching procedures to get your heart racing.

Like many low-time pilots, I'd never been very comfortable with night flying. It seemed that such skills might prove handy on such an adventure, so I took some after-dark training to prepare myself should the need arise. Further practice came through moonlit dinner flights with Jean to the Mattoon, Illinois, airport steakhouse. The food was terrific there, but so were the crosswinds, I soon learned. After several hair-raising experiences taking off and landing there in strong winds at night, I reengaged my flight instructor for professional help. That additional practice would prove useful on the upcoming trip.

With paying for our travel a growing concern, Howard invited his friend, Steve, to fly commercially from Houston and join us in Palm Beach for the Bahamas portion of the trip. That seemed like a great idea until I made weight-and-balance calculations. Even with the most optimistic of projections, our little airplane could not be expected to safely lift four of us along with fuel, luggage, life preservers, and a raft.

This presented an insurmountable dilemma for cash-starved students like ourselves, until someone suggested meeting Steve at Freeport on Grand Bahama Island, instead of Palm Beach. Flight through the Bahamas would be limited to island-hopping after the initial crossing. Therefore we could check our life raft in Freeport, reclaiming just enough carrying capacity for Steve to climb aboard. To save weight, we negotiated luggage at two pairs of shorts apiece, along with two t-shirts and a bathing suit, all carried in soft bags. Only one of us would bring a camera.

When college and the control tower finally released us for that long-awaited spring break, I thrilled to crossing the Ohio River and entering Kentucky as a pilot for the first time. Then, after refueling at Smyrna, Tennessee, we made several hours' use of my freshly honed night flying skills. The three of us were elated.

Up to this point, skies had been cloudless and the weather perfect for flying in every respect. But of increasing concern as we flew south was a cold front ahead, accompanied by low clouds and rain. Although forecast to quickly clear our route, it was barely past Atlanta when we landed there that evening.

After sampling Atlanta's nightlife, we awoke next morning to find that the front had all but stalled across our route. With the snow encounter still fresh in my memory, I was not interested in taking chances. Following long hours of waiting, we finally took flight behind the slow-moving front, trailing as close behind it as we dared. We made only Alma, Georgia, that afternoon, and then later in the day, Waycross. There we spent the night.

Spirits were low that evening. We'd traveled only a little over 200 miles from Atlanta and our precious vacation seemed to be hemorrhaging away. It didn't help when the folks at flight service said the front had gone stationary and might obstruct progress for days to come. Frustrated, Howard phoned Steve and told him we'd be at least a day late to Freeport, if not more. Waycross nightlife wasn't on a par with Atlanta, either.

I learned a bit about the fickleness of weather upon awakening next morning—and the futility of worrying about it much ahead of time. To our astonishment, the front had zoomed away totally and unexpectedly overnight. Again jubilant, we proceeded to Stuart, Florida, to rent survival gear.

Charles Lindbergh could hardly have felt more trepidation before his epic flight than did I as a recent pilot, facing my own tiny slice of the Atlantic in our single-engine 172. Along with worries of going down mid-crossing, we had long harbored concerns about missing those islands that appeared so minuscule on the chart, and blundering blindly past them into the open Atlantic. Shark stories liberally peppered our conversations, and we speculated as to whether our route fell within the Bermuda Triangle or not.

Hours of prior deliberation back in our campus apartments had generated our transatlantic strategy. We would fly down the coast to the point of shortest crossing, in the process climbing as high as possible to extend gliding range in case of engine failure. That would reduce our ditching exposure to a slightly shorter time period mid-crossing. (Never before had I become so intimate with the gliding distance chart in my aircraft operating handbook; ultimately the page had to be taped back in due to excessive handling.) Radio and radar coverage would be available to us most of the way across; hopefully, if we went down someone would be able to find us before we drowned or were eaten by sharks.

Taking off from Stuart, we climbed to 9,500 feet before turning eastbound over Palm Beach. Before us lay nothing but pale blue ocean silvered by sunshine. Howard, Al, and I looked at each other, laughed nervously, and shook hands. Al had taken a few flying lessons in the past, and so had some inkling of the process for reaching our destination. Who knows what Howard was thinking, however, as he helplessly turned his life over to some college kid from across the hall.

"Safer than two-block motorcycle wheelies down Green Street in campus town," I said, upon observing the expression on his face.

"You've got a point there," said Howard. "If we make it back, I'll do another one to celebrate."

So long as mainland Florida remained visible behind us, there was much joking among us. But when land disappeared entirely and the expected warm blanket of radio voices declined to answer my calls, our confined quarters became silent. The navigational station at West End on Grand Bahama was coming in clear ahead, however, as was that of Palm Beach behind us. What's more, the course they agreed upon matched my precalculated heading.

"What if we lose our radios?" asked Howard, watching me twiddle the knobs.

"For backup I'm employing the method Lindbergh used," I explained. "I computed compass heading and flight time in advance, based on forecast winds. Theoretically all I do is hold this heading and we should get there." For the moment, I neglected to name this navigational method— under the circumstances, *dead reckoning* didn't seem like a term Howard would appreciate. "So long as the engine keeps on running," I continued, "we should be okay."

Then puffy cumulus clouds began appearing at our altitude. This was alarming because I'd read that over water in these latitudes there should be few clouds in good weather, except for those crowning land. Clouds, in fact, should hopefully guide us to land should we lose other navigational capability. Now I was faced with the choice of weaving our way among clouds, thereby surrendering careful control of our heading, or *descending toward the water* to get beneath them. Explaining my actions so as not to alarm my passengers, I descended first to 7,500 feet, then 5,500.

"What does this do to our glide range if the engine quits?" asked Al.

"I'll figure it out later," I replied.

Following what seemed like an eternity out of sight of land (actual flight time was under forty minutes, shore-to-shore), we spotted larger fair-weather clouds over Grand Bahama Island. Faces brightened and joking returned to the cockpit as we closed the distance to Freeport.

That evening we met up with Steve to enrich the nearby casino, then island-hopped the next morning to our final destination. Ninety miles over red reefs and sparkling turquoise waters delivered us to Great Abaco, one of many Bahamian "out islands" accessible only by boat or light aircraft.

This flight was much different than our first day's leg across open water, as we never left the reassuring sight of land. Pristine beach lined the shores of each island, while the interiors were luxuriantly foliated in trees. The sight could hardly have been more different than the familiar flat farm fields of central Illinois.

This sense of paradise was diminished, however, when we approached our destination of Marsh Harbour Airport and radioed for landing information. According to the booming voice answering our call, a powerful crosswind assailed the narrow landing strip cut between tall trees.

At fifteen knots, the crosswind was at the very limits tested for this type of airplane, and as a relatively new pilot I was uncertain of my ability to safely deal with it.[2] I discussed these concerns with Al and Howard. With the object of our long journey in sight below and no nearby alternates for landing, none of us was enthused at the idea of turning back. Then there was the question of how to change our landing destination within the Bahamian regulatory system. We had filed a flight plan with specific arrangement to clear Customs at Marsh Harbour.

Further queries of the airport radio operator indicated that although strong, the crosswind was steady and therefore relatively predictable. After a good deal of discussion with my passengers I decided to approach for landing, but be prepared to abort and go elsewhere if the situation proved uncomfortable.

As it turned out, the wind was indeed challenging at first, but dropped away when we dipped below treetop level. Still, I was grateful for my Midwest crosswind landing experience when we touched down.

Parking facilities were primitive at Marsh Harbour, so we tied down our Cessna among tall weeds, using tent stakes

---

[2] Since wind velocity is always reported to pilots in *knots,* it is presented that way by the author. A common unit of measure among pilots and mariners, 1 knot refers to a speed of 1 nautical mile per hour, where 1 nautical mile equals approximately 1.15 statute miles. With the exception of wind, all speeds and distances in this book are expressed in statute miles, as familiar to U.S. drivers.

and ropes brought along for the purpose. Much veneration was felt for the old airplane, having brought us so far to our destination. After patting the Skyhawk's nose, we balanced our one camera on a rock and snapped a commemorative picture.

Having safely completed the long journey, we balanced our one camera on a rock and snapped a commemorative picture.

The booming voice on the radio proved to be that of Mr. Strong, a charming and affable Bahamian official who ran the airport and also served as Customs officer. Bedecked in a perfectly creased uniform, his powerful physique matched both his voice and his name. Our conversation took on a time-delay character, given our unfamiliarity with the man's thick local dialect.

"How will you get to town?" Mr. Strong's basso voice rumbled, after he filled out the requisite paperwork.

"Taxi?" someone answered, following a moment's processing time.

"It just so happens I run the taxi," he said. "Hop in."

After learning we'd made no reservations, Mr. Strong asked whether we were interested in renting a house.

"My wife cleans houses and acts as rental agent," he said. "Let me show you one." The house was heaven, on a narrow spit with beach on both sides; we signed up on the spot.

"What are your dinner plans?" he then asked, as we retrieved our traveler's checks.

"We heard that food is expensive here," said Al, "Our plan was to buy groceries and prepare our own meals."

"I have a much better idea than that," said Mr. Strong. Countering student frugality with tales of luscious island food, he offered "the best cook on the island," to prepare us dinner right there in our beachside lodging. That cook turned out to be Mrs. Strong.

The price seemed reasonable enough and Mr. Strong had already guided us well, so the four of us shrugged at one another and accepted. With ocean sunset as a backdrop, we dined that evening on fresh grouper, homemade conch chowder, and key lime pie. It was a gourmet dinner I'll never forget, and the Strongs proved entertaining hosts as well as good business people. For years afterward I kept in touch with them through referrals and holiday cards.

The next few days were spent snorkeling in crystalline waters amid scarlet reefs and colorful schools of tropical fish. At sunset we wandered remote beaches, then returned to our veranda to relax before a moonlit ocean. It was life in a perfect aquarium; we were so relaxed and satisfied that we never visited anywhere else on the island.

Not until departure day did we communicate with the outside world. Mr. Strong picked us up by prearranged appointment; at the airport we paid a few dollars departure tax and called for weather by radiotelephone. And even when time came to depart Paradise, we relived the joy by overflying coral reefs and teeming turquoise waters.

After dropping Steve at Freeport to catch his Houston-bound flight, we aimed our nose westward across open water. The trip didn't seem so daunting this time, given our newly acquired experience, and in any case the coast of Florida would be tough to miss. We cleared U.S. Customs at Palm Beach International Airport, returned our rented survival gear at Stuart, and then steered northward over sun-bleached beaches toward home.

Meeting darkness near Jacksonville, we had some trepidation about overflying Okeefenokee Swamp at night—talk of alligators entered that discussion—but despite those concerns we landed uneventfully at Macon, Georgia.

Next day was bumpy in strong headwinds; I experienced my first mountain turbulence over the Smokies near Chattanooga. But nothing could discourage us now. We touched down at University of Illinois-Willard Airport eight days and twenty-four flight hours after departing, astonished at what three average college students had just accomplished.

Bikinis? Hard as we looked I don't believe we ever saw one. But we found plenty of beautiful beaches and wondrous travel by flying carpet to places few classmates would visit in a lifetime. To this day I doubt many would understand how our spring break could be more memorable than all their parties put together.

Test-Pilot Territory

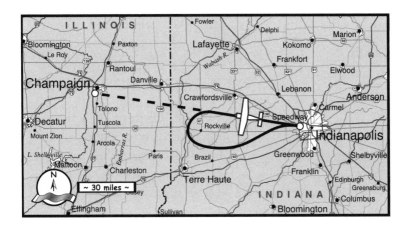

Mastering flight by little needles is challenging, exhausting, and not inexpensive. But the ability to fly in marginal weather without seeing the ground tremendously increases the safety and utility of being a pilot. Flights like that from Decatur to Champaign would have been trivial with an instrument rating, and over spring break my friends and I would have made the Bahamas a day earlier. So when Jean and I married and moved to Indianapolis, becoming an instrument pilot was high on my list of priorities.

My new wife was supportive of this endeavor. We'd flown often together while dating, and she saw that airplanes offered easy access to skiing and other recreational activities. Perhaps more importantly, she had deduced that trips I might otherwise resist—such as visiting the in-laws—became exciting to me when flying was involved. Therefore, with her encouragement I began taking instrument flying lessons not long after our wedding.

I was maybe halfway through training when I received a call from an old college friend, a nutty English girl named

19

Corrine. Over many a campus-town beer, we'd analyzed important topics like why it's okay for British girls to borrow a "rubber" from classmates, and why "Randy" is not a popular name in the U.K. I'd even taken Corrine and her girlfriend flying. So when she called to say she was back in the U.S. visiting for a few weeks, Jean and I invited her to join us for a weekend. We even volunteered to fly to Champaign after work and get her.

The day we were to pick Corrine up, I awoke to cloudy winter skies. Based on the forecast, I could see that visual flying conditions were unlikely that evening, and therefore it might not be possible for me to fly over and get her. Driving would be an option if the weather remained bad after work, but then I had another idea.

I phoned my flight instructor, Dave, told him the situation, and asked about prospects of making the trip an instrument flying lesson. Dave thought it was a great idea, as we were just wrapping up the basics and I was ready to start learning practical skills. The flight would be about a hundred miles each way, and with instrument approaches through the clouds to landing at each end, it would make an excellent lesson.

Before leaving work that afternoon, I phoned for a weather briefing. The clouds were indeed too low for me to fly alone from Indianapolis to Champaign in visual conditions, but the surface weather sounded perfect for an instrument lesson. Clouds were reported at 700–1,000 feet overcast along the route, with excellent visibility underneath. (Clouds 1,000 feet above ground is the legal minimum for most visual flying, though 3,000 or 4,000 is a safer practical limit, especially for night flights like this would be.) Winds aloft were strong from the west. Turbulence was expected, however, and surface temperatures in the low forties.

When the briefer got to pilot reports, however, I quickly became concerned. Accumulation of ice on the wings had been reported by many aircraft, including several "moderate icing" reports by airliners. This often occurs when planes fly through clouds or precipitation at temperatures near freezing.

Ice accumulation on an airplane is dangerous for many reasons. First, ice weighs a lot, and can tax a plane's ability to carry it. Also it forms irregularly, unpredictably changing the shape of the wing. This decreases the wing's lift, while increasing drag. Finally, ice forming on the propeller reduces its ability to pull the airplane. In short, icing works against the pilot in every imaginable way. I had read about these effects, but never seen them at work. Larger, more sophisticated aircraft have effective systems for dealing with this problem, but our small airplane did not. Even to a novice like me, this did not sound like good flying weather for a lowly Cessna 172.

When I reported these findings to Dave by telephone, he pooh-poohed my concerns. "It's well above freezing temperature on the ground," he said, "so if icing becomes a problem we can always descend into warmer air, if climbing above it won't do the trick." I was only fifteen or twenty hours into my instrument training, but he was a seasoned pilot with a day job flying a high-tech twin-engine airplane. *Who am I to judge?* I thought. I arranged for Jean to meet us at the airport, and phoned Corrine with details for our meeting.

It was already dark when Dave met Jean and me at Speedway airport, a peaceful uncontrolled airport not far from Indianapolis International. We picked up clearance instructions for our instrument flight plan, bundled Jean with her book and flashlight into the back seat, and took off. As we climbed from the airport, streetlights spread comfortingly before us. The instant clouds cloaked our view, however, ice began to accumulate. By the time we reached our filed altitude of 4,000 feet, the wing leading edges were coated with a growing ridge of ice.

Worried, I tried to concentrate nonchalantly on my navigation, while Dave peered into blackness out the window, monitoring accumulation with his flashlight. "We'd like a climb to 8,000 feet," he radioed the air traffic controller, who promptly cleared us to do so. Ice continued to build, however, so long before reaching that altitude Dave again queried the controller.

"Where are the cloud tops?" he asked. Word came back a few moments later, after the controller surveyed other aircraft.

"There's an aircraft at niner thousand who says he can see the moon occasionally," said the controller, "figures tops are at ten or eleven thousand." Dave's strategy was to climb into clear skies above the clouds, where ice would cease to accumulate.

By this time our small craft had struggled up to 6,700 feet, and due to its accumulating frozen burden, could climb no further. The level of cloud tops had become academic. Onward we chugged, the surrounding blackness perforated only by the intermittent red glow of the rotating beacon reflecting off the inside of our own personal cloud. The icy ridges on the wing leading edges continued to grow, as did lumpy formations coating protruding probes and antennas. Although we were carrying full power, the airplane soon began to slowly lose altitude.

"Cessna One-Five-Five," squawked the radio, "You are cleared to 8,000 feet. Are you continuing to climb?"

My instructor peered silently out his window.

"Dave," I said, surprised at my mentor's uncharacteristic silence, "don't you think we ought to go back?"

"Yeah, well . . . " he said after a long pause, "I guess so."

Dutifully, he notified the controller of our decision to turn back, and requested descent to 3,000, lower as soon as it was available. Then, as I turned gradually toward home and increased our rate of descent, the plane began to shake. This was not a minor vibration, but rather violent, rhythmic quaking of the entire aircraft. I turned to Dave in horror.

"Just some ice on the prop," he said, expressionless, then turned his flashlight back outside. I gripped the shuddering control wheel and held my breath.

Mercifully, we descended out of the clouds to find our-selves within sight of our little airport. With strong westerly winds working against us, we had covered little ground dur-ing the outbound leg of our journey, then had rocketed back within minutes thanks to what had now became a tailwind.

"Keep our speed up," said Dave as I entered the traffic pattern, "we're in test-pilot territory with all that ice on the wing." The windshield being almost totally iced up, I made my approach twenty miles per hour faster than usual while peering out through a two-inch peephole melted by the defroster. On short final for landing, enough ice cracked off the prop so the vibration almost stopped, and after a bounce or two we were on the ground.

My knees would barely support me when I climbed out the door. The little Cessna carried ice on its wing leading edges approaching 3/4 of an inch thick, along with large chunks remaining on the prop and the still mostly glazed-over windshield. The lesson had proved a powerful one, if not in the manner my instructor originally intended.

While Dave stood silently by, I reached into the plane and took Jean's book from her hand, then helped her from the back seat. Looking around in confusion after getting out she asked, "What? Are we back at home?" I'd been so absorbed in our perilous situation that I'd never thought to say a word to her about what was going on. And she'd been too absorbed in her book to ask.

"Jean," I said, "We'll have plenty of time to talk about it on the drive to Champaign."

Alone in the Soup

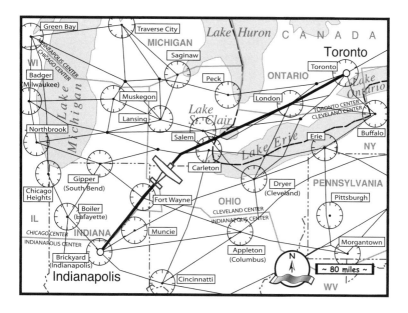

A wet blanket of stratus raced menacingly over our heads, so low that we all but felt the urge to duck. Clearly the winds were strong and the cloud layer thick to generate such an evil appearance. My wife and I had long anticipated this trip from Indianapolis to visit my aunt in Toronto, but the low-skimming clouds were scary enough to give me second thoughts about going today.

The resilience of human emotion is amazing—despite the icing experience of six months earlier, I had gone on to earn my instrument rating. But only a month had passed since my flight test, and if we chose to proceed, this would be my first venture into the clouds without an instructor.

"Don't you think we'd better get going?" asked Jean.

"I must admit," I replied, "that this weather has me nervous. The clouds are solid all the way to Toronto, with tops way above 12,000 feet. There's no way we could climb above them. We'd be in the soup the whole way."

"So?" she said with increasing irritation, "that's why you got your instrument rating, isn't it?"

"Of course, Jean, but look up there. See how fast those clouds are moving? And how dark they are?"

She didn't reply.

"The weather at Toronto is only 800 feet overcast," I added, "and not expected to improve all day. For that matter, the ceiling is between 600 and 800 feet overcast the whole way."

"So," asked Jean, "are you saying it's not safe to fly today?"

"Well, not exactly. Toronto has an instrument landing system that can take us down to 200 feet, and there are plenty of good alternate airports along the way. The freezing level is high, so icing shouldn't be a problem. No thunderstorms, either. It's just that . . . "

"Greg," my wife interrupted, "If it's your professional opinion as a pilot that flying today is not safe, we'll go another time. But if it *is* safe to go today—well, we've just spent all that money on an instrument rating, so I say *let's get going!*"

Later I'd recognize the wisdom of this challenge—in fact I still use it as counsel today. Like every new instrument pilot, I was justifiably nervous about charging off into the clouds without my instructor. But rationally, I had to admit that based on the hard facts presented by flight service, there was no reason why it shouldn't be safe to go, given my newly acquired instrument flying skills.

So after checking the weather one last time, preflighting the airplane yet again—and convincing myself that my repeated bathroom needs were from "butterflies," not terminal illness—I collected our clearance. We rolled down the runway at Speedway Airport and almost immediately entered the clouds, not to emerge again until 2–1/2 hours later.

Things went pretty smoothly at first. My flight planning had been thorough and I had a good deal of experience in the flying club Cessna 182 we were flying. Slightly larger than a 172 Skyhawk, the 182 Skylane was faster, more powerful, and more stable.

But this plane had no autopilot. Between distractions of navigating, reading maps, and operating the radio, I often looked up to find us banking one way or another, or drifting off heading. It seemed like we were all over the sky. But whenever I looked over at Jean, she was absorbed in her book as usual. Despite the surrounding whiteness, she didn't seem to have a care in the world. *Everything's cool,* I kept telling myself. *Just stay focused and we'll arrive in good order.*

Periodically, the clouds opaquing our windows would thin for a moment, and I'd peer desperately downward for a glimpse of terra firma. I never saw it, but well into the flight I did penetrate the haze for a second, only to see . . . water!

Water! Despite my careful navigation, that could only mean we were far off course—somewhere in the middle of Lake Erie. Or Lake Huron. I turned to Jean in panic. "I just saw *water!*"

"So?" she said. Either not reading my consternation, or ignoring it, Jean went back to her book. I was smart enough to drop the subject. Why had the air traffic controller not told me we were so far off course? There had to be a way to check without giving away my confusion.

"Cleveland Center," I radioed tentatively, "Five-Victor-Yankee—radio check, please." My logic was that by bringing attention to my blip on his radar screen, the controller would say something if I was indeed in the wrong place.

"Loud and clear, Victor-Yankee, how do you read?"

"Loud and clear," I replied. The guy seemed unconcerned, so again I pored over my maps. Carefully, I calculated radio navigation position from my instrument chart, then transferred it to my sectional chart depicting visual landmarks. Several times I countered self-induced airplane rock and roll during the process.

"Whoa!" I said out loud. Jean jumped.

"What?" she said with alarm. "Is something wrong?"

"Oh, ah . . . no," I replied. "Turns out that water was just Lake St. Clair, this little lake near Detroit. See? We're right on course!"

"Fine," she said, "but try not to scare me next time." With momentary annoyance she returned to her book, and I to my perilous mission.

Actually, having confirmed we were on course, I had to admit that this instrument-flying stuff was making pretty good sense to me. Better yet, although I was still working hard, my stomach had calmed down and panic now threatened only occasionally.

Toronto weather had dropped to 600 feet overcast and three miles visibility by the time we arrived, still well above legal limits, but below forecast and low enough to get the attention of a novice instrument pilot. I studied my approach charts, set up the radios, and began preparing myself mentally to avert disaster. For once I even remembered to memorize the missed-approach procedure.

Instrument flying was designed to allow pilots to fly when weather obscures the view of the ground. Long ago it was learned that without some sort of visual reference, it is physically impossible for pilots to maintain aircraft control by feel alone. ("Seat of the pants flying," that's commonly called.) Among the reasons are that our sense of Earth's gravity is obscured by the effects of other forces of flight. Then there's the issue of knowing where you are when you can't see outside.

To fly by instruments, pilots use a collection of cockpit displays to level the plane, turn it, climb, descend, and direct its course. Having completed the en route portion of our flight, we would now transition to an "instrument approach" for landing. These published procedures guide pilots through a series of steps leading from en route airways to landing position just short of the runway. There are several different types of instrument approaches, but the most precise and common at busier airports is called an instrument landing system, or ILS.

To create an ILS, two radio signals are projected from the airport—one a vertical plane aligned with the runway (the localizer) and the other an intersecting horizontal plane tilted 3° upward from the end of the runway (glideslope). My assignment was to fly the intersection of these two signals, which would lead me on a descending path to the end of the runway. Executed properly at Toronto, this ILS would deposit our airplane 200 feet above the ground, lined up with our assigned runway to land.

Not only would I have to precisely track two intersecting needles representing localizer and glideslope, but on the chance that the runway might not appear when I reached the decision point, I must be prepared to climb on a memorized "missed approach" procedure back up toward the safety of open skies.

As it turned out, the training paid off. Although my performance was far from perfect, those needles stayed more or less where they belonged on the face of the instrument, and we broke out of the clouds perfectly aligned with the runway. As if by magic, we'd materialized precisely over our destination, not having seen ground since takeoff. (I preferred to forget the sighting of water.) It was like sitting in the hangar for two hours, then opening the door to find Toronto.

Along with the kick of actually arriving at our chosen destination came the realization that despite seemingly constant wanderings, I'd actually done a journeyman's job of navigating by instruments. Never once during the flight had I departed the assigned airway or altitude envelopes (or perhaps the air traffic controllers were too polite to say anything).

"How was your flight?" asked my aunt, when she picked us up from the airport.

"It was great!" said Jean. "We were in the clouds the whole way, but it was no big deal, because *Greg is an instrument pilot.*"

"I am *very* impressed!" said my aunt, with melodrama that might otherwise have been annoying. But I didn't care. I indeed felt for the first time like an instrument pilot, and without Jean's urging I wouldn't have—not yet, anyway.

My instrument flying skills and confidence were honed on the flight home two days later; my logbook shows 2–1/2 hours in the clouds, with an instrument approach to 400 feet at Indianapolis International Airport. There we cleared U.S. Customs, but the weather was too low to reposition the plane five miles home to Speedway Airport; we had to leave it at International and call a friend to pick us up.

I didn't mind in the least. For the first time I felt like a true all-weather aviator, with a whole new world of flight opened to me. Plenty of learning adventures still lay ahead, but that single trip stimulated a fascination with instrument flying that would remain with me forever.

"Hey! We're in the soup!" I'd never be the same again.

Eclipse
Sun Worshipping in Winnipeg

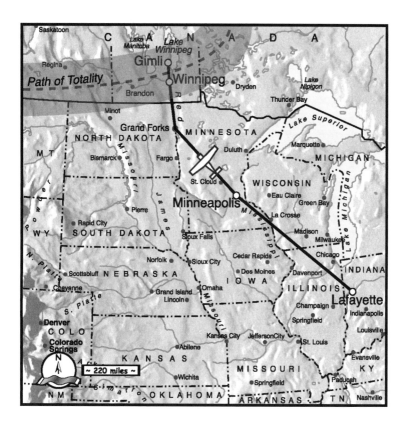

It was gray November in Indiana when I opened the battered campus mail envelope. I anticipated a meeting announcement inside, or other bureaucratic blather. But instead there was a note from Art Winfree, biology professor and fellow member of the Purdue Staff Aero Club. Jean and I had joined the group after moving up the road from Indianapolis to Lafayette.

"What are you doing in February?" asked Art. "There's a solar eclipse in Winnipeg and I'd dearly love to enlist an instrument pilot for the trip."

I admit to swelling with pride at the words, "instrument pilot," but frankly, wasn't very interested in going when I first read the note. I'd seen eclipses before, and pursuing one to Canada in dead of winter seemed hardly worthwhile. But Art being a sharp guy, I suspected there must be good reasons behind his enthusiasm.

"I'm skeptical," I wrote back, "but tell me more." This would be a rare total solar eclipse, I soon learned from articles he sent, and therefore unlike the partial eclipses I'd seen in the past. With the sun entirely blocked by the moon, no special filters or glasses would be required to view it. Although the eclipse would be partial over most of North America, totality would occur over a narrow 195-mile-wide band arcing through the U.S. Northwest and Canada. Winnipeg would be the closest place for us to observe it.

Before long Art convinced me to reserve the club Cessna 210 for the trip, "in case we decide to go." The clincher came when a Purdue astronomy professor volunteered to join us.

"You're hesitating?" she asked, when I questioned her about the details. "There won't be another nearby total solar eclipse for decades!" Then she tantalized me with talk of "Baily's beads," the "diamond ring effect," and other mysterious eclipse phenomena. Soon I found myself touting the expedition to others, and before long we'd filled the airplane's six seats.

Our original plan called for departing to Winnipeg the day before the eclipse, but two days before the celestial event Art and I noted a major weather system approaching Indiana from the southwest. The potential for wintertime icing appeared significant, and could very possibly force us to scrub the trip.

Quickly the two of us took to our telephones, begging, cajoling, and arm-twisting our passengers to drop everything for departure yet that afternoon. Fortunately everyone was as motivated as we were, and within hours we were airborne toward Minneapolis for the night.

Our strategy worked. Next morning the threatening weather passed well south of us, and we sailed frigid blue skies northwestward from Minneapolis. I'd never flown northern Minnesota skies in wintertime before, and was surprised at how different the terrain appeared than what I was accustomed to just a few hundred miles away.

The land was pancake-flat here, and below us treeless fenced farm fields were frosted by snow into stark geometric relief. Adding both beauty and mystery to the scene was the absence of moving vehicles on the ground, or even signs of plowing. I wondered where the residents might be, imagining them gone away for winter or perhaps provisioned for long stays barricaded at home before a cozy fire. Soon we crossed from Minnesota into North Dakota, and upon reaching Grand Forks followed the Red River north into Manitoba.

Winnipeg, when we arrived, was crowded with eclipse-watchers, but to our surprise almost every store and restaurant in the city was closed. Apparently once-in-a-lifetime February tourists didn't justify opening on a Sunday. I was also intrigued to see electrical outlets at every parking space. Given the severe winters, plug-in engine heaters are mandatory for restarting cars in cold weather there.

After wandering—freezing—through town we finally found shelter and entertainment at the city planetarium's eclipse show. The excitement of our little group was tempered, however, by the weather forecast; clouds might obscure tomorrow's celestial event.

Next morning Winnipeg was indeed overcast. Panic set in as we and thousands of other eclipse enthusiasts contemplated coming all this way for nothing. TV meteorologists recommended points west and north for possible better viewing, encouraging auto travelers westward onto the Trans-Canada highway to Brandon.

To avoid the crowd, we decided to fly north to Gimli, on the shores of Lake Winnipeg. Time was running out, however—the 147-minute eclipse was to begin at 8:36 a.m., with totality occurring mid-morning. If all else failed, we hoped for a clear view from the air above the overcast.

With the weather so cold, we had to preheat the airplane's engine before starting. By the time we did that, obtained takeoff clearance, and topped the clouds, the show had already begun. Hurriedly, we scraped frost from our windows using credit cards. Then, guided by our onboard astronomer, we punched pinholes in index cards to project the still-partial eclipse on scraps of paper.

At this point the skies were still bright enough that, had no one informed us of the event taking place overhead, I doubt anyone would have noticed. We could see clearly on our pinhole projectors, however, that the sun had already been trimmed to a crescent by the moon's overlapping silhouette. Yet none of us could be sure whether the perception of slightly dimmed daylight outside our windows was real or imagined. Amazing the power of the sun, that even when largely obscured it should be so bright.

Fortunately, Gimli was clear when we arrived. We landed to find the airport's ramp peppered with observers, tripod-mounted telescopes, and cameras. Not knowing what to expect, we set up our own equipment, then watched on our pinhole projectors as the moon's silhouette overtook the sun's orb. I think it was Art who discovered that binoculars turned backward could project the show at a larger scale.

Only in the closing seconds before totality did the daylight finally dim dramatically and unnaturally. Then, suddenly, this bright sunny morning turned black. In an instant, stars appeared, birds stopped singing, and temperatures plunged twenty degrees.

Someone discovered that binoculars could project the show at a larger scale than our pinhole projectors.

The crowd gasped in a single note—then was silent. It was as if our chests had been crushed, and as near to the end of the world as I ever hope to experience. Where bright blue had illuminated just a moment before, black night skies now dominated overhead, tinged only by unearthly purplish light ringing the distant horizon.

Overhead in place of the sun, licks of flame ringed a dark circle like snakes on the head of Medusa. With the moon now covering the sun's disk, we were observing solar flares normally invisible in daytime brightness. Millions of miles long, they revealed themselves as streamers of orange fire in a pale white halo. Anyone who doubts the force of the sun in powering our Earth, need only hear what happens when it suddenly disappears. The silence was oppressive.

We didn't see much of Baily's beads—bits of sun glinting from between mountains at the edge of the moon. But while seeking them, I was startled by the sense of daylight racing up from behind us. Before I could comprehend that it was

Art views totality from beyond the propeller.

departure of the moon's shadow, light burst from one edge of
the orb overhead. It was the diamond ring effect, when the
sun first peeks again from behind the moon.

Then, just as suddenly as it had left us, sunlight returned.
Birds sang and the sky turned blue. We were alive! Although
it seemed like eternity, totality had lasted a mere two minutes. Only then did I realize how cold I'd been. Temperatures
when we arrived that morning had hovered around ten
degrees; during the eclipse they dipped below zero. The
thought prodded me to hurry my passengers along and start

the airplane's engine; no preheat was available here and the oil might congeal if allowed to get too cold.

Quickly we gathered our gear and navigated through the still-stunned crowd. The Cessna's engine sputtered to life, and while we waited, shivering, for the airplane to warm up, I turned to Art and shook his hand. Eleven hours in the air had proven a small investment for two minutes I'll remember for a lifetime. I applied power for takeoff, and as our passengers monitored the show's conclusion through their pinhole projectors, I set course southbound toward full-strength sunlight and home.

A Bit of an Expert

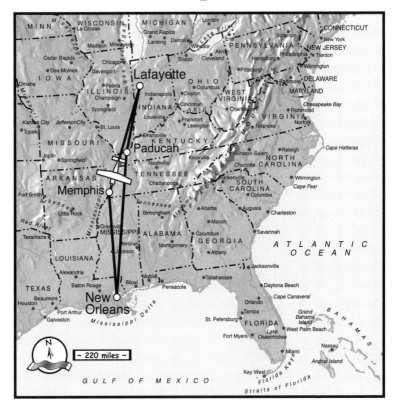

"I'm a bit of an expert on airplanes," said George, when we met for the first time at Purdue Airport. He and his wife, Diana, were joining us for a weekend getaway to New Orleans.

Jean and I had originally planned this vacation with just our close friends, Jan and Bernie. But the only available airplane was a six-place Cessna 210, so we'd invited an additional couple to share the adventure and the expenses.

"How about Diana from work?" Jean had suggested, "I've never met her husband, but she's so nice that I'm sure we'd have fun." George and Diana happily accepted.

We gathered on a Thursday after work, and following introductions, took off into clear skies. Lively conversation soon filled the cabin as the occupants got to know one another. We'd been friends with Jan and Bernie for years; they were interesting and great fun to be around. Diana was reserved but charming.

Based on his surprise at finding our Cessna's wings mounted on top, George was not the aviation expert he'd claimed to be. He seemed like a nice-enough guy, but spoke monotonously and perhaps a bit too much about himself. After enduring a lengthy demonstration of his new camera we learned that George was also "a bit of an expert" on photography. "*I'll* be the official trip photographer," he announced.

Dusk fell as we crossed southern Indiana, and thunderstorms began to appear. Although massive, they were largely isolated. So rather than cause much worry, they entertained us with glowing internal pulses of yellow and orange against a velvet sky.

While the rest of us sat silently engrossed, our noses pressed against the windows, George talked. I don't remember what he spoke about, but the rest of us were too filled with wonder at what lay outside to follow it very closely. I did notice, however, that throughout the incredible sky show, his vaunted camera never left its case.

Reaching Kentucky in starlight, I learned that multiple cloud layers were forming ahead, alarmingly peppered with embedded thunderstorms. Memphis was shrouded by low ceilings but clear of storm cells, so I made that our destination and filed instruments for the approach.

Soon a cloud deck materialized beneath us, bathed like a dance floor in flickering flashes from distant thunderstorms. We joined the instrument approach and descended into nothingness. No amount of encouragement from tiny fluorescent needles can keep your heart from thumping when descending through nighttime clouds. Even George was silent. Bursting from blackness at 800 feet, we found the airport drifting tranquilly ahead of us amid city lights.

We departed Memphis early next morning, and by noon were skimming Lake Pontchartrain on final approach to New Orleans Lakefront Airport. There we were welcomed in typical out-of-towner fashion—bilked on our brief cab ride downtown. "It's right there," said the taxi driver, pointing to the exorbitant "airport fare" displayed on his dash. Only later did we deduce that the posted fare referred to Moisant International, the commercial airport some fifteen miles away.

That small setback was quickly forgotten upon our arrival at the French Quarter. Dixieland music filled the air, while everywhere signs and barkers trumpeted auditory, culinary, and carnal delights. Being in the Crescent City at lunchtime, we got right down to business sampling seafood gumbo and crawfish étouffée. Even George's unsolicited advice in selecting entrees couldn't dull the flavor. That evening we grooved to jazz at Preservation Hall and Pete Fountain's club, and next day toured the city.

For the grand finale of our weekend, the six of us dined Saturday night at a landmark New Orleans restaurant. Attired in formal finery, we sat among crimson bougainvillea blossoms in a century-old courtyard filled with elegant diners. A waiter in coat and tails promptly appeared with the wine list.

"I'll take that," said George. "I'm a bit of an expert on wines." Then he explained how he'd once read a book on the topic and been to a wine-tasting. Next came lengthy dissertations on how to check the bouquet of a fine wine, proper etiquette for tasting samples, and how to return a bad bottle. Mercifully, the waiter soon returned.

Then, as the maitre d' stood elegantly by with the traditional cloth folded over his arm, George brandished the wine list and turned to order. Mustering his most sophisticated voice for everyone to hear, he loudly proclaimed, "We'll take the *bo-jayz'-layz.*"

After a silent instant of disbelief, Jean burst hysterically into laughter, knocking her silverware clattering onto the tile. The rest of us snorted and clutched our sides in futile attempts to suppress our own mirth. I can only guess what nearby highbrow diners thought, enduring five of us laughing until tears rolled from our eyes.

The maitre d' was truly a pro. He never flinched at George's order—nor during our subsequent outburst. There was just the obligatory "Thank you, sir," following which beaujolais indeed appeared at our table. As for George, any concerns about hurting his feelings were fortunately unfounded. Throughout the uproar he never missed a beat on his wine lecture until it came time to pontificate on appetizers. Funny that such a character should deliver our most memorable moment in New Orleans.

Sunday morning after brunch we sailed home through clear skies, refueling at Paducah, Kentucky. We met George only once more after the trip, when he came to our home with Diana to share his photos. Jan and Bernie joined us for the occasion, and Jean prepared a special dinner. After dining, our "official photographer" produced a large, fancy portfolio, and with everyone gathered around to relive our trip, he opened it with great fanfare.

If only George had been smart enough to capture our faces at that moment, he would indeed be a famous photographer today. Inside the portfolio when he opened it there were no New Orleans photos at all—just thirty or so oversized living room portraits taken of himself.

No Fuel
and a Dented Wing

By this time, I'd been flying for eight years. With some 600 hours in my logbook, I figured I had become a valuable repository of aviation knowledge, and was ready to pass it on to others. Over several months of training I earned my commercial and flight instructor certificates, then went shopping for students who could benefit by my talents. As so often happens in life, I soon found that my anticipated teaching expertise was far exceeded by what I still needed to master.

We quickly learn a good deal about human nature, for example, when teaching nervous would-be pilots thousands of feet above the ground. Among my first revelations was that it's not advisable to instruct your own spouse, even if she is the one person gullible enough to become your first student.

I determined this after the first few lessons, when introducing stall recovery procedures. (The term "stall" in airplanes does not refer to engine failure, but rather means that the wing ceases to fly.) Stalls and recovery from them, while trivial for experienced pilots, are not well-loved among flight students. The airplane tends to buck and plunge dramatically until the student masters the technique.

"Pull back gently on the control wheel," I said to Jean, after explaining and demonstrating the procedure. "When you feel the nose fall, just lower it a bit more to regain flying speed."

Gently she pulled back.

"A little bit more . . . " I encouraged. By now the stall warning horn was sounding alarmingly. Jean hesitated, as most pilots do when learning this maneuver.

"Keep pulling back on the wheel," I cajoled, "You're almost there."

"No," replied Jean, through her teeth.

"Seriously," I offered, "just pull back a little more and you'll be done with it."

"No!" said Jean forcefully, looking me square in the eye. "I won't do it!" Astonishment must have been written all over my face. "Here," she said, "You fly."

Nowhere in the flight training handbook does it explain what an instructor should do, when told "no," by a spouse while practicing a maneuver. Although Jean later went on to solo and become skilled as a pilot, we returned home early that day.

Not long after that, I offered my services to my brother, Alan, who had earned his pilot's license before me. He was just completing graduate school and had not flown for some time. With the glow of new instructor wings shining brightly in my mind's eye, I phoned with a generous offer.

"I know you haven't flown for a few years, Alan, and your birthday's coming up. Why not come down for a visit, and I'll give you a flight review for your present? That way you'll be legal and current to fly again."

An enthusiastic private pilot, Alan was delighted at the offer, showing up just a few weeks later for his flight review. On his arm was his new girlfriend, Lesley. There were introductions all around, and the three of us walked out to look over the airplane.

"Are you a pilot?" I asked Lesley.

"No," she replied, "but I've always wanted to go up in a small plane."

"That's great," I said. "Why don't you relax over a soda in the pilot lounge while we do our maneuvers. Then, when we get back, Alan can take you up for a ride."

"Oh no," said Lesley, "I want to go along with you guys now."

"We'll be doing some stalls and steep turns; I . . . "

"Come on!" interrupted Alan, indignantly. "Lesley won't have any problem with the maneuvers. She loves roller coasters. This'll be *nothing* for her."

Clearly this was something they both wanted to do, and after all, it was Alan's birthday gift.

"Well okay," I said. "Just let us know, Lesley, if you become uncomfortable anytime during the flight and want to come back."

Alan preflighted the plane under my supervision; we buckled in and took off. Then we flew to a nearby practice area and reviewed various standard flight maneuvers including stalls, steep turns, and slow flight. I also simulated engine failures by pulling the throttle to idle so my brother could practice emergency landing procedures.

Several times during the flight I looked back at Lesley to see how she was doing. Each time she smiled and waved.

Alan did a credible job, considering how long it had been since he'd flown, and upon completing the air work we cruised back to the airport to practice landings. As we prepared to enter the traffic pattern, I turned to ensure that Lesley's seat belt was secure for landing. Her face was green.

Alan squeaked the landing; we taxied back, and Lesley ran into the ladies' room. I was concerned about ruining their day, but Alan shrugged the whole thing off.

"She'll be fine in a few minutes," he said, laughing. Lesley said the same thing, after re-acclimating to terra firma.

I learned my second flight instructor lesson that day, though much time would pass before I fully appreciated the impact of it. Lesley and Alan continued dating, and eventually went on to get married. That was many years ago, and Alan has not piloted an airplane since, partly because Lesley won't go up in them. Until recently she required coaxing even for airline travel. I'll never know for sure if our lesson that day was the cause of her phobia, but the possibility has resulted in a recurring dull ache whenever I see them. Never again have I taken an inexperienced passenger along on that sort of training flight, no matter how strong the argument.

My most chilling flight instructor lesson occurred about six months later. In the meantime I'd begun polishing my rough edges and had accumulated a pretty good clientele of paying flight students. Despite the challenges, this sort of training is richly rewarding, because most aspiring pilots have dreamed of flying for years. Therefore they are generally enthusiastic, highly motivated, and diligent.

I had also begun soloing flight students. It's hard to overstate the emotions of a new instructor signing off neophytes to pilot an airplane alone for the first time. On one hand, there's the elation of knowing that first solo numbers among the most memorable days of any student's life. As with me and my own primary instructor, Bob, no pilot ever forgets the person who first delivers the key to flight. On the other hand, every instructor carries the burden of knowing that something terrible could happen to his charge, while he or she watches helplessly from the ground.

To the uninitiated, it might seem that the scariest part of teaching people to fly would be preventing them from crashing the plane with you in it. However, if the instructor thinks ahead and remains alert, that's not a particularly big risk. Solo flight, however, carries with it the unpredictable factor of student decision-making. Weakness in flying skills can almost always be overcome, but judgment goes to the very core of a person and is much harder to impact.

This particular lesson I learned the hard way from a young college student, Phil, whom I had successfully guided through initial training and solo. Next I'd introduced him to cross-country flying, the art of navigating from one place to another. Together we flew on several cross-country training missions; then he completed such a flight alone. Phil was now to make a long solo cross-country flight, defined by regulation at the time to include landings at three different airports, at least 100 miles apart.

On the morning of Phil's departure, we met at the airport to review his flight planning and check weather, which proved ideal for the trip. We agreed that at each stop he would refuel the airplane, have his logbook signed, and phone me with a progress report.

He then took off on his flight, after which nothing more was heard from him for the rest of the day. Alarmed when Phil's expected phone calls did not come, I frantically called the airports along his route trying to establish whether he had passed through. No one remembered for sure having seen his airplane, and since none of the airports had control towers, there was no other way to check his progress. Not until late that afternoon did I determine that Phil had ultimately returned to our home airport, quietly parked the airplane, and gone home.

The real excitement didn't begin until the following morning. I had just arrived at the flight school office when an airplane fueler walked in.

"Hey everybody," he announced. "I thought you'd want to know that one of the Cessna 150s out there was almost bone dry—there was hardly a drop of gas left in it."

"Which one?"

"The one with the big dent in the wing."

After everyone rushed outside to look, we instructors urgently investigated who had last flown the plane. It turned out to be Phil, of course, on his long cross-country flight.

The young man initially denied involvement, but since he was the only one who had operated the aircraft on the day in question it didn't take long before the truth came out.

When it did, I contemplated quitting my short career as flight instructor—*forever.*

Phil's mom was paying for his lessons, it turned out, and their arrangement was for the flight school to bill her directly each month for his flying. Now when Phil landed at his first stop and prepared to purchase gasoline, he was confronted by the revelation that if the plane was refueled, he would somehow have to pay for it.

Phil did have a credit card with him, but decided against buying fuel due to concerns that his mother might not reimburse him for charge-card expenses. Of course he was faced with an identical situation at his next stop, too. So he did what only a cartoon character on a hangar bulletin board would do. He took off without refueling—twice.

To properly appreciate this, you should know a little about the aircraft he was flying. The Cessna 150 is a tiny two-seat training plane that carries enough fuel, when topped to the brim, to fly for about 3–1/2 hours before running out. Now, consider that Phil's trip had three flight legs of maybe 110 miles each, in a plane that flies 100 miles per hour.

During the interrogation afterward, I asked Phil if he'd calculated the fuel required to get home before taking off on the last leg of his journey.

"I figured I probably had enough," he said.

Then, as my future flying career flashed before my eyes, he told me about the dent.

"I was taxiing around at one of the airports [he couldn't remember which one], looking for the fuel pump [even though he didn't refuel]. There were some of those big light poles around, and I ran into one with the wing."

"Did you have a mechanic look at it?"

"No, I didn't tell anybody."

This guy had completed one or more flights exceeding 100 miles each in the airplane, with a big dent in the wing, and without refueling.

These events caused me (and my supervisor) to look back at my prior experience with Phil, and to try to determine how I could have predicted his behavior before he'd risked his life, the flight school's airplane, and my future flying career.

Phil had been a lackluster performer from the beginning. He rarely prepared for his lessons ahead of time, so we spent an inordinate amount of time reviewing things he should have learned before coming to the airport. It had been difficult to get him to take seriously the preflight preparation and attention to detail that marks a good pilot. He was also sloppy in every sense of the word, neglecting to bring necessary items for lessons and routinely leaving candy wrappers, pop cans, and other trash in the airplanes. Phil did an adequate job flying the airplane, but he was not inwardly driven to excel.

In short, I'd been uncomfortable with the guy's attitude throughout his training, but since he'd completed all of his maneuvers and training requirements within parameters, I had tolerated his performance as passable. There would be other interesting characters in my future as flight instructor, but never would I allow anything like this to happen again.

JOURNEYMAN
AVIATOR

Coyote Hunting
Small Adventures Under a Big Sky

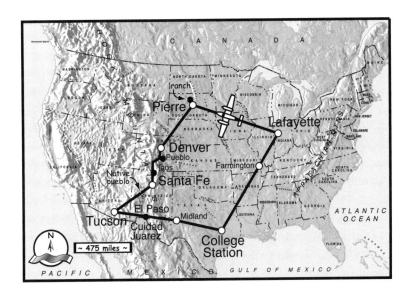

We bumped along a barren South Dakota hillside, three of us in a battered pickup truck, our feet riding a twelve-pack and me squeezed in the middle.

"Ever been coyote hunting before?" asked the driver, Jerry, as he offered me a beer. (They don't pronounce the "e" in "coyote" around these parts.)

"No," I replied, waving off the beer at least until lunchtime. "I've only shot a gun once or twice in my life." I glanced back at the rifle rack.

"Oh, we won't need guns," said Jerry, popping a can for himself. "Larry, didn't you fill Greg in on this?"

"Not yet," replied our other passenger, grinning. "For starters, Greg, we need to finish this beer before going home, so you'd better get to drinking."

Larry was one of my more interesting flight students. A Purdue graduate student, his research involved analyzing forest and crop data collected by satellites and airplanes. While I taught Larry to fly, he enlightened me to Earth's mysteries out the window.

One day after a lesson, the subject of Christmas vacation had come up. "I'm making a road trip out West," Larry told me, "but it's pretty ambitious. I hope there's time to get out of the car."

"Where are you going?"

"First to South Dakota to visit my family," said Larry. "Then on to Denver with my brother."

"From Indiana that *is* a long drive."

"That's just the beginning," he continued. "After Denver I'm heading to Tucson to visit my old girlfriend. And on the way back, I'll stop at Texas A&M in College Station to check out the doctoral program."

"Too bad you won't have your pilot's license by then," I said. "That would make a terrific flying trip." Larry's eyebrows lifted.

"You wouldn't be interested in going along," he asked, "would you?" Within minutes, our charts were spread across the table—the lure of touring the West from a pilot's seat was too much to ignore. At the time I didn't really believe I could go; the trip was over New Year's and there would be family obligations. But when I learned Jean had to work over the holiday, I phoned Larry and volunteered to accompany him. I reserved a Piper Seminole for the journey, a small twin engine plane with four seats.

With paying for such adventures always an issue, we enlisted another grad student to join us. Alex, a young Romanian, seized the opportunity to photograph the U.S.

from the air. (Larry's brother would fill the fourth seat, between South Dakota and Denver.)

We launched from Indiana just after Christmas, and late that afternoon found ourselves approaching Pierre. It was my first visit to South Dakota, and as we descended I was struck by the starkness of the place—treeless rolling hills with hardly a blade of grass, all dominated by the biggest, bluest sky I had ever seen. Add harsh shadows from the low wintertime sun, and for a moment it seemed we were landing on the moon.

"Odd, that there's no snow at this time of year," commented Larry as we taxied in. "I'd heard there was a drought, but had no idea it was this bad." His folks were waiting at the airport to pick us up, and greeted Alex and me like long-lost children.

The warmth of Larry's family to strangers somehow emphasized the remoteness of their ranch northwest of Pierre. Over steak and potatoes that evening, we learned it was sixty miles to the nearest doctor and ninety miles to the nearest public hospital. The community had invested in emergency medical technician training for the local veterinarian's assistant to deal with trauma cases. Yet clearly the remoteness was something Larry's family treasured.

Next morning while wandering near the barn, Alex and I discovered the ranch equivalent of a flight simulator. This "bucking barrel" was saddled and suspended on chains between poles. Alex had just climbed aboard to try it when Larry and his brothers unexpectedly showed up. With three strong men manhandling the lines, the would-be Romanian cowboy soon hit the ground.

It was then that Larry's uncle and his cousin Jerry invited me coyote hunting. Proudly each introduced his hunting dogs, then herded the animals into large wooden boxes built into the beds of two pickup trucks. Subconsciously I noted small doors on the sides of each box, presumably for ventilation. Rope lanyards ran from each trap door to the driver's

Alex rides the ranch equivalent of a flight simulator, while Larry mans the chains.

window of each truck. Jerry and his dad tossed beer into the cabs, and off we drove through isolated rangelands.

"So if we're not using guns," I continued, "how do we get the coyotes?"

"See how my dad is paralleling us on the next ridge?" Jerry gestured toward the other pickup. "Any coyotes along here will run for cover into the dry wash between us. Then . . ."

At that moment, the dogs behind us began yelping wildly.

"There's one now!" said Jerry. Slamming on the brakes, he signaled the other truck. Both drivers tugged rope lanyards, opening trap doors in the boxes mounted in each pickup. Barking hysterically, dogs bounded from both trucks into the dry wash.

"Now what?" I asked. "The dogs corner the coyote and we go get it?"

"Oh, that's not necessary," said Jerry, popping another beer. "There won't be much left of the coyote once the dogs get a hold of it."

That took a moment to sink in. Values here were as different from my own background as that big, big sky was from the cloudy Midwest.

"Let's get out," said Jerry. "Bring your beer." We climbed from the truck onto the barren hillside, then stood 'round with hands in our pockets, discussing the drought. Sweeping their arms across endless bare dirt vistas, Larry and Jerry told of the snow normally covering the grazing land at this time of year, and of green grass normally expected in spring.

"Now you know why the coyotes are so active this year," said Larry. "The predators are as hungry as the cattle." The two complained of hardships afflicting local ranchers, while I tried uncomfortably to ignore shrieking and howling in the wash.

Fortunately for my city-boy sensibilities, the coyote escaped that afternoon, and we spotted no more. The remainder of the day was spent cruising dry grasslands and telling stories. When the beer was gone we turned homeward toward the ranch.

Next day we launched with Larry's brother for Denver, where we celebrated New Year's Eve. Then we were off to Arizona. It was only my second time flying out West, and the first for my companions. En route we thrilled to mountain passes near Pueblo, overflew rugged ski areas near Taos, and lunched in old Spanish Santa Fe.

We had just passed Albuquerque en route to Tucson, when I looked randomly down at remote desert terrain— and then rubbed my eyes. There, atop a lonely mesa in an isolated canyon, appeared an ancient adobe city, seemingly untouched from its primitive origins. Had we somehow passed through a time warp? Entranced, I pointed out the site to my companions, but could find no evidence on my charts as to the community's identity.

"Albuquerque Center," I radioed. "Do you have time for a question?" I knew the controller had been following our progress on radar.

"Affirmative," came the reply. "Go ahead with your question."

"We're looking down at what appears to be an old adobe city. Any idea what that might be?"

"Not offhand," said the controller, "though there are several Native American pueblos in that vicinity."

Unfulfilled, I thanked the controller and returned to my chart. There I noted Acoma Intersection on the Victor-190 airway we were traveling. I knew from past experience that such radio navigation intersections are often named after features on the ground—it proved to be just the clue I needed. Later I'd determine that the mysterious city was named Old Acoma Pueblo, and that due to its spectacular mesa-top location, it was also known as "Sky City."

"I'm going to visit that place some day," I told Larry, filing the location in the back of my mind.

I remember little about our visit to Tucson, except that the beauty of cactus-studded trails helped counter Larry's lack of success in rekindling the dormant romance that had drawn us there. On the flight from Tucson to College Station, however, we experienced another memorable image.

Our route took us over El Paso at 11,500 feet. Anticipating an old Western town from the famous Marty Robbins song, I looked down and instead saw a metropolis sliced in two.

On one side was the modern city of El Paso, with its bustling streets, freeways, and skyscrapers. On the other lay its Mexican neighbor, Juarez, marked by winding dirt paths and hovels. Dividing wealth from poverty in this single large metropolis was just a razor-thin line—the contrast was stunning, especially from such a great altitude. Never have the effects of a political border on the everyday lives of people been more striking to me from the air.

Following a day at Texas A&M University, where Larry was considering further graduate work, we took off toward home. For the first time on our long journey the weather was less than perfect—we flew in the soup all the way back to Indiana. Larry was uneasy piloting in such weather, and in his face I saw my own discomfort with instrument flying just a few years earlier. It takes time to appreciate the intellectual rewards of navigating unseeing over long distances. I'd even learned to relish the damp insides of a cloud, at least when everything was working properly and the windshield wasn't leaking.

Funny, that with the many interesting places and adventures of that long-ago journey, some of my most vivid memories should be of cruising barren grasslands to the music of barking dogs, a cold beer in my hand, and the warm companionship of a South Dakota ranch family. Perhaps it was because those people were so unassumingly part of the land.

I remember that we'd barely arrived back at the ranch after coyote hunting when orange began welling from the horizon, reddening as it conquered the oversized sky. Purple reinforcements appeared overhead, and under colorful assault the ground retreated from dusty brown to black. Then, violet heavens faded to streaks of gray and surrendered to star-studded velvet. Spellbound, Alex and I clicked innumerable pictures of that Western sunset, all while Larry's relatives stood by scratching their heads.

"No need to burn up all that film, fellas," said Larry's uncle when it was over. "Same sunset we get here every night."

Talking Spirits

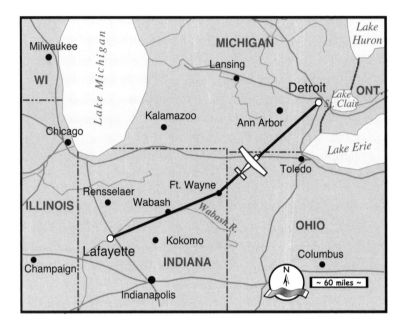

Damp gloom saturated the airport as I tugged the airplane from its hangar. The weather had been dismal for weeks—endless low clouds and that aching dullness of mind and spirit that comes from long periods without sunlight. I was en route to Detroit to attend a weekend ground school, and although not relishing long days in a classroom, the prospect of flying promised rejuvenation. Best of all, this gray morning offered grand prelude to blue skies. With the cloud layer reported as only a few thousand feet thick, I would quickly climb to long-missed sunshine on top.

Eagerly, I plunged after takeoff into the dark underbelly of clouds. With just a thin membrane of plastic and metal between me and outside, the soggy smell of fog instantly enveloped my cockpit. Droplets gathered on forward surfaces of the plane, then streamed back over windshield, struts, and wheel fairings. I noted an isolated rivulet traveling the inner surface of the rear window, soon to drip on my luggage. *At least this Cessna doesn't whistle in the rain like so many others do,* I found myself thinking.

Bang! I jumped as the right side cabin air vent departed its housing and blew before me across the windshield. Trailing behind like the tail of a comet came a spray of mist to moisten my face. These cylindrical pullout vents are a quaint feature of older single-engine Cessnas. Why they should be more prone to such outbursts in clouds I don't know, but invariably that's where they always launch.

The gray of my windshield grew lighter and lighter, until without warning I burst into blue skies above. Sunlight warmed my face and joy filled my heart. A spectrum of just two colors now dominated the world beyond my cockpit— featureless cloud carpet of white trapped by translucent dome of blue.

Leveling at 9,000 feet, I set course for Detroit. I was flying a Cessna 182 on this day, had tried to find someone to go along and share the cost, but without success. Funny how travel begs company, but once on the way alone, the sky's rich solitude fills an aviator's soul with music. With no outside landmarks to show progress toward my destination, my thoughts soon turned inward to the voices assaulting me from my headset.

Voices could be heard coming from everywhere—busy voices, relaxed voices, angry voices, commanding and timid voices. Yet in a sense, all came from nowhere. It's part of the strangeness of removal from the earth. Only a few times during a flight do you see another airplane, yet the seemingly empty sky is filled with people's voices, like the sounds of a city without buildings, or a twilight zone inhabited by spirits. Sometimes the voices are occasional and random, other times they back up in a traffic jam. Voices rush from point to point, then stall circling over imaginary locations that have names but no physical reality.

When driving, you can see the people in other cars, guess their moods, ponder the music they might be listening to, imagine the nature of their destinations. But most of the time they can't be heard.

In the air the phenomenon is reversed. You hear the voices but cannot see the people. There's impatience and there's calm, some are ahead and some are behind. I wonder what the owners of those voices might look like, and try to visualize their faces based on timbre and tone.

This radio call comes from someone calm and strong, a gentleman from the country South. A city voice soon interjects—aggressive, hurried, and impatient. That draws a chuckle from some third spirit; clearly she's at peace with the world and unhurried by the rush. Subtleties of expression identify the spirits who love flying—those who are sociable and those who are loners, and those in the cockpit strictly for business.

Perhaps that's one of the great mysteries of flying; you can distinguish the marks of people, but not the people themselves. On a clear day, phantoms seen from the air in warm sunshine prove the existence of people and their industry. At day's end, long shadows cast shapes of things on the ground, their vertical profiles painted on the terrain in detail unmatched by any artist. The contents of every rail flatcar, the true shape of every roof is distorted onto the earth's surface, while the thing itself is invisible. It reminds me of Plato's world of the ideal.

When flying instruments on a day like this, however, clouds obscure all cues from the ground. Only voices in a headset and the occasional moving instrument needle suggest that other people might exist.

Approaching Detroit, I was returned to the physical world by the one other airplane I would actually see on this flight. It was an ancient DC-3 airliner, gleaming silver 2,000 feet below me against an endless sea of clouds. Desperately, I trolled for the pilot's transmissions amid all the radio chatter. No luck.

This was time travel. Who could say for sure what the date might be beneath those clouds? DC-3s are hardly faster than the Skylane I was flying. Not wanting to lose my transport through time, I followed the path of that shining craft for what seemed like an eternity, straining to keep it in sight. It was like turning up the volume of a favorite song as it fades away. Is something special hidden there, where it disappears? At what instant does it truly end?

I arrived at my hotel after dark that Friday evening. A clean and formal place, it struck me as somewhere I could largely enjoy my upcoming weekend of classes. The registration desk was located in a towering atrium, packed with people. Those in line were cordial and polite as I waited, but something seemed strange, which at first I couldn't identify. Then it struck me—even with so many people around, the place was nearly silent. A faint rustling could be heard of people moving about, and scents of perfume and cologne wafted gently by. But there were no voices.

"Is there a convention going on?" I asked the desk clerk when I reached the front of the line.

"Yes," she said. "It's some sort of meeting of the hearing-impaired." Upon closer examination I then recognized hand signing between people in the room. Given the quietness of the lobby, I cheered myself with the thought that if I must study in a convention hotel, this was the place to be and still get some work done.

There were surprises later that evening, however, when I climbed into bed. My neighbors on both sides had guests, sharing boisterous conversation over televisions turned up loud. Then the clinking of glasses was enlivened by crashing bottles. More and more, this convention sounded like a party crowd, as ultimately my neighbors entertained visitors throughout the night. Several times I thought my door was being knocked down when revelers mistakenly pummelled mine in lieu of my neighbors'.

The following night I transferred to another room, but the experience was no better, perhaps even worse. I hardly slept at all. When time came to check out after completing classes on Sunday, I stumbled to the registration desk, prepared to share woes for the second time with the proprietor. The clerk noticed my blackened eyes long before I reached him.

"I see that you, too, are a victim of the Deaf Bowlers' Convention," he said, offering a discount on my room. "We're still cleaning up the ballroom this morning. At least things calmed down a little once we got the strippers out of there last night."

I dragged myself to the hotel restaurant, there to load up on coffee for the flight home. The place was packed, and after finally finding a seat I noticed a woman sitting quietly near me in the corner. She was signing with her hands, apparently to no one in particular. I scanned the busy restaurant, trying to determine who, if anyone, might be engaged in silent conversation with her. No one.

I sipped my coffee, ate breakfast, and rose to pay the bill. Only then, at the far corner of the restaurant, did I observe a solitary man, signing. I looked back at the woman. The two were having a private conversation, spanning sixty feet or more. No one else appeared to have even noticed. The potential for intrigue was so delicious that I found myself wishing I could sign to others across the room myself.

Armed with a fresh perspective on voices to ponder while flying home, I paid my bill and headed for the airport.

Powerless
Soaring with Hawks

"The box," a Schweizer 2–22.

"Man, are we close to that airplane," said Larry, as we rolled down the runway at the end of a towrope. Most pilots spend their lives trying to distance themselves from other airplanes, so trailing this close behind is an eye-opener the first time they experience it.

"We may not be able to stay up for long," I observed to Larry. "With that thin bit of cloud cover shrouding the sun, there won't be much lift today."

"That's okay," he replied, "I'm just thrilled to be here."

Ever since I'd described soaring on our trip West, Larry had been eager to try it. But in this part of the country flying gliders is a warm weather activity. Six months had passed before a conjunction of weather, ground crew, and tow pilot allowed me to invite him for a flight.

Gliders compare to powered airplanes as sailboats do to speedboats. (For that reason, today's high-performance gliders are commonly called sailplanes.) Although a few models are self-launching "motorgliders," most have no engines and are towed skyward by powered airplanes, winches, or automobiles.

Together Larry and I had pulled the Blanik sailplane from its hangar. Then I'd introduced him to Buck, pilot of the Piper Super Cub that would tow us aloft.

"You may not be up for long with those high cirrus clouds blocking the sun," Buck had told us. "I'll drop you near the smokestack, then stick around for awhile in case you want to go up again." I'd then buckled Larry into the front cockpit and adjusted his rudder pedals.

"Let me borrow your hat," I said. Surprised, Larry watched me cut the button off the top with my pocket knife.

"Why are you doing that?" he asked.

"That button could make a bad impression on you," I replied, "if you bump your head on the canopy in turbulence."

Soon we were rolling down the runway, assisted by a volunteer running our wing until we approached takeoff speed. On climbout I demonstrated use of the rudder to keep our Blanik centered behind the towplane.

"Use the yaw string to keep the nose straight," I said, referring to a bright yarn scrap taped to the canopy. "Here, you try it." Flying tow is the hardest thing to learn in gliders. When we reached the agreed-upon altitude of 2,000 feet, I yanked the red rope release. Our tow pilot Buck banked left, while we peeled right.

"Wow!" said Larry, as we slowed to forty miles per hour and wind noise dropped off to nothing. "How long can we stay up here?"

"Depends," I said. "On a good day we could fly forever, but with those thin cirrus clouds diluting the sun, we'll be lucky to get fifteen or twenty minutes." We watched Buck spiral down in the Super Cub and drop the tow rope before landing.

"Buck's a bit of a legend around here," I said. "He flew a single-seat Schweizer 1–26 from here all the way to St. Louis."

"Lafayette to St. Louis nonstop in a glider? That must be 200 miles."

"Sounds about right—took him six hours, I understand."

"How could he stay up for so long?"

"If only this were a better soaring day, I'd show you." Quietly we coasted through air smooth as glass. Pointing out a 200-foot-per-minute descent on our variometer (sensitive vertical-speed indicator), I directed Larry toward a nearby smokestack. "Hope you don't mind the smell of soybeans," I said. "Maybe we can find some lift over the factory parking lot."

You might logically wonder how engineless aircraft can stay aloft, much less climb. The simple answer is that in calm air, they cannot. On overcast days with stable air, gliders simply coast casually to the ground. Atmospheric turmoil is required for sailplanes to gain altitude and fly for extended periods of time. In mountainous terrain, for example, wind flows over ridges like water over stones in a brook. Glider pilots find lift along the upwind side of each ridge, or in mountain waves that form downwind.

In flat country like northern Indiana, lift results only from unequal heating of the air. This occurs because sunlight heats not the atmosphere, but rather the ground beneath it, which in turn warms the air. Surfaces like asphalt and dry dirt fields radiate a great deal of heat into the air, while forests, lakes, and green fields absorb it. As a result, columns of air rise from warm surfaces, while all around them cooler air sinks. Sunlight is the engine that powers it all, and therefore our glider.

"Those rising columns of air are our soaring tickets," I said to Larry. "We call them 'thermals.' Another way to spot them is on otherwise clear days when cumulus clouds form on top."

"You mean like that one, Greg?" Before I could look, I sensed the left wing rise ever so slightly.

"I've got the controls!" I said, lowering half flaps and banking sharply into a steep left turn.

"What's happening?"

"That rising wing hints of a thermal. They're cylindrical in shape, and I'm turning to center us in one. Look at the variometer." The instrument for the first time showed a climb instead of a descent. With a "whoosh" our stomachs dropped and we began rising like an elevator.

"Greg, we're climbing at 1,500 feet per minute—without an engine!"

Surprised at the thermal's strength on such a day, I looked up. The cirrus layer had unexpectedly retreated from the sun, replaced instead by the scattered cumulus clouds that mark a perfect soaring day.

"Each cloud caps a thermal," I said, "Try to picture where the thermal originates for each cloud—think of it as a balloon on a string."

"This cloud above us must come from the parking lot," shouted Larry, elated. "How high can we go?"

"To wherever the lift runs out, short of the clouds themselves. Then we make a beeline to the next thermal and climb again. That's how Buck made St. Louis. 'Cloud streets,' we call 'em, when they're lined up properly."

"You mean Buck circled in steep turns like this for hours on end?"

"That's right. Altitude is traded for distance cruising from one thermal to another through areas of 'sink.' Then you must climb again by thermaling. In flat country like this, thermals are the only way for sailplanes to climb."

"What if you can't find another thermal?"

"Then you land in a field, haul out the glider, and try again another day. It happens less often than you might expect."

"How did Buck get back from St. Louis?"

"That's a little less glamorous. His wife followed him by car, and they trailered the glider back."

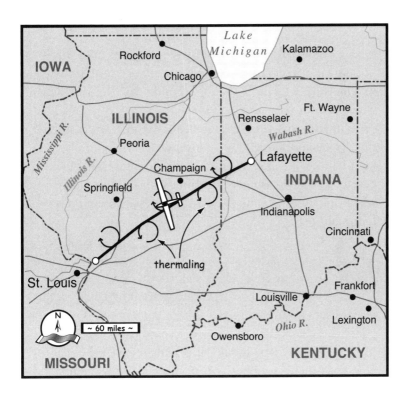

Soon all was silent except for the gentle whistling of cabin vents, whoosh-and-wheeze upon entering each new thermal, and an occasional few words when switching off on the controls. Each of us retreated to private thoughts in the rich company of sun and deep blue sky.

Jean and I had earned our glider ratings two years earlier, in an aging fabric-covered Schweizer 2–22 marked with red lightning bolts. Hangars being in short supply, the beast resided in only half a hangar stall, meaning the wing had to be removed at the end of each flying day and reattached before the next flight.

While piloting the machine, we soon saw the irony of those lightning bolts. The glider's red-line "never-exceed speed" was a leisurely ninety miles per hour, though none of us would dare fly it anywhere near that fast. Official stall speed was only thirty-four with two occupants, and thirty-one solo. Since stall speed diminishes with decreasing aircraft weight, my petite wife claimed honors for slowest flight while soloing.

Our authoritarian flight instructor, George, was skeptical that Jean could actually fly as slow as twenty-eight miles per hour without stalling. She rubbed it in for months, knowing he had no way to disprove her claims without riding along—which, of course, would increase aircraft weight and, therefore, stall speed.

Although the 2–22 was notorious for its poor glide performance—George had nicknamed it "the box"—it handled docilely and was a good trainer. Better yet, those who learned to find lift in that primitive machine could climb like rockets in anything else. Like a homely old dog, that glider had character, and we soon learned to love it.

The Blanik I flew today with Larry, on the other hand, was constructed entirely of metal and fully aerobatic. Although heavy on the controls, it was comfortable and far more capable as a soaring machine.

"Look!" said Larry, interrupting my thoughts. "Off our wing!" Three hawks banked shoulder-to-shoulder with us, sharing the same column of rising air. "Incredible—to think of birds flying formation with us!"

Jean's flight instructor was skeptical that she could fly at twenty-eight miles per hour without stalling.

You never know what effect any given flight will have on your passengers. Years later, after Larry took a position at the University of Alaska, we reminisced about this particular flight.

"When taking graduate students up into the Tundra," he told me, "we often see sandhill cranes spiraling overhead in thermals. Other birds will spot them from as much as twenty miles away, and fly over to join them. As I explain this to my students, it always comes back to me, thermaling in the company of hawks over a little airstrip in Lafayette, Indiana."

In my memory, that wonderful, lazy afternoon soared on forever. We climbed, swooped, and then climbed again. Not until bladders pressured us did we consider coming down. Gently I applied spoilers to kill lift over the wings, but even when fully extended they showed no effect in bringing us down. Only when I kicked the rudder opposite our direction of turn and sideslipped did we finally descend from our rightful place with the birds. We landed to discover the tow-plane lodged in its berth, the hangar doors closed, and Buck long gone.

"I had no idea we were up for so long," said Larry, checking his watch after climbing out. Unwittingly, we'd flown for 3-1/2 hours, climbing repeatedly as high as 6,400 feet. Not bad for an engineless aircraft over flat Indiana farm fields. This day our flying carpet had transported us far from Earth, yet covered no physical distance in the process. Our destination had been simply the pure joy of flight itself.

"What do I owe you?" asked Larry as we manhandled the ancient hangar doors.

"Two dollars and fifty cents," I replied.

"Seriously, Greg, I agreed to pay for half, and to me this flight was worth every penny of whatever it cost."

"That is half, Larry."

At that time our soaring club charged $2.50 per thousand vertical feet to tow the glider aloft, with no hourly rental rate. We'd released from the towplane at 2,000 feet above ground, for a total bill of $5. Memorable as that flight was, at my share of 71¢ an hour it was also the cheapest of my life. Larry invested a bit more than that, however. He insisted on buying the burgers on our way home.

Over the River and
Through the Woods . . .

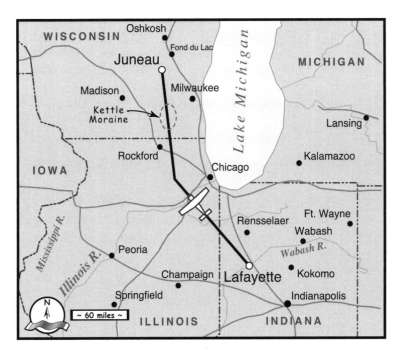

We'd always joined my in-laws for Thanksgiving. The whole family would be there again this year, Jean's folks, her brothers and sister, uncles and cousins. But behind the scenes, Jean's paternal grandmother had always pummeled us with her gravelly voice, "When are you coming to *my* house for Thanksgiving?" Family politics be dashed, this year we were finally doing it, flying up to Grandma and Grandpa's to celebrate an old-fashioned holiday.

They were everything grandparents should be, Shorty and Lulu, living in a big old house in the small Wisconsin town of Juneau. The two were loving but just a little bit tough, opinionated but accepting. When I was new to the family and an outsider, they'd welcomed me with open arms, believing so much in their granddaughter that I got to be their grandkid too.

By now Jean and I had two young children, Hannis and Austin. We loaded our little boys into the flying club 172, and took off from Lafayette for the glacier-cut Kettle Moraine of central Wisconsin. It was unusually warm for November, and our little family bounced among clouds over Indiana farmlands, and then above Chicago suburbs teeming with holiday traffic.

"I need a sack!" cried our older son, Hannis, urgently and unexpectedly. We looked back in alarm. Never before had either boy become sick in the air. Frantically, we searched the plane for relief sacks, probing around cooler and home-made pies to no avail. Finally, Jean requisitioned a retired cookie bag from the trash. But Hannis lingered in opening it.

"C'mon," I said, fearing "regurgitative" cockpit disaster, "Hold the bag to your face!" Slowly, our young son opened the bag, and peered inside.

"Very funny!" he said, grimacing. Jean and I looked at one another, confused.

"I want a snack!" repeated Hannis. Laughter displaced in-flight emergency as we fished for more goodies.

It was now late afternoon over southern Wisconsin, and the shadows of glacier-sculpted contours transcended human boundaries of farms and dairylands below. From the ground the Kettle Moraine appears like no more than rolling hills, but from the air its true heritage becomes apparent. You can see and almost feel where primeval ice carved parallel furrows through the soil. Over them flows farmland like a tentative veneer. From the air in places like this, human efforts seem no more than appliqué on Mother Earth.

There's comfort in that. We peered ahead through dimming light for Juneau's ancient brick water tower.

Grandpa waited in his old Pontiac when we touched down. "I saw you fly over," he said, dentures clicking through an expansive smile as he shook my hand. He admired our sky-blue steed, then chauffeured us to the smells of food baking in a big old warm house with fallen leaves in the yard on a cold autumn evening.

Next day we ate turkey and Syrian kibbe, cranberries and pie. In the meantime, rain began in the manner so appropriate for holidays and gradually changed to sleet and then snow, all while we gathered warm and laughing in Grandma's bright kitchen.

Grandpa regaled us with stories of a past incomprehensible within the short span of our overlapping lifetimes—growing up on a farm with horse-drawn vehicles.

"I remember the first airplane I ever saw," he said, "a barnstormer that landed over by Mayville." He paused for a bite of pie. "And the first car, too, a Badger made right here in Wisconsin." He'd garnered a ride from its owner one day, leading to celebrity among school friends.

Grandpa told, too, of his days as a "speed cop," riding hand-shift Harleys on gravel county roads, and of courting Grandma up at Fond du Lac in his Model T. Proudly, Grandma produced scrap albums detailing her husband's adventures as Dodge County Sheriff in the thirties. Yellowing newspaper clippings boasted of periodic prostitution crackdowns—"to make the politicians look like they were doing something," interjected Grandpa—and a memorable Montana train excursion to collect a fugitive.

Grandpa was a great storyteller, and although others sometimes joked about his reminiscing, I never grew tired of it. But even Jean tuned in when Grandpa told of putting her uncle "in the pen" during his days as sheriff.

Grandpa told of his days as a "speed cop," riding hand-shift Harleys on gravel county roads (1926 photo).

"You arrested one of Mom's brothers?" she asked with surprise.

"He was just a teenager at the time," said Grandpa, "got in with a bad crowd. There was an armed robbery in a bar, when someone started shooting and a man died. Talk was that Capone might have been involved—that he hired a bunch of naive kids to pull off the heist."

Dark images of that long-ago night flooded my mind, but were soon displaced by something even tougher to fathom. I tried to imagine the scene when Grandpa and Grandma later met their son's fiancée, only to realize she was the sister of someone Grandpa had jailed for a barroom shooting. Jean had the guts to ask about that, though neither of us dared press further about her uncle's specific role in the crime.

"Your uncle was much older than your mother, Jeannie," said Grandpa. "She was just a little girl when it happened. So when your Dad brought your Mom home to meet us, Grandma and I just tried to remember that plenty of young people make mistakes. I won't say it was easy at the time, but after he was released your uncle turned out to be a good man, when everything was said and done with." I noted that Grandpa had waited for Grandma to leave the room, before telling this particular story.

Then, Grandpa changed the subject to his usual questions about my "Blitzen Benz," and how it was running. I had an old Mercedes diesel car at the time, and he always delighted in asking about it. Not until years later did I learn that "Blitzen Benz" wasn't just some grandfatherly name he'd made up, but rather a famous racing car from the early days of motoring.

"You kids aren't going home tomorrow," called Grandma with feigned disappointment from the kitchen window. "It's snowing out there to beat the dickens!" Sure enough, an Arctic storm was driving in from the plains. But there are worse places to get stuck than at Grandma's on Thanksgiving weekend. We slept soundly and happy that night, in the big old bed with homemade quilts upstairs in the spare bedroom.

Next morning dawned blizzardy with eighteen inches of snow on the ground. Flight service said it would end before noon so Jean and I built a snowman with the boys while Grandpa watched from the porch. Then as the sun peeked tentatively through the clouds, we packed our bags and bundled off to the airport. ("Take some turkey!" insisted Grandma.)

Skies were cobalt when we got there—that deep, dark blue seen only after a snowstorm—and at the airport office sat a man in red flannel shirt, sipping coffee. Unbroken white stretched out the window.

"The runways haven't been plowed?" I asked, disappointed.

"No problem," he replied, "I'll call the county and they'll take care of it." Being a city kid I was astonished when sure enough, a plow materialized on the runway fifteen minutes later. Before we'd even finished scraping snow and ice off the airplane, the runway was clear. So was a short stretch of taxiway for getting there.

Tears filled Grandpa's blue eyes as we loaded the kids and said our goodbyes; we started the engine, and taxied for takeoff. It was slippery, as the original rain had frozen under the snow and covered the ground with glare ice. A spot rough with snow served for engine run-up, but at the end of the runway I couldn't turn around for takeoff—every time I added power we skidded closer to the snowbanks.

So I shut the plane down right there at the end of the runway, and with the two little boys sleeping bundled in blankets in the back seat, Jean and I slithered it around manually. Then we cranked up the engine, and departed skyward from our one-and-only most special Thanksgiving ever at Grandma and Grandpa's house in Juneau, Wisconsin.

Grandpa could still be seen at his Pontiac when we took off, waving and bundled against the wind in his trademark Fedora hat, so I waggled the wings goodbye and turned toward home over that now long-gone brick water tower. Some special flights you get to make just once in life.

Oh, if only we could go back . . .

Happy Feelings of Progress

Among the most challenging and yet rewarding aspects of piloting is that you rarely feel total and lasting mastery of it. You might feel competent, of course, but despite each acquired degree of skill, new challenges constantly present themselves. Therefore the healthiest pilot attitude is preparedness, rather than cockiness. The rare souls who consider themselves masters of the air are usually setting themselves up for a fall.

Over time you learn that by planning ahead, imagining the worst that could happen and anticipating it, safety can be attained. Rarely do you hear seasoned pilots bragging about their accomplishments. More often their stories are about situations that almost didn't work out. The result is a peculiar combination of confidence and humility among experienced aviators.

This is such a gradual and imperceptible learning process that it's hard to measure your own growth as a pilot. Very slowly you metamorphose from bumbling student to hopeful novice to cautious journeyman to confident captain. Feedback comes rarely, if ever, and when it does, the most meaningful is usually delivered by your passengers.

It was Baraboo, Wisconsin, temperature near zero. Bitterly cold winds drove snow down my neck at thirty miles per hour.

Jean and I were preparing to return home after a wedding, and although the weather was flyable, I could see immediately that conditions would make preflighting the airplane miserable. Quickly we loaded our bags into the luggage compartment; then Jean trekked hunched against the wind across the ramp for a final pit stop.

"Hang out inside and stay warm!" I yelled over the gale. "I'll come get you when we're ready to go." I then ordered an engine preheat due to the low temperatures, and while that frigid hunk of metal slowly warmed, began my deliberate progress around the vehicle.

Removing frost from an airplane is always time-consuming, especially on a top-wing Cessna, but it's something that must be done. Even the slightest coating of frost, ice, or snow on an airplane can degrade its ability to fly. I was well along with my scraping before realizing that the quart of oil I'd planned for the engine should be added immediately—with the container cold from sitting outside, the molasses-like oil could take twenty minutes to pour.

Interesting how a process that seems so trivial on a warm sunny day becomes such an ordeal on a lousy one. After what seemed like hours, I got the frost and snow removed from the wings, the oil installed, and the prop pulled through to limber the engine. The preheat unit was weak and the cold wind so strong that I still questioned whether the engine would start anytime before spring. Although still cool to the touch, the engine seemed as warm as it would get. I disconnected the preheater.

Concerned that all hope of starting would blow away in the wind, I sprinted across the ramp to the office. There I sipped hot coffee while quickly paying the bill.

"Mighty cold out there," said one of several local pilots hangar-flying at the coffeemaker.

"You bet!" I replied, rubbing numb hands together.

"Windy, too," volunteered another. He shook my hand as Jean and I braced to go out the door. "You folks have a safe trip."

To my relief the engine turned over easily, and after a bit of sputtering and stuttering, burst to life. Setting the throttle at idle to allow warm up, I removed my gloves and fumbled with numb fingers for my charts.

"Ooh!" said Jean, sharply, "These headsets are cold!" Our flight gear had chilled in the cockpit all weekend.

"Seemed like nice guys there in the office," I said, adding power to taxi toward the runway.

"Well, they were okay," she answered hesitantly.

"What do you mean?" I asked. "Did someone give you trouble?"

"Actually, they were kind of annoying, making fun of you."

"Really, Jean? Why?"

"Oh, they were watching you out the window, and saying stuff like, 'I can't believe that guy is doing such a careful preflight on a day like this.'"

"Did you say anything?" I asked, surprised that any sane pilot would question thorough preparation before flying, especially given the frigid weather.

"Yup," said Jean. "I told them, 'Listen, my husband and I have flown safely all over the country in every kind of weather, and it's all because he exercises that kind of thoroughness no matter what the conditions.'"

"What did they say?" I asked.

"Oh, they were pretty quiet after that."

Jean gave me a marvelous gift that day, by defending me against my detractors and then telling me about it. Looking back at those warm coffeepot handshakes, I could see the effect of her words on their attitudes far beyond anything I might have said myself. More important was the effect on my own attitude.

It was a relief to learn that my acquired thoroughness as a pilot was not an annoyance to others, as I'd feared it might be, but rather something passengers could admire in me. Now I understood why Jean had flown unperturbed with me through so many challenging situations. Such words could never be stronger, I suppose, than when coming from your own spouse.

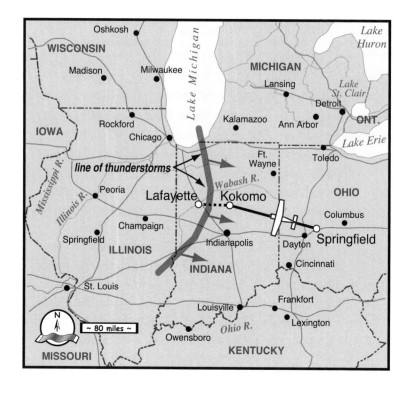

Another experience several months later reinforced these happy feelings of progress. I had flown with my business partner, Ron, and an employee to meet with a client in Ohio. We were now on our way home to Lafayette.

Ron was a serious and creative individual, deeply thoughtful, and among the smartest people I've ever met. I respected him tremendously. He was in the process of earning his own private pilot certificate, and had flown many hours with me on business. Like Jean, Ron had experienced many aviation weather challenges at my side, and although occasionally asking my reasons for doing things, never expressed any concerns about riding with me.

On this particular day we had just crossed into Indiana from Ohio, when we learned of developing thunderstorms obstructing our route to Lafayette. While proceeding across Indiana, I repeatedly queried weather briefers and air traffic controllers as to the best way around or through this line of thunderstorms. After tackling the problem from every possible angle, I lost hope of finding a safe way past the weather.

"We'll land at Kokomo," I told my passengers with some disappointment, "and wait until the thunderstorms either pass or dissipate."

Once on the ground, Ron took me aside to talk. Although a quiet and private fellow, this was not his normal manner. I was alarmed that perhaps I had done something wrong.

"Greg," he said, almost gravely, "I want to tell you something that's been bothering me. I've always felt you were an excellent pilot, but sometimes feared that you might be a risk-taker. Whenever weather has threatened our trips, you seemed to rationalize a way to proceed anyway. Frankly, it's made me nervous more than once."

He looked me straight in the eye.

"Today, for the first time ever," he continued, "I saw you decide that it was not safe to proceed, and land instead. I cannot express how much that increases my respect for you, and my confidence in you as a pilot. You do have limits and are not afraid to act on them. Knowing you can indeed say 'no,' I can now believe in you when you say 'let's continue.' Thanks to your actions today, I doubt I'll ever fear riding with you again."

An old saw among aviators is that passengers judge pilots based exclusively on landings. "Fly them skillfully through life-threatening situations," says common wisdom, "but all they'll notice is whether or not you make a smooth landing."

While that may sometimes be true, these two small incidents taught me that perceptive passengers do indeed notice more than landings. More importantly, I learned that the respect of a pilot's passengers is earned through caution rather than daring. That lesson would serve me well on flights to come.

Bowling Alley Hot Dogs

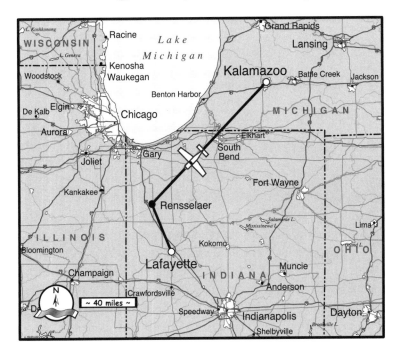

By now, flight instructing offered some of my most rewarding flying. Not only did I enjoy introducing others to the skies, but my own piloting skills benefited in the process. Opportunities arose to master many different types of airplanes, and after journeying with Larry to South Dakota and Arizona, I found myself increasingly in demand to travel with my students. Best of all, in teaching others to fly I met many interesting and colorful characters.

So far there had been relatively few scares while teaching. Most students respond predictably to various flight situations, I'd quickly discovered. I'd also found that similar errors can be expected of most students when learning any given maneuver. It helps that in airplanes, mistakes rarely happen fast enough to require hair-trigger response. The majority of flight training is done far from the ground, meaning that instructors have the luxury of time when correcting mistakes. (For this reason, I'd much rather teach in airplanes than cars.)

Nasty surprises do sometimes occur, however, when students do something dangerously unpredictable near the ground, or in a few other critical situations.

One of my best flight students, for example, quit the controls during a night touch-and-go landing, on a narrow runway edged by snow banks. I'll never know why the otherwise confident student chose that moment to throw up his hands and stop flying, but in any case I grabbed the wheel barely in time to avoid clipping a wing on a snow bank.

Then there was the time during a flight review, when an older pilot released the rudder while practicing power-on stalls in a Cessna 210. Instantly we entered one of the most vicious spins I've ever encountered, putting me for the second time of my career into test pilot territory. Fortunately I was able to recover uneventfully.

A surprising number of emergencies are pilot-induced, like the time I was instructing an experienced pilot in the traffic pattern at Fort Wayne. We had flown there on a night training mission, and after grabbing a bite to eat, took off again to practice landings. Barely had my student leveled the plane in the traffic pattern when a loud and vicious banging began, suggesting that the plane was either falling apart or someone was trying to get in the door. So resonant was this noise that we could feel it through our seats, as well as hear it.

I advised the control tower of our problem, and asked permission to circle for a few minutes while we tried to figure out what was wrong. This being a retractable gear airplane, I didn't want to attempt landing without knowing whether all three wheels were extended. At the same time, we had no urge to linger aloft, in case either a failing engine or some structural problem with the airplane was causing the noise.

While taking turns at the controls, the two of us tried frantically to identify the source of the banging, but without success. All we could determine was that the noise diminished whenever we slowed the airplane. After a low pass in front of the tower to confirm that the landing gear was down —you can't see the nosewheel from the cockpit on this model —we were cleared to land. We touched down uneventfully, at which time the banging stopped immediately.

We taxied off the runway to where emergency vehicles were waiting, and shut down the engine. There, upon opening the door, I discovered the source of the noise that had so alarmed us. Hanging out the bottom of my cabin door lay the shredded sleeve of my new windbreaker, which Jean had bought me just the week before for Christmas. Inadvertently I had closed the door on the coat, leaving the sleeve dangling outside to slap rapidly against the fuselage in the slipstream. Similar distractions sometimes result from seatbelt straps being closed in an airplane door, but this had been so much louder that I never made the connection. We secured the coat in the back seat and took off for Lafayette. The worst aftermath of this scare came at home, when Jean saw the remains of my new Christmas coat.

One of my more colorful flight students owned a pristine Piper Cherokee, low-wing counterpart of the Cessna 172. John, a would-be fighter pilot, actually wore a military flight suit and flying gloves to instrument flying lessons in his small single engine airplane. Despite the unusual outfit (or perhaps because of it), John proved to be an outstanding student of blind flying. He arrived thoroughly prepared for each lesson and exhibited exceptional powers of concentration, making for performance far better than average in this difficult art.

John was a neatness and organization fanatic well beyond the actual flying of the plane. On any given Saturday he could be found at the airport vacuuming the newly upholstered interior of his Cherokee, touching up minuscule paint imperfections, and polishing microscopic bugs from the wing leading edge. This was a man who invested much of every weekend scrubbing seams and rivets on the underbelly of his airplane with a toothbrush, and who disassembled the instrument panel to scour joints and corners where invisible bits of grime might accumulate.

John and I breezed through his instrument training with few setbacks, and I found myself consistently impressed by his rock-steady performance under the training hood. No disturbance or simulated emergency I could contrive succeeded in distracting him. Clearly, if the guy was going to dress like a military pilot, he also intended to fly like one; certainly I couldn't fault him for that.

A cross-country lesson is required of every training instrument pilot, and when time came for John to do that, we decided to go somewhere special. We waited for a good cloudy instrument-flying day, loaded up the Piper's back seat with John's teenaged son and his son's friend, and took off for Kalamazoo, Michigan, to visit the warplanes museum on the field.

The first leg of our flight went well. John piloted us through clouds the whole way, and at Kalamazoo made the first of three instrument approaches required on this lesson. As usual, he was organized, thorough, and unflappable throughout the trip. Upon landing, the four of us spent several enjoyable hours at the airplane museum. Then we headed across the street to consume hot dogs at a nearby bowling alley before taking off for home.

The weather had deteriorated during our visit, so upon departing Kalamazoo we endured not only immersion in clouds, but a wet and bumpy ride as well. Rain now assaulted our diminutive craft, and the cloud vapor obscuring our windows oscillated wildly between shades of darkness and daylight. It was the perfect training environment for a soon-to-be all-weather aviator, and my prize student met the challenge admirably by maintaining course and altitude. Unlike many new instrument pilots under such difficult conditions, John even seemed to be enjoying himself. He shot his second required instrument approach at Rensselaer, then turned us southward toward Lafayette and home.

Nearing Purdue Airport, we were cleared for our third and final approach through the clouds for landing. As usual, John had organized his charts well in advance. He studied them yet again (John always pored over likely approaches before coming to the airport) and tuned the radios as required.

This particular approach is different than the instrument landing system (ILS) described earlier, in that there is no glideslope leading the pilot down a slanted path to the runway. Rather, John was to descend a fixed course in a stairstep manner, first to "stepdown altitude," and then to "minimum descent altitude" where we would stay until the airport hopefully came into sight.

Using flawless technique, John made the appropriate radio report and began our descent toward the stepdown altitude. We would soon be home. I put my hands behind my head and relaxed, taking seemingly well-deserved pride in my student's excellent flying, and in my own expert instructing.

We were just a few hundred feet above the stepdown altitude, descending rapidly through the clouds and ready to begin level-off, when the only disaster that could possibly phase my unflappable flight student occurred.

I guess the combination of greasy bowling-alley hot dogs and two hours of bumping around in the soup hadn't done much for the two forgotten teens in the back seat. First one boy and then the other began vomiting violently on the new upholstery.

When John realized what was happening, he turned suddenly around and began yelling at the boys. Gripping the control wheel as he turned, he unknowingly rolled the plane into a steep bank, veering our plane off course and accelerating our descent. Down we plunged.

By the time I'd untangled my hands from behind my head and lunged for the controls, we were plummeting obliquely through our stepdown altitude toward the ground. Probably it took only seconds to regain control and climb back on course, but to me the process took an eternity—grab the control wheel, mentally process our flight attitude from the instruments, level the wings, raise the nose, apply power, climb, turn, level off, intercept course. Since we were still enveloped by clouds, John in his distraction didn't even realize what was happening.

Once I safely reestablished our plane on course, emotion and logic began battling for my attention. *The only thing scarier than seeing yourself plummet toward the ground,* I found myself thinking, *is plummeting toward ground you cannot see.* Rationally, I knew we'd approached nowhere near the ground, but emotionally, I'd been within millimeters of it. *How close were we?* Certainly it would have taken less than a minute to get there, but that would still be plenty of time to recover. *Who among parents has not yelled at their kids for a full minute?* I looked at my student, who was still focused on events in the back seat, then banished further speculation from my mind.

Twice I urged John to retake the controls, but the man was so flustered that I elected to complete the flight myself.

Throughout the approach, landing, and taxi to the ramp, he continued berating the boys and attempting to clean up the mess.

Not until we shut off the engine and got out, did John calm down enough to admit that he shouldn't have allowed himself to be distracted from flying the plane.

"What would have happened had you been alone with the boys?" I asked.

Silent for a moment, John then replied somberly, "I don't know." He paused again. "Good thing you were there, I guess." After gradually reestablishing communication, we talked long and hard about what had happened.

In visual flying conditions, John would have noticed immediately the steep turn he'd caused and corrected it, but in clouds even the most experienced pilot must rely on instruments to control the airplane's attitude. That's why breaking concentration even for a moment can be deadly when flying instruments.

Then there's the fact that sudden head movements cause vertigo, as I had so effectively learned those many years before when flying motorcycle parts home in the snow. John's sudden turn to face the boys had added to his disorientation. Once losing control, odds do not favor the pilot in regaining it.

It's provocative to consider how many accidents happen due to minor distractions like a flapping coat, an open door, or a sick passenger. Again I was reminded that pilots who live to learn from their errors, rarely make the same mistakes again. After overcoming the trauma of such lessons, I was always pleased that the student experienced them for the first time with an instructor on board, even if the experience was stressful for me.

"Aren't you glad this happened?" I asked John, after we'd relived the incident from every possible angle.

"Yeah," he replied hesitantly. "I guess I'm glad it happened." His voice strengthened. "I'll certainly never make a mistake like that again."

"Good," I said, "then it was a worthwhile lesson in every respect."

Now it began drizzling. Quickly we agreed on the date for our next lesson, and walked briskly toward our respective cars.

"I am going to buy 'sick sacks' for the airplane," said John as he walked away. "Can't believe I didn't get some before."

I waved, and wanting to stay dry, kept walking.

"Greg," called John as he entered his car. Covering my head with my jacket, I turned to look.

"Ever price seat covers?"

Bad Omen

"Do you hear that noise in the radios?" asked my friend, Pete.

"You mean that faint staticky buzz?" I replied. "Sometimes dirty alternator brushes will do that." We were over western Missouri, flying Pete's airplane to Kansas, late at night.

"Could the weather cause it?"

"I suppose so, with all the electrical activity around here."

I imagined the view out Pete's side window, now daubed opaque by the insides of a cloud. A massive line of thunderstorms lay some thirty miles south of us, and for two hours we'd watched pulsating clouds battle with lightning bolts against a jet-black sky. Then we'd entered a stratus layer, blotting out the view. Despite our distance from those thunderheads, our cockpit continued to flash alarmingly, from within what seemed like our own cloud. So intense was the lightning that our faces flickered more with light than dark.

"Hopefully the lightning itself can't travel this far," said Pete, his face ghoulishly illuminated by a particularly bright flash.

"Maybe we should climb on top of the clouds," I said. "Shall I ask?" Pete was flying, and I was working the radios.

"Sure," he replied, turning up the instrument lights to compete with the light show.

I waited for a break in the conversation, given all the aircraft requesting vectors around the thunderstorms; then I keyed the mic. "Kansas City Center," I said, "Seven-Niner-Charlie with a request, over." Another aircraft broke in before the controller could reply.

"Can't get a word in," I said to Pete. "I'll keep trying."

"No rush," he replied. "I need the cloud-flying practice, anyway."

The ride was smooth, so despite the light show we settled into that sense of peace that comes with night flight. Even the radio chatter smoothed into unobtrusive rhythm below our levels of consciousness. Air traffic control was clearly busy, and there seemed no urgency in requesting clearance for the climb.

"That buzzing seems to be getting louder," said Pete, after some time had passed. "Hard to tell if it's the radios, or something else."

"Had any trouble with them recently?" I asked.

"No, but you know how finicky radios can be in bad weather." Again the windshield illuminated, as if to punctuate his remark.

"Ever seen St. Elmo's Fire?" I asked, referring to the mysterious electrical phenomenon sometimes found around thunderstorms.

"No," said Pete, "I thought that only occurred with ships. Have you?"

"Yes, but only twice. Once, when flying a twin-engine Piper Navajo in similar weather, I looked up to find the windshield glowing electric green."

"Any danger associated with it?"

"Not that I could tell—everything in the airplane continued to work properly. Fortunately I knew what it was, or it might have scared the heck out of me."

"I understand that on sailing ships, St. Elmo's fire sometimes coated the rigging," said Pete, "A very bad omen."

"There are stories of it covering whole airplanes," I said, "but I've never seen that myself. My only other experience was in a 210 like this one—halos shrouded the antennas and ringed the propeller."

Again I tried contacting Center, but with increasing background noise we could no longer be sure if anyone was answering or not.

"Gotta have these radios looked at in Lawrence," said Pete. "Let's try another frequency."

"Good idea," I said, "got the next chart?"

Not until Pete turned to look for it did we notice the bright light glowing from the map pocket near his knee.

"What the heck?" he said, reaching in.

"Is it a flashlight?" I asked.

"No," he said, directing the beam at me.

"Sure looks like a flashlight, Pete."

"It's a cable—for my remote antenna!"

"What do you mean?"

"I have a battery-powered portable radio transceiver, for emergencies. This cable connects it to an external antenna on the belly of the plane. Look—the connector is glowing!" He touched the illuminated end. "Shit!" he shrieked, throwing the cable to the floor.

"Are you okay?" I said, alarmed.

"Heck of an electric shock . . . "

As if to emphasize the seriousness of our situation, the buzzing in our headsets now multiplied into swarms of angry bees. Louder and louder the noise grew, with no moderation as we frantically changed radios, set new frequencies, and wiggled headphone and microphone jacks. Pete and I tried everything —cycling the alternator, pulling circuit breakers—all to no avail. Ultimately, the din became so alarming and so painful that we tore off our headsets and threw them to the floor.

"We've got to get out of here!" yelled Pete.

"Let's descend, now!" I replied.

"Without asking anybody?"

"There's no choice." I said. "If we stay here we might lose the whole electrical system—fry the radios, and short out the flaps and landing gear. Climbing above the clouds is no good either. It could mean getting stuck on top without electrical power. Let's start down!"

Without needing further convincing, Pete trimmed the nose down, while I confirmed terrain clearance on the charts. The whole concept of instrument flying is for every plane to maintain its preapproved route and altitude, so as to remain clear of other aircraft and the ground. Therefore, descending through clouds without permission is traumatically unnatural for anyone trained in the art. Fortunately, this was flat country and we could safely descend many thousands of feet —providing no other airplane crossed our path.

"Not many light aircraft flying, tonight," yelled Pete hopefully over the noise of the engine, "due to the weather." I suspect he was crossing his fingers, as I was. Odds of colliding with another aircraft were slim, but certainly it was not beyond the realm of possibility. Resisting panic, we came down through the clouds at a conservative 500 feet per minute. I couldn't help but remember my recent experience with John in his Cherokee. At least we were descending under control this time, and for the moment anyway, remained farther from the ground.

"Any idea where the cloud bases are, Greg?"

"I haven't checked for awhile, but last I heard ceilings were at least 3,000 feet above ground, except near the thunderstorms."

Now silent, we descended lower and lower. We had yet to experience a break in the clouds, and although still well above minimum altitude for instrument flying in the area, I couldn't help but think of the tall broadcast antennas in this part of the country.

What if our altimeter is wrong, and we're lower than we think? I had no reason to suspect such a problem. But such is the effect of descending unseeing through opaque clouds, when not following an air traffic control clearance or a published instrument procedure. It's like sliding into a dark hole with little sense of how far down the bottom is, and no idea at all of what awaits you there.

"The tallest antennas near here are 2,000 feet," I added nervously, "so let's hope the ceilings haven't come down."

"What should we do if we reach minimum instrument altitude without seeing the ground? I have no idea how well the nav radios are working."

"That's a good question—do we stay in the clouds and risk total electrical failure? Or continue descending below minimum altitude and hope we don't hit anything? That's a tough one. Let's hope we break out before then without having to make that decision."

With nothing else to do but sweat, I continued studying my sectional chart. Knowing the surrounding terrain should give us more options if low descent was required. Five hundred feet per minute is standard for instrument descents in light airplanes, but it felt painfully slow under the circumstances. In our minds, each blind second seemed to heighten our exposure to danger, yet two full minutes were required to descend each thousand feet. I didn't ask Pete, but I suspect the urge to lower the nose and plunge downward was a strong one. Doing that, however, would have been suicidal.

Four eternal minutes later, we burst mercifully into the clear, nowhere near minimum altitude and still several thousand feet above the ground. Friendly lights beamed welcome from cars and houses 100 miles away. Although the lightning was more intense than ever, the line of thunderstorms from which it spouted had retreated even farther south. We were in the clear.

Shaken, Pete and I looked at each other, then gingerly retrieved our headsets from the floor. They were dead silent. Tuning our last assigned radio frequency, we cautiously turned up the volume. To our great relief, the voices had returned.

"Kansas City Center," I transmitted, "Seven-Niner-Charlie here. Do you read me?"

"Loud and clear," said the controller.

"We've changed altitude," I told him, suppressing the quiver in my voice, "after losing radio communications due to the electrical activity."

"No harm done," replied the controller, "the closest traffic near your altitude is forty miles away. Contact the next sector on frequency 120.5 for approach into Lawrence, and have a good night."

Later we'd learn our nemesis had been precipitation static—flight through certain weather conditions causes buildup of static electrical charge on an airplane's skin. But for the moment, all we cared about was surviving it. Relieved and rejuvenated, we set about preparing to land. Pete arranged his approach charts, and I retrieved the checklist.

St. Elmo having now departed our airplane for bigger adventures, I pointed to the again-inanimate antenna cable lying on the cabin floor.

"Pete, aren't you going to coil that up?"

"Not now," he replied, nursing his still-sore finger. "Remember that business about the bad omen? Well, I'm not touching that thing again until time for the flight home tomorrow."

WESTERN SKIES

New Lives Ahead

Not until I rolled into the first steep turn did it strike me how new and different my experiences would now become as a pilot. Strangely brown earth and low craggy mountains lent an extraterrestrial character to the land below, notable after so many years traversing green patchwork farm fields. But the big surprise came upon entering this precision turn —there was no horizon, not as I'd known them in the past, anyway.

I was taking instruction to qualify for aircraft rental, in our new home of Scottsdale, Arizona. All had gone well until the instructor asked me to demonstrate steep turns. When I rolled into a 45° bank, the flat horizon that had for so many years provided reference for the maneuver was nowhere to be found. High mountains northeast and low desert southwest generated a roller coaster of visual cues when turning so steeply and rapidly. I would soon learn to "see" the horizon in such terrain, but that sloppy first steep turn in Arizona enlightened me to new learning experiences ahead.

Jean and I had grown up in the Midwest. In Indiana we'd resided in a hardwood forest populated by flaming maples, oaks, and hickory trees. Our neighbors were fox and pos-sum, robins and blue jays. Fresh eggs came from the farm family up the road, along with sweet, newly picked corn. Mosquitoes were the pests; ice storms and winter snows sometimes confined us home on our country lane.

While living there, flying for me had been lifeblood transportation—like a car. In Cessnas, Pipers, and other small aircraft, Jean and I had traveled the East and Midwest to far-flung places like Maine and Vermont, Florida, and Texas. Closer destinations—such as Chicago, Cincinnati, Louisville, and Buffalo—seemed no more than short hops from home. Even with dozens of travel destinations to make per year, I had traveled by airline only two or three times since earning my pilot's license.

We'd visited the West only a few times, however, merely whetting our palates for more. The opportunity came when Jean sought to expand her professional horizons. With a new graduate degree to her credit and our young boys just entering school, it seemed like the perfect time to change our lives.

We flew ourselves to interviews in North Carolina, Chicago, and Wisconsin—Jean received offers at all of them. Then came an opportunity in Arizona. The job appeared professionally exciting and, just as importantly, offered new worlds for our family to explore. Jean pretended to weigh her choices objectively for a few days, but from the moment we set foot in Arizona her glowing eyes told me where we'd be moving.

I thought of the adventurer, Halliburton, that hot spring morning when I first flew from Scottsdale. So far as I was concerned, we'd just been plunked in Timbuktu, desert and all. Surrounding us as far as my mind could see, were unexplored territories on my personal map of the air. Longtime fascination with big rivers, Eastern seaports, and British-French heritage was now to be replaced by snow-covered mountains, Native American culture, and Spanish-Mexican roots.

Temperatures exceed 100° a third of the year here, so heat would be our climatic enemy, rather than cold. Gila woodpeckers, cactus wrens, and hummingbirds would populate our birdfeeders. Two-hundred-year-old saguaro cacti would displace 100-year-old oaks in our yard; javelinas instead of possums would eat Jean's plants, and scorpions would replace mosquitoes as pests. I'll never forget the first time we saw a tarantula—the insect was so large we swerved to avoid it while traveling gravel at thirty miles per hour.

(Tarantulas are benign, it turns out, and we'd learn to appreciate the furry creatures.)

Flying southwestern skies would prove as radically different as our new lives on the ground. From Indiana we'd been within a few hours of most destinations east of the Mississippi, even in the slowest of airplanes. But other than Tucson, the nearest major cities to Phoenix were hundreds of miles and many flight hours away—Albuquerque to the east, Las Vegas to the northwest, San Diego and Los Angeles to the west. What would be our destinations here? And our incentives for traveling such great distances?

Then there were the mountains. At the most visceral level, it's thrilling just flying over and around them. Traversing flat lands in the East, you lose all sense of height within a few hundred feet of the ground. But peering down thousands of feet over a mountaintop ridge cuts straight to your soul. No matter how often you experience it, there are still gut-wrenching occasions when you imagine that precipitous fall to the valley floor below.

Next was the effect of mountains on weather. From the Great Plains east, weather is primarily generated by large-scale systems traveling cross-continent. Pilots can often see trouble coming days ahead of time and plan accordingly. Such systems impact the Rockies, too, but much mountain weather is locally generated, based on some combination of moisture and airflow over specific terrain. With such localized effects and relatively few reporting stations, flying in the West presents many mysteries about what lies beyond the next mountain pass.

Clear skies dominate Arizona and surrounding states, especially in summertime. Where ten miles had been good flight visibility in Indiana, views of fifty miles or more are common here. That makes for excellent flying conditions, most of the time. But when weather does turn bad in the mountains, light aircraft generally have no business there; high terrain generates icing conditions and thunderstorms. Therefore instrument flying, which I had labored so diligently to master, would rarely prove useful here, except when navigating stratus layers along the Pacific coast.

Finally, there are significant effects of high terrain on aircraft performance. Many western mountains are taller than average light planes can climb—flying up dead-end canyons in such country can truly mean a one-way trip. Few small aircraft are turbocharged, meaning that their performance suffers in the thin air of high elevations. Add low clouds or strong winds to the mix, and conditions can become overwhelming for light planes and their pilots.

I had studied such effects in my training, but until now experienced few of them in real life. There would be new mistakes to make and new lessons to learn, but overall the challenging confluence of weather and topography would lead to rich new adventures.

Jean and I couldn't wait to explore this vast new territory, so just a few days after my checkout we departed on a family flying weekend to visit a friend in Santa Fe. There, already, I experienced my first mountain-flying lesson.

"Something's wrong," I said to Jean, holding my breath after takeoff from Santa Fe. "This plane isn't climbing at all!"

"I know," she said, clenching her teeth. Fortunately there were no obstacles to clear, and following several stressful moments we eventually labored our way up to safe altitude. Not until the perspiration dried off my brow in level flight, did I recognize what had happened. Air density decreases with warmer temperatures, and when that effect is added to the already thinner air found at high elevations, the combination can be deadly.

Santa Fe's airport is located at 6,300 feet above sea level, where takeoff performance is already marginal, and the four of us had departed late morning on a warm summer day. I later calculated that with air temperatures in the upper 80s, the "density altitude" at takeoff had been around 9,500 feet, meaning that our Cessna 172 had performed as if taking off at that much higher elevation. A few degrees warmer outside and our low-powered airplane might not have climbed at all. Never again would I take off fully loaded at midday from a high-elevation airport in summertime, in such an airplane.

Riding the Cumbres & Toltec steam train.

Spiced by such learning experiences, flying the Southwest immediately proved to be great fun, and more flights would follow as finances permitted. Among the most memorable was a flight to Alamosa, Colorado, to ride the Cumbres and Toltec narrow-gauge steam train. This one-day rail excursion transported us from a warm mountain valley over the Continental Divide through snow-covered mountains in summertime. The train stopped for lunch at a remote high-mountain ghost town, where residents lodged there solely for the purpose served up tacos and enchiladas Mexican-style.

Not only was the trip scenic, but Jean and I would remember it for more personal reasons. By now our children, Hannis and Austin, were old enough to take active part in our flying adventures, despite small-boy stature. Although neither was tall enough to reach flight controls from the front seat, they took turns flying us home from Colorado from a standing position. Somehow it seemed appropriate, the young boys sailing us ship-captain style into the uncharted skies of new lives ahead.

Race Against No One

Money was tight for our young family, so I decided to subsidize our travel adventures by instructing at a Phoenix-area flight school. This would also help familiarize me with flying conditions in the area and stimulate new friendships with other pilots.

There were many interesting characters instructing at the flight school. One of them, an older fellow named Earl, had lived and flown in the area for many years. One day when we had time on our hands, Earl toured me by air over numerous Native American ruins surprisingly close to metropolitan Phoenix. These were difficult for the uninitiated to find and identify, so seeing them was quite a thrill.

A former Indian Health Service pilot, Earl also knew the back roads on various Indian reservations, and perhaps even more importantly, claimed tribal permission to go there. An avid off-road enthusiast, Earl offered Jean and me an open invitation to join his family for a backroads tour of Monument Valley, on the Arizona-Utah border. Monument Valley is one of the most spectacular sites in the country and also where many early Westerns were filmed. We were excited about taking him up on his invitation.

One day Earl approached me at the flight school. He had just returned with his family from the very route we planned to experience together, and had photos of the trip to show me at his desk. I was eager to see them, and the two of us departed my second floor cubicle for his office. On the way, Earl talked glowingly of panoramic views from a remote overlook visited by few people other than the Navajo residents themselves.

As we descended the stairs, Earl patted me on the back, looked me in the eye with great sincerity and said, "Greg, there's something you need to know before I show you these pictures."

"Of course, Earl," I found myself replying. What could possibly be so delicate that he needed to give me this heart-to-heart talk? We reached the bottom of the stairs and turned down another corridor toward his office.

"Not many people know this Greg, but I recognize that you're a person with discretion so I can share it with you."

"Well, sure, Earl."

"You see, my family and I are naturists."

"You mean as in outdoors people? Jean and I are wilderness campers, too."

We turned into his office and he closed the door behind us.

"No Greg, we're nudists." He then pulled out these photos showing spectacular views from back roads of Monument Valley—with himself and his family prominently stationed in the foreground of each and every one.

Now you would think that the wonders of such a renowned place could not be dimmed by anything. But the sight of this all-too average family staring back, nude, from each photograph made even Monument Valley pale by comparison. (Or maybe it was the other way around . . .)

We never did make that trip to Monument Valley with Earl. It wasn't that Jean and I had a conceptual problem with his family's lifestyle, but we weren't sure if we were prepared to experience it firsthand. There was also some question about whether we'd be expected to join our hosts *au naturel,* if we did accept. Considering the potential for sunburn in sensitive places, we let the issue rest and it never came up again.

One nice feature of this particular flight school was that the operators often organized group fly-ins to out-of-the-way places. When a weekend trip was planned to raft Marble Canyon on the Colorado River, Jean and I eagerly signed up to take the boys.

Just downstream from Glen Canyon Dam, Marble Canyon leads the Colorado River into the Grand Canyon, and accordingly features spectacular scenery. A fly-in group of about fifteen airplanes was organized, and lodging was reserved at remote Marble Canyon Lodge, which has its own airstrip.

Most pilots making this trip would be flying fast airplanes, including high-performance 210 Centurions, Bonanzas, and some twin engine models. But we were on a budget and among the last to sign up, so what remained for us was a 172. After taking some good-natured ribbing about being a flight instructor flying such a slow airplane, I decided the opportunity was ripe to wreak a bit of vengeance.

A departure briefing was arranged for the morning before takeoff, so my older son was surprised when I arose early to collect weather and do my own preflight planning.

"Can't you get that stuff at the meeting?" asked Hannis.

"Yeah," I said, "but I'm doing my homework ahead of time so we can be first to Marble Canyon."

He looked at me quizzically and walked away.

At the airport we preflighted the plane, then dropped by the planning meeting at the appointed time. As always when traveling with such a diverse group, some pilots were well prepared but many others were not. Numerous discussions could be heard around the doughnut table, addressing such topics as the best route to take and who would call whom on air-to-air radio frequency after takeoff.

Another group pondered what luggage to leave behind, after realizing they'd brought too many bags for their airplanes to safely carry. Still others had just opened their maps for the first time, discovered the need to fly corridors over the Grand Canyon, and were now trying to determine how to do it.

Noting with pleasure this state of confusion, I waved a friendly hello to my detractors, collected an information packet and a bag of doughnuts, and proceeded discreetly out the door. In the hallway two more pilots "guesstimated" their on-course headings, then speculated on who would reach our destination first—the Bonanza pilot, or the one flying a twin engine Cessna 310.

"What's the big rush?" asked Jean with irritation, once we'd left the building on the way to the airplane.

"Call it a guy thing," I said. "But we're going to see if we can beat everyone else to Marble Canyon by doing our homework properly, instead of fudging like at least half these other pilots are doing."

"We're going to get there first, flying a 172?"

"That's my game. Think we can do it?"

Suddenly Hannis and Austin were all ears at the prospect of a "race." We were just taxiing out, as the first of the other pilots approached the ramp. Hoping that no one else had grasped my plan, I completed engine run-up and took off.

The boys were all ears at the prospect of a "race."

Along with departing promptly, my strategy was to take advantage of shifting winds and precise navigation over ground landmarks to gain advantage over lazier pilots. Based on morning weather reports, I'd carefully precalculated headings and altitudes for each leg of the trip. Most other pilots I knew would simply pick altitudes by habit and zigzag over widely spaced navigational radio stations. (This was before the days of GPS navigation.) My approach was low-tech, but as in the past, I figured if dead reckoning and pilotage worked for Lindbergh, they would work for me.[1]

Using my best guerilla tactics, I collected not only forecast winds aloft, but also those on the ground. This was a long shot, but with much of our route over high plateau, knowledge of surface winds not far below us might be used to our advantage. I'd noted a weak weather front and associated wind shift that morning between Scottsdale and our destination, and planned an altitude adjustment along the way to capitalize on it.

Despite these efforts, I knew that odds were not in our favor to "win." Marble Canyon lay over 200 miles away, and some of our competitors flew planes almost twice as fast as ours.

We cruised along at a blistering 120 miles per hour in our Skyhawk, monitoring on air-to-air frequency the "I'll get there before you" discussions of those behind us. I kept silent, of course, not wanting to hurt our chances by giving up our game. Even if we arrived last, it would be worth every

---

[1] Three types of aerial navigation are commonly used in light aircraft. *Dead reckoning* relies on time, speed, and distance calculations over a known course and distance, adjusted for forecast winds. *Pilotage* refers to the art of navigating by features on the ground. The third type is *radio navigation,* which figures prominently in instrument flying and is also widely used in visual conditions.

bit of effort based on the broad grins and silver-dollar-sized eyes worn by Hannis and Austin in the back seat.

As planned, I changed altitude about halfway through the trip to capitalize on the wind shift. I'd also calculated exactly how far from our destination we should begin descent. After reaching this predetermined point, I began gradually descending to reach traffic pattern altitude precisely upon arrival at Marble Canyon Airport. Our speed would be optimized by coasting the final miles "downhill."

The kids were on the edges of their seats as we approached Marble Canyon. Heck, I was too, as the four of us scanned for aircraft gaining on us from behind. It looked more and more like we might just "win" this informal race no one else knew we were in.

As it turned out, a turbocharged Centurion descended from above to join downwind just ahead of us, paralleling the runway for landing. (That model cruises seventy miles per hour faster than the Skyhawk we were flying.) Then the pilot of a twin engine Cessna 310 (eighty miles per hour faster than our plane) ignored proper procedure and cut in front of us in the traffic pattern.

The boys weren't happy about "losing," but certainly I didn't mind. We had played the game well and as a result were number three to land. Rather than walk immediately across the highway to the lodge, we secured the plane and seated ourselves prominently in front of it. Victory was found in the surprised looks on each subsequent speedster's face when taxiing in, only to find us parked, unloaded, and waiting before our lowly 172.

Lost over Utah

Beyond the exhilaration of flight itself, nothing is more rewarding for an aviator than granting the gift to others. In fact for many pilots, the joy of sharing flight ultimately surpasses the fundamental pleasure of handling the controls.

Always in the back of my mind had lingered the people who introduced me to flying and nurtured my skills along the way. I had now been flying long enough to begin seeing my own impact in inspiring others. Of course most prominent in my memory were the pilots I had trained from first lesson to last. Many have continued to fly for pleasure, and others went on to become airline pilots. I'll never forget opening my aviation magazines one month to discover a long-ago private pilot student smiling back at me. The young graduate student who once bicycled to the airport for flying lessons with me had now earned a place on the championship U.S. Women's Aerobatic Team.

Along with those I've trained as pilots are many others with whom I made just a flight or two, never guessing the long-term impact I might have on them. Learning their exploits afterward is always rewarding and sometimes entertaining.

Among those I'd first introduced to flying upon moving to Arizona was our new neighbor, Joe. Several years later I was delighted when he phoned to tell me that as a result of our flight together, he'd gone on to earn his pilot's license. He had a story to tell, too.

Shortly after passing his flight test, Joe was approached by friends who knew of his accomplishment and hoped to attend a family reunion in southern Utah. Would he be interested in flying them there and joining the party? Joe saw immediately that this would be an ideal trip by light airplane. It would also offer true adventure for a new pilot, requiring several hundred miles of flight over remote mountainous terrain. Enthusiastically, he had accepted.

Well in advance, Joe reserved a Piper Archer to rent for the trip. This four-place Cherokee model sported an upgraded 180-horsepower engine, and would be capable of carrying pilot and passengers, light weekend luggage, and adequate fuel to make the flight nonstop with reasonable reserve. It was a good choice for the trip, given the skill level of a new pilot. Careful planning would be required, however, due to the combination of high terrain along the route and summertime heat.

The reunion was to be held at Parawan, Utah, but early in the planning process Joe decided he would land instead at

Cedar City. Given Parawan Airport's 6,000-foot elevation, Joe was concerned about departing there safely for the return trip home with four occupants in summertime heat. "I knew we'd be taking off pretty heavily loaded," he told me, "and didn't want to take any chances with high density altitude." Only twenty miles away, Cedar City was 400 feet lower in elevation and offered a longer runway with unobstructed approaches. A navigational radio station at Cedar City made it also easier to find.

Joe did an admirable job on his preflight homework. He identified alternate airports along the planned route from Phoenix, and made preliminary takeoff calculations for the return trip so he wouldn't over-fuel at 5,600-foot Cedar City. Then he made his first mistake.

In the heat of Southwest summers, knowledgeable pilots plan early morning flights; otherwise, afternoon turbulence can make lightplane occupants feel as if they're riding in a martini shaker. This pilot didn't want to inconvenience his passengers with an "o-dark-thirty" departure, so he arranged to meet his passengers at a Phoenix area airport at 10:00 a.m.

Even that would have been a late start, but upon arriving at the airport that morning, Joe was horrified to discover that the Archer was grounded with mechanical problems. The only other available airplane was a Piper Warrior—similar to the Archer but with thirty fewer horsepower. Being both slower than the Archer and capable of carrying less weight, the Warrior would be a marginal performer for this trip. Frantically, Joe recalculated flight plan, fuel consumption, and takeoff performance.

To his relief, he determined that the flight was still feasible, but to meet weight criteria with the smaller engine, fuel onboard would have to be limited. Therefore he targeted St. George, Utah, as a possible fuel stop if necessary on the flight from Phoenix. On the return trip landing for fuel would be mandatory, due to the weight limitations of taking off in summertime from Cedar City's high elevation.

By the time Joe completed these revised calculations, it was high noon in Phoenix, on a hot desert July day. Joe loaded his three first-time passengers into the Warrior and took off. Despite 100° temperatures, the flight proved uneventful until the vicinity of the Utah border.

There, Joe became uncertain of his position and made mistake number two—he deviated off course. You might assume that pilots should know at every moment exactly where they are, but over trackless terrain that's not always possible. Sometimes nothing is visible below to precisely confirm position. With experience, however, you learn that maintaining a properly computed heading will almost always lead to the next expected landmark. Compare this to driving on a highway—between crossroads, drivers rarely know exactly where they are, but it's only a matter of time until reaching a recognizable place. Turn off the highway in the middle of nowhere, however, and you've got a problem.

That's exactly what Joe had done. The more he turned, looking for landmarks, the more lost he became. "By now fuel was getting a little low," he told me, "so I followed a road to St. George. Then I realized I'd actually flown over the St. George Airport while I was lost!"

By this time Joe's passengers had endured heat and turbulent air for hours, and the faces of all three were buried in sick sacks. "When we finally landed at St. George," he told me, "a lineman ran out to meet us. I assumed he was there to help tie down the plane, until he started yelling something to us. I hadn't even shut down yet.

"'The FAA is looking for you!' the man shouted over the sound of the engine. It turned out we were overdue on our flight plan due to getting lost, and flight service was calling airports throughout a three-state region, looking for us."

After straightening that out and getting his bearings, Joe regrouped, refueled, and proceeded with his passengers on the short remaining flight to their destination.

"Joe," I said, remembering the unfortunate flight review with my brother, Alan, and future sister-in-law, Lesley. "Do you think your friends will ever fly with you again?"

"They wouldn't have," he replied, laughing, "except for one thing."

"What's that?"

"Parawan is in the middle of nowhere, and there was no other way for them to get home after the reunion."

Fortunately for Joe's friendships and reputation as a pilot, he did not make the same mistakes on the return trip to Phoenix.

"This time we left early in the morning," he said, smiling. "I stayed on course the whole way, and the flight was smooth as glass. If I'm lucky those friends just might fly with me again one day . . . after some time has passed."

Mountains Crowned by Fire

The Rio Fire. (Photo by Arnie Dworkis.)

"Dad!" blurted young voices from the telephone, "Are you and Mom okay? We heard the whole town was on fire!" Only a few hours earlier the two boys had rushed to hug me at Payson's mountain airport, their Boy Scout uniforms grimy from outdoor adventure.

It was a trip I treasured every summer—shuttling Hannis and Austin from Camp Geronimo to Northern Arizona University at Flagstaff. Scout camp always ended on the same day summer music camp began, and it was my enviable duty to make that transfer by airplane.

The route was a 200-mile triangle over mountainous terrain: northeast from Scottsdale to collect the boys at Payson, then northwest to drop them at Flagstaff, and finally due

119

south for the return flight home. Although the distances weren't great, planning was required to fly a planeload of kids and baggage out of high-elevation airports in Arizona's summer heat. Along with the past week's camping gear, fresh clothing had to be carried for each boy, plus instruments for music camp.

Accordingly, I arranged an early morning departure when the plane would perform better in cooler temperatures. To minimize weight, I carried just enough fuel to complete the trip with a safety margin. Back in the Midwest, my general policy had been to carry as much fuel as possible. Here in the mountains, however, excess weight could make the difference between climbing successfully off the runway or going off the end. Every pound lighter on takeoff would improve climb performance.

"Beautiful day for flying," said the briefer that morning, when I called for weather. "Just the usual scattered flight restrictions due to summer firefighting." Dutifully I noted their locations and launched in clear skies from Scottsdale, climbing on course to cross the McDowell Mountains a few miles away.

Reaching the ridge, however, I was surprised to encounter a thick sea of smoke dammed on the other side. Eyes and nostrils burning, I turned away and radioed Phoenix Approach for radar guidance.

"We're too busy to help you," came the reply, "but the valley northeast of the McDowells is crowded with firefighting aircraft. You'd best proceed twenty miles north before turning east toward Payson." Following that advice I skirted the perimeter of the smoky haze, then rendezvoused with the boys and their scoutmaster at Payson.

Quickly we dined on omelets before temperatures became too hot for takeoff from the 5,000-foot elevation air-

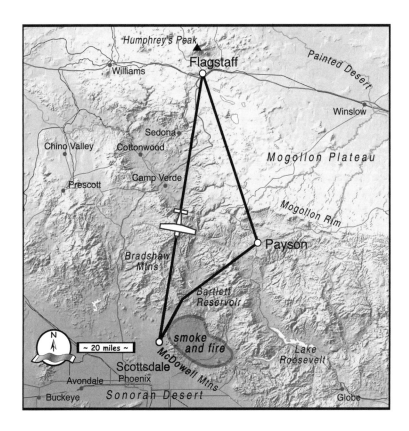

port. Then I loaded kids, backpacks, keyboard, and guitar into the airplane, along with clothes and goodies sent by Mom from home. Maneuvering after takeoff to avoid rising terrain, we staggered aloft toward Flagstaff.

Now came my favorite leg of the trip, tracing softly forested edges of the Mogollon Plateau. Morning sun silvered mountain lakes off our wing, and before long Flagstaff materialized ahead. There we dined vegetarian-style at a favorite café, and wandered pine-shaded streets before delivering the boys to music camp. Takeoff from Flagstaff came at dusk, with darkness falling on the way home.

Finding no haze reflected in the landing light and little scent of smoke, I assumed with relief that any remaining fires must be under control. Scottsdale Airport soon appeared at 12 o'clock, cloaked by its mantle of city lights. But something was wrong as I entered the traffic pattern. Glimmering weirdly to my left were lights that shouldn't be there. Increasingly confused while descending, I watched those strange lights climb and then hover supernaturally over my wing.

"What's going on?" I radioed the tower, disoriented. I wasn't even sure what question to ask.

"Fire on the McDowells," came the reply. After a moment to process the implications, I understood. Normally black and invisible at night, mountain peaks 2,000 feet above me were flickering with jewels of flame. Fires had jumped from the valley beyond and ignited the ridge. Complementing the usual blue-and-white airport illumination when I landed, was the bizarre orange glimmer of firelight.

The McDowell mountain range extends some ten miles northwest to southeast, with Scottsdale Airport nestled beneath the northwest end. Driving around the west side toward our town southeast of the mountains, I was relieved to see the ridgetop flames receding behind me.

Not until turning north toward home on the other side, did I grasp the magnitude of the fire. There, to my shock, the sky glowed with firelight 1,000 feet high, concave in smoke like the inside of a red balloon and squeezed by blackness from above. Those ridgetop glimmers near the airport had granted no hint of the inferno on the other side. Worst of all, the north edge of town with our home appeared to be in flames.

Brighter and yellower grew the sky as I struggled homeward through streets clogged with gawkers and emergency vehicles. Hundred-foot flames consumed fully half the horizon, tinting our neighborhood orange like fires from hell. Smoke choked the air, and ash coated the streets like snow. The boys I knew were safe at camp. But what of Jean, and our home?

Fortunately, the house still stood. Rushing panicked through empty rooms, I almost missed a ghostly shadow on the back patio. It was Jean, resisting fate with a garden hose. We embraced, soaking in sweat.

"I couldn't imagine you flying in this," she said, crying.

"And I thought the house was gone with you in it," I said through tears of my own.

We sweltered on that patio in the red-hot glow of flames, wishfully watering the roof and wondering what would happen next. The fire department had already been by, Jean told me, warning residents to be prepared to evacuate. The entire valley north of us was on fire, with northerly winds blowing the conflagration in our direction. We threw a change of clothes into the car trunk, and contacted friends for a place to stay. Sadly we contemplated losing our home and all we'd worked for.

That's when the phone rang and it was Austin and Hannis, caring about our safety and underlining our bright future. The tide seemed to turn when we heard those young voices, reminding us that material possessions don't matter.

Late into the night Jean and I lingered on the patio, not daring to sleep lest the flames overtake us, yet resisting evacuation until all other options had failed. Between moments of panic we held hands and talked. It was one of those precious occasions for sharing deeply personal feelings about the past, the future, and what's important in life.

Near midnight the air cleared somewhat, heralding a wind shift away from town. Slowly the fires receded, and we fell into fitful sleep until awaking next morning to tanker planes bombing slurry along the dry wash behind our house. The inferno lasted several more days and threatened other communities to the north, but thankfully for us the danger was over.

Time dulls the memory of that fire, but Jean and I are still reminded of it every time we hike the desert north of our home; scars in this parched landscape will remain for hundreds of years.

Deeper are the marks on my soul. Even today I relive those nightmarish scenes—crossing the McDowells after takeoff into that valley filled with smoke; the blood-red cavern of sky upon turning my car homeward; and especially, holding Jean drenched and choking amid hellish flames on our normally tranquil patio.

Then there's the loving phone call to remember, from two worried little boys. It was the beacon of hope for a father who'd landed disoriented on an unnaturally black night, in the flickering shadows of mountains crowned by fire.

Airline Pilot at Age Twenty-Six

"Twenty-six years old! And I'll be flying right seat of a Boeing 737 for a major airline! Can you believe it?"

If the news had come from anyone but Danny, I wouldn't have thought it possible. Just about every pilot dreams at least once of getting on with the airlines. It's tough, and to be hired at such a young age is quite a feat.

Danny's story proved almost as amazing as his accomplishment. Although very different than Joe's tale, it started around the same time with another of those casual intro flights I'd delivered shortly after moving to Arizona. One of Jean's friends from work knew I was a pilot, and had phoned one evening with a request.

"My little brother, Danny, is coming to visit me in Phoenix," she said, "and I'm looking for some good things for him to do while he's here. Any chance you could take him flying?" She talked a bit about Danny, how he was studying at his hometown university but was discouraged with school, and about how tough it is for young people to make career decisions. "I just want him to have fun while he's here," she said.

"I'll be glad to take Danny flying," I replied.

Soon afterward, young Danny and I found ourselves exploring blue skies north of Scottsdale. Although our flight was intended to be little more than sightseeing, it quickly became clear to both of us that Danny liked airplanes. He tried his hand at climbs, turns, and descents, but he didn't want to stop there, so we sampled steep turns and stalls, too.

Two weeks later Danny surprised me with a long distance call from college.

"Hey, Greg," he said, "I'm coming back to see my sister this weekend. Any chance we could fly again?" That Saturday found us winging toward Prescott in a Cessna 172. I don't remember much about the trip except that it was a beautiful day, Danny did most of the flying, and he peppered me with aviation questions throughout the flight.

Once more, Danny returned home and I forgot about him. Then, several months later the phone rang again.

"Hey, this is Danny. Remember me? We flew together," he gushed. "I finally know what I want to do—be a pilot! I'm gonna drop out of school for awhile and concentrate full time on my flying career. My private license is almost finished already!"

We talked for a long time. Like many in aviation, Danny had wavered in the career planning department until he discovered flying. Now he had a mission. I tried to convince him that while becoming a professional pilot was a great decision, dropping out of school might prove to be a mistake. "It's awfully tough to go back later," I said, trying not to discourage him. "Better to slow your progress on ratings a bit, and finish up that degree now."

This was not what Danny had called me to hear. For the first time in his life he had a plan, and two more years of school was not part of it. I explained the importance of a degree for succeeding in any field, including aviation. Danny didn't seem convinced, but thanked me anyway in his usual enthusiastically gracious manner before hanging up.

Several years passed before I again heard from Danny.

"Guess what!" he then called to tell me. "I'm moving down your way to find a job!" He had just earned his commercial pilot certificate, and much to my delight, had graduated from college with a four-year degree.

Danny and I talked more frequently once he moved to Phoenix. He first worked fueling airplanes at a local airport, while studying to become a flight instructor. Then, after several months teaching others to fly, he took a job flying long hours of pipeline patrol between Yuma, Arizona, and El Paso, Texas. Periodically he phoned to share the finer points of patrolling the pipes. Soon Danny graduated to freight runs, flying a twin-engine Cessna 310.

A handsome young man with square jaw and bright eyes, Danny proved to be one of those unusual people who successfully mixes modesty with energy and enthusiasm. With each advancement in his career he was already planning for the next. "It's probably too much to hope for," he told me one evening, "but I'd sure love to fly for a major airline one day."

Danny took his next job with a courier operation, delivering packages around Arizona. Each day the routine was similar—fly out from Phoenix early in the morning, unload the plane, sit for the day, reload with inbound packages, and return at supper time. Most waiting hours were spent at an outstation at Page, Arizona, on the Utah border.

Other pilots might have spent that free time sunning at nearby Lake Powell, but not Danny. He carried books along each day, and invested those long hours between flights studying for his next step up the career ladder. Then one day Danny had a brainstorm, justifying yet another breathless phone call.

"Have I got a great idea!" he raved happily from a pay phone. "I'm applying for a part-time ramp job with a regional airline, here in Page. After I unload my courier packages every day, I'll just head over to the airline and work there until time to go home. In the process I'll prove I'm a good employee and meet some of their pilots."

Danny's objective was to get hired into the right seat of a turboprop.[2] Although he barely met the airline's minimum

---

[2] *Turboprop* refers to an airplane powered by jet engines driving propellers, as is common in small regional airliners. Although also propeller-driven, the smaller general aviation planes flown by the author in this book are powered by piston engines related to those found in cars.

pilot experience requirements at the time, this plan seemed to him like it might work.

Within weeks, Danny had befriended several captains at the airline and traveled to company headquarters to introduce himself to the pilot-hiring coordinator. Apparently it worked, because nine short months later, Danny was hired as first officer (copilot) on a nineteen-passenger airliner. Still I'd hear from him every few months.

"I've been talking to the hiring department at one of the big airlines," he told me. "They give preferential interviews to current employees, so I took a ramp job with them on my days off." Nothing had come of that connection when I next saw Danny. But he had bigger news, an interview with the "dream major" he'd always wanted to work for. And he had a story, one that would be too incredible for anyone but Danny.

"I'd been in touch with the airline for quite awhile," he told me, "and over time gotten to know one of the chief pilots pretty well. He's a neat guy and I'd been stopping in to see him every couple months for the last year and a half. Needless to say, I was thrilled when one day he said, 'You're the kind of guy we want working here.' He told me to expect a job interview, and even gave me the date it was scheduled to occur."

Several days later Danny received a letter from the airline. Filled with excitement, he opened it. But instead of confirming the interview, as he'd expected, the letter stated that he did not qualify for a position and could not reapply for one year.

"I contacted the chief pilot about the letter," Danny told me. "He sounded very surprised, and said he'd look into it. Then, when he called back later, I could tell he was concerned." Danny repeated the conversation he'd had with the chief pilot.

"Dan, you don't have an ATP—an airline transport pilot certificate," the pilot told Danny. "That's required to qualify for an interview."

"But the application said passing the ATP written test was all that's required," Danny responded.

"Apparently they've recently changed the interview requirements. Now you need to have taken the flight test and earned the actual license itself. Sorry, Dan, there's nothing I can do about it."

"Today is Wednesday," Danny told the senior pilot, "and my interview was scheduled for a week from today. I'll go get the ATP. When do I need to have it?"

"If you can complete the training and fax me your ATP certificate this weekend, I'll see what I can do about reinstating the interview."

"I'll earn my ATP by Saturday, and fax it to you by Sunday," Danny told his contact.

I knew this was a gutsy offer. The airline transport pilot checkride is an instrument flight test flown to very tight standards and laced with simulated emergencies. Although it's feasible to earn one in a few hours of intensive training, plenty of applicants require more than that to avoid failing the first time around.

Next morning was Thursday, and Danny found a flight school willing to train him on Friday and Saturday. The flight test was scheduled for Saturday afternoon. Training would take place in a Piper Seminole, like the one I'd flown with Larry to South Dakota. Since Danny had been flying professionally on a daily basis, he was confident that he had the basic skills to pass the flight test.

Switching from a high-tech airline cockpit to a small piston-powered twin might prove daunting, however, given the few training hours available. Crossing his fingers, Danny calculated how he'd supplement the few dollars of credit remaining on his charge card to pay the bill, and made the appointment.

Friday afternoon was Danny's first lesson in the Seminole. The flight went well, so he met with the examiner to prepare application paperwork for the following day's check-ride. The examiner looked things over, then turned to Dan with visible irritation.

"Your ATP written test results have expired," he said.

"I know it's more than two years old," replied Danny, "but I've been flying continuously for a scheduled air carrier. According to regulations that keeps the written test results current."

"I hate to tell you this," said the examiner, "but I'm pretty sure those rules have changed." He then called the FAA to confirm his conclusion. It was true; as of January that year, ATP written tests no longer remained current beyond two years on basis of employment. The ruling was so new that it didn't yet appear in the printed regulations.

At this point most normal human beings would have acquiesced to fate. By now it was Friday afternoon at 4:35, and Danny's airline pilot certificate was to be faxed to the airline by Sunday morning. Once the shock of the moment had passed, Dan informed the examiner that he'd have fresh written exam scores "in time for tomorrow's flight test."

With only minutes to spare before closing time, he scheduled an appointment with a local computer testing center for the following morning, then bought a test-prep guide and went to work. After studying all night, Danny appeared at the testing center first thing Saturday morning, took the written test and passed.

From there it was off to the airport for more lessons in the Seminole, followed by oral and flight tests with the examiner. Despite having been up all night, Danny succeeded in walking out the door Saturday afternoon with a brand new Airline Transport Pilot certificate in his pocket. He faxed it to the chief pilot Sunday morning, then resumed studying for the hoped-for airline interview.

I learned of all these events when Danny phoned on Monday to brainstorm in preparation for Wednesday's interview, which had just been confirmed by the airline. "I'll phone you afterward, and let you know how it went!" he promised at the end of the call.

Well, Danny didn't call Wednesday night, nor Thursday. When the weekend arrived I knew that things couldn't have gone well, or I'd have heard from him. Not until late the following week did I finally learn the outcome, when I saw Danny at a birthday party for his sister.

"What have you been up to?" I asked, not wanting to risk hurting his feelings with direct questions about the interview. Surely the unstoppable young man had mapped out some new strategy, like maybe flying the space shuttle.

"Didn't I tell you?" replied Danny, "I got hired!" He cranked my hand. "Sorry I forgot to call, but I've been busy. Spent the week contacting all my friends at the airline to see if I can get into an earlier training class; better seniority, you know." In the airlines, everything from work schedule to where a pilot lives is based on date of initial training. Danny was again working ahead to improve his odds.

"Congratulations, Danny!" I offered in surprised admiration, and raised a toast in front of his friends. This young man was now a Boeing pilot at age twenty-six, and accomplishing it was far from a matter of luck. He had personally made it happen through grit and determination every step along the way. Seemed like only a few months before that I was demonstrating steep turns to a nineteen-year-old kid over the Bradshaw Mountains. Now he was a pro, and I was thrilled to have had a small part in it.

"Thanks for all your help," said Danny later, when time came for me to leave the party.

"My pleasure, Danny," I replied, shaking his hand. "Let me know when you begin ground school!" I reached for the door.

"Oh, and Greg, can I ask you one last favor?" said Danny, taking me aside and lowering his voice.

"Sure," I replied, turning back to face him. "Anything."

"If you don't mind, how about calling me 'Dan,' these days—you know, just in front of the other pilots."

"Watch Out for the Fountain!"

Balloons depart Fountain Park.

Kaleidoscopic dragons awakened all around. Inhaling and rising from the earth, their fiery breathing filled the air.

I gripped our basket as pilot Mary Woodhouse activated our own burner in harmony with those gargantuan neighbors. A colorful bag of hot air rose gracefully above our heads, then coaxed us slowly from the ground. Around us rose other balloons, a herd of great beasts struggling from rest. Slowly we drifted toward the adjacent pond.

"We'll skim the water," said Mary, "just for the sport of it."

A longtime hot-air balloon pilot, Mary had invited me on this flight only a few days earlier. "We're doing the race at Fountain Hills," she'd offered, "and I thought you might like to join us."

Knowing that most balloon passengers earn their first flights only after crewing for the pilot, I jumped at the opportunity. Only after hanging up the phone did I wonder whether acrophobia might be more of an impediment in balloons than in airplanes. Jean had always found it humorous that I should be so comfortable in airplanes but uneasy about heights elsewhere. The question in my mind was whether ballooning would be more like flying, or more like staring down uneasily from a tall ladder.

I arrived at Fountain Park at 7 o'clock Saturday morning, only to find that early rising crews had been there for hours beforehand setting up. Mary's balloon was already rigged and spread along the ground, with a giant fan inflating the bag. With three of us perched precariously in a tiny wicker gondola barely reaching our hips, Mary activated the propane burner. Next thing I knew, we were floating ghost-like over Fountain Lake.

It seemed so alien to me—in airplanes we rush from the ground, always with an eye out for safe places to land. Yet our balloon was drifting slowly over a body of water at an altitude of only inches, and in fact descending to touch its surface. And descending, and descending . . . When water began filtering through the weave of the basket, I wondered if I should have worn other shoes, not anticipating that balloon flight would wet the new ones I was wearing.

"Isn't this fun?" asked our smiling pilot. But as my shoelaces submerged, new determination captured Mary's face, her formerly relaxed touch changing to firm grip as she again activated the burner. Water climbed our ankles as we slogged into the pond, defying the best efforts of burner and our collective will to rise.

Suddenly the murmur of spectators turned to a roar, with the crowd on shore shouting and pointing at us.

"Look out!" came cries through the uproar, "The Fountain!"

I then realized that more than our impending immersion was attracting attention. Although we'd finally arrested our submarine descent and begun rising skyward, directly ahead in our path lay "The Fountain."

As you might gather from the names of the community, the park, and the lake, their respective namesake is no run-of-the-mill peeing statue. In fact, town fathers claim this fountain to be tallest in the world, a single huge spout of water rising vertically some 550 feet from the surface of its pond. Seriously, this fountain is so big it's a reporting point for Phoenix airspace—check your sectional charts, pilots—and by the time I turned to see what all those fingers were pointing at, we were headed directly for it at the grand elevation of five feet.

The crowd's roar grew deafening as we approached the fifty-stories-tall fountain, then fell dead silent as all eyes focused on our hapless craft. Mary just hung there on the burner control, saying not a word. Finally we began to rise, but clearly it would be impossible to outclimb the geyser. What would be the effect, I wondered, of a 500-foot-tall column of water striking a paper-thin bag of hot air? Surely I wasn't the only one musing on the topic.

At what seemed like the last nanosecond of this slow-motion crisis, our balloon drifted ever-so-slightly to the right. Gentle spray cooled our faces as the craft kissed the fountain, then rose briskly to join company with its heaving-and-sighing brethren.

"Wonder why they don't turn off that fountain for the balloon ascension," said Mary, in what seemed ultimate understatement. "Didn't mean to skim quite that low either." A hint of smile crossed her face. (The following year a balloon did indeed drift into the forceful waters of The Fountain. Ignominiously deflated, it dumped its passengers into the reclaimed effluent of Fountain Lake. Only ego-based injuries accompanied the soaking.)

Having escaped the treacherous spout, we soon found ourselves drifting low and silently above homes and streets. Regally, we received waves of smiling spectators from their backyards, while uninvited voices joined us eerily from unseen conversations below. Reaching open desert, we observed deer and coyotes fleeing our great shadow, the sounds of their foot-steps through the brush clearly audible. Now came my one tinge of acrophobia—I just couldn't make myself lean back-ward out of the basket to photograph my companions against their colorful backdrop of balloons, mountains, and desert.

At walking pace we drifted southward, then southwest. "Good thing we're going this direction," said Mary. "Northeast is too rugged for chase vehicles to get us out, and we'll avoid Phoenix, with its air traffic and lack of landing sites."

Other balloons drifted in synchrony nearby. Being part of the same air mass, they departed our company only grad-ually as pilots sought differing winds at other altitudes. Ours was a distance race, to see who could travel farthest from the starting point.

"I don't care about winning," said Mary, as we watched the group dissipate. "We'll just stay low and enjoy the ride." Silence was now punctured only occasionally by blasts from our burner to maintain altitude. Our reverie was broken by Mary's handheld radio.

"Sheriff's deputy just came by," announced a staticky voice from our ground crew. "Said the balloons do not have permission to land on the reservation. I guess the race orga-nizers forgot to ask ahead of time."

"Oh goody," said Mary, looking to me for guidance. "Where is this reservation?"

"All around us," I observed, with a grand sweep of the hand. "The only other open land is way over there, by the community college." I pointed west, which was not the direction our wind was taking us.

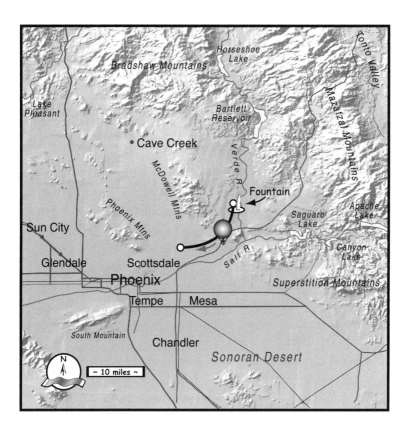

To raise our spirits, Mary then cheered us with tales of hapless aeronauts greeted by guns, jail, and fines for landing on valuable crops and in exclusive neighborhoods. The most hair-raising punishments were, of course, reserved for those dropping in unannounced on Indian reservations. Setting aside visions of night in a tribal jail, I concentrated instead on surrealistic views of hue-saturated balloons dancing across brown desert and green fields.

Ultimately, there was no choice but to put down on the reservation anyway. Coordinating with our chase crew to minimize waiting time on the ground, Mary selected an open field free of crops or other damageable property. We would land near an intersection, so driving off-road for retrieval would be avoided.

"Hold on tight," instructed our pilot. We dragged and bumped to a halt in the unplowed field, escaping with no more attention than the watchful excitement of young Native American neighbors.

My hour-and-a-half initiation into the mystical world of hot-air ballooning was over. We'd covered only 8 or so miles in that time, instead of the 200 I was accustomed to. Low and silent passage over the ground had granted perceptions that pass you by in an airplane—smelling the smells, hearing the sounds, and sensing the lives of those below. It was like casually bicycling the countryside instead of rushing past by interstate highway. Rather than marveling at covering ground at 160 miles per hour, I'd gained new perspectives at a groundspeed of 5.

Under Mary's supervision, we heaved deflated bag and basket into the chase crew's pickup truck, then refueled propane tanks at a nearby gas station. Our day was not yet over, however. Ballooning tradition calls for pilots to host the chase crew after flying. Returning to Fountain Park, we indulged ourselves in celebratory gourmet brunch, followed by dousing of first-flight neophytes with champagne. Bubbly dripping from my nose, I pondered new meaning brought to me this day for the unceasingly fascinating act of "flying."

High School Hero

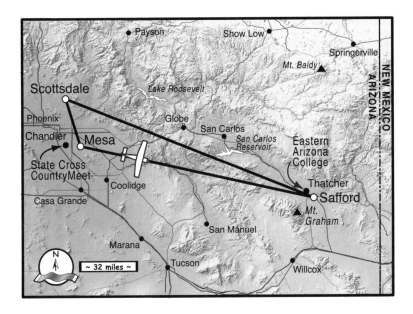

"You've *got* to help!" implored Ms. Patterson over the telephone, her voice cracking with emotion.

"Me?" I replied, "But how can I help with the marching band?"

"You *must* persuade your son to be in the Marching Band Invitational."

"But Austin loves band," I said, "why would he not participate?"

"There's some sort of track meet that day, but you need to convince him that band is more important. We have only thirty-eight marching band members, and several already can't come. Without Austin we'd have only four trumpets."

I knew better than to second-guess my son on what was apparently a volatile topic, but promised the band director I'd check into it.

"Austin," I said, when he arrived home from high school, "what's the deal with Ms. Patterson and the marching band competition?"

"She just doesn't understand!" he said, with irritation only a teen can muster. "There's no way I'm skipping the state cross-country meet."

"The state meet?"

"That's right," he said, "I know the band competition is important, but so are the cross-country finals." It turned out that the cross-country coach had also been contacted by the band director, and Austin was now under pressure from both of them.

"When are these things happening?" I asked.

"A week from Saturday," he replied, "I just can't believe they're on the same day."

It turned out that the marching band competition was scheduled for 2:45 p.m. at Eastern Arizona College near Safford, on the New Mexico border. By bus that's some three hours from Phoenix over two-lane roads, so the band was scheduled to depart at 10:00 in the morning.

But Austin was already registered to run in the Arizona State Cross Country meet at 11:30 a.m. that same day, in the Phoenix suburb of Chandler. It wouldn't be over until 12:30 or 1:00, at the earliest.

The situation sounded impossible, but on the chance flying might offer a solution, I retrieved my aeronautical charts to have a look. As it turned out, flight time from Phoenix to Safford should be no more than an hour by Cessna 182. That offered hope, but the question was could we make the logistics work.

As little as 45 minutes would be available to accommodate ground transportation at both ends of the flight. That ruled out flying from our home airport, an hour's drive from the meet. Maybe if Austin and Jean could hitch a ride after the meet to the closer Williams Gateway Airport, I could fly the plane from Scottsdale ahead of time and be there waiting to pick them up.

I was also pleased to learn that Eastern Arizona College was only seven miles from the Safford Airport, and that the nice folks there were willing to loan us their courtesy car. I laid out these plans for Austin to consider later that evening. He was concerned about the quality of his trumpet performance, after running three miles in state competition and making this rush trip, but he was game to try. And needless to say, once Ms. Patterson got over the novelty of our plan, she was all for it.

As the big day approached, a new crisis arose. On Thursday Ms. Patterson phoned again, more distraught than ever. Two other band members, Andrew and Spencer Markey, were to attend a family wedding in Scottsdale at 6 p.m. Saturday. With the band competition not expected to end until 4 p.m., there was no way they could compete and still make it home.

"Is there any possibility," pleaded Ms. Patterson, "that you could fly the Markey brothers home in the airplane?"

I wasn't sure how Mrs. Markey might feel about her sons flying halfway across Arizona in a small airplane, but I proposed the plan to her anyway. As it turned out, she was delighted that her kids might march in the band and still make the family wedding. The only downside was that since Jean wanted to come along and watch the band performance, Austin would have to ride the bus home from Safford, because the plane seats only four. With his political problems solved, however, he was happy to help out.

All of us waited with bated breath to see if this complex plan would work; I became particularly concerned when Saturday's forecast called for a cold front to cross the state. (Of course I'd informed all parties that if Arizona's normally benign weather proved problematic, all bets were off.)

Fortunately, Saturday dawned flyable, though hazy. After an initial panic when Jean's ride to the cross-country meet didn't show up, I repositioned the airplane from Scottsdale to Williams Gateway Airport.

Jean and Austin met me there at 12:45, allowing just enough time for a quick sandwich before launching for Safford at 1 p.m. Austin flew—it was the least I could offer since he'd be riding the bus home. After skirting 10,700-foot Mt. Graham we spotted Safford in the fertile Gila River Valley, touching down around 2:00 p.m. Quickly, Austin changed from running shorts to band uniform, and after dashing madly from the airport, intercepted the band at Eastern Arizona College just in time for warmup at 2:45.

The trumpet section.

Our high school band played well in competition, and while ratings were being tallied Jean and I relaxed to a demonstration performance by the Eastern Arizona College "Marching Gila Monsters." (Find *that* mascot anywhere else.)

As soon as band photos were shot and awards dispensed, it was time for Part Two of our plan. Leaving Austin at the band bus, we rushed Andrew and Spencer back to the airport. Departing at dusk, we climbed back into sunlight after takeoff. On their first-ever airplane flight, the Markey brothers would watch the sun set twice.

Jean assumed pilot duties for the flight home. On the way, sunset-reddened skies deepened to silhouette the Sierra Ancha Mountains in purple, then turned black as we overflew the McDowells inbound for landing at Scottsdale. I radioed ahead to phone the boys' father, which led to the only glitch on our trip—Mr. Markey went to the wrong location on the airport. He found us at the terminal just before 6 o'clock, and rushed his boys off to the wedding.

Mission accomplished! Ah, the glory of being a pilot . . . for a few days I even got to be a high school hero. Hey, better late than never!

Dumb Dads Club

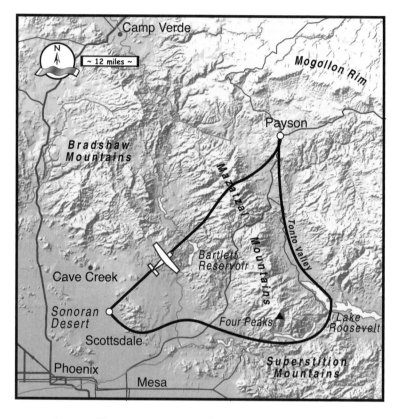

It was Christmas vacation from school, the Arizona air crisp, cool, and blue, when Austin raised the subject at the breakfast table.

"Hey Dad, think we oughta go flying?"

"Today?"

"Yeah, why not?

"Well," I said, "let me think about it for a moment." I'd been struggling with a difficult project for weeks, and in turn, frustrated those around me.

"C'mon, Dad, it's vacation and I don't have anything to do. You always say you want to fly more often, so let's get with it!"

Parents of fifteen-year-olds quickly learn that their formerly affectionate kids have little patience with them. Now that I'd unwittingly joined the "Dumb Dads Club," invitations to do things with my kids had become disturbingly rare. This opportunity to spend a pleasant day with my son was too important to miss.

Setting my project aside, I phoned the airport to arrange rental of a diminutive Cessna 152. Austin and I loaded water bottles, collected our charts and headsets, and headed for the airport.

We plotted course that morning for the quiet mountain town of Payson. It would be a short but scenic flight, and as my son pointed out, the airport restaurant there offered many flavors of homemade pie to occupy us upon arrival. As usual for such weekend adventures, Austin claimed pilot duties for the trip. I would back him up on the radio, help with navigation, and offer occasional (if uninvited) professional advice.

Upon arriving at the airport, Austin transformed as if by magic from typical high school sophomore to dedicated professional pilot. Without a word from me, he preflighted the airplane, organized the cockpit, and worked his way through the start-up checklist. Then he taxied us toward the runway, centering our nosewheel on the yellow taxiway stripe better than I ever seem able to do. Quietly, I was proud.

"You know, Dad," said Austin after completing the engine run-up, "Now comes one of my favorite parts of flying."

"What's that, Austin?"

"I love to taxi out onto the runway and line up with the center line, knowing we're about to pour on the coal and take off."

Smiling, I radioed the tower for takeoff clearance.

"Taxi into position and hold," replied the controller.

"That's even better," said Austin, applying power to comply with our clearance. "Now we get to sit on the runway for a minute and enjoy the view!"

"Cleared for takeoff," said the tower. Smiling, Austin advanced the throttle.

Arizona is roughly divided into two parts, topographically. The southwestern portion of the state is mostly low desert, hot, and populated by giant saguaro cacti. To the north and east lie mountains and high plateau. Phoenix lies in the desert near the junction of the two, thereby offering divergent views and weather depending upon direction of travel.

On this day we climbed northeastward out of the Sonoran Desert. Overflying boat-speckled Bartlett Reservoir, Austin wove us between white-dusted summits of the Mazatzal Mountains. The combination of snowy peaks, cobalt sky, and sparkling water displaced all thoughts of our world left behind, and we soon gazed silently out our respective windows. Clearing the ridge, we penetrated a green valley cut deep by the thread of Tonto Creek far below.

Now there was something to talk about. Playing detective, Austin noted glittering tinsel among distant pines beyond the valley—sparkling windows offered clues to our destination long before we could positively identify town or airport.

Beyond those reflections loomed the Mogollon Rim, edge of the gigantic Colorado plateau that consumes northeast Arizona and stretches unbroken all the way to the Great Plains. Snow-covered at this time of year, the densely wooded Rim towers some 2,000 feet almost straight up, northeast of Payson. Most incredible to former flatlanders like me is that such rich variations of terrain should occur in a mere sixty-mile flight.

We soon identified the airport north of town. There being no control tower here, I radioed Payson unicom frequency for information on winds and active runway.[3] Today my call was answered by someone working the fuel shack, but fondly I remembered the days when inbound pilots made radio contact through the kitchen of the airport restaurant. After receiving landing advisory, you could reserve a table and even order breakfast.

Although the cook no longer answered Payson unicom to the sound of frying eggs, a wonderful family atmosphere still pervaded the place. Despite my personal origins 2,000 miles away, it always seemed like returning home when flying here.

We joined downwind leg parallel to the runway for landing, and following discussion about winds and the dip in the runway, Austin set down the Cessna in good form. As he turned us from taxiway to restaurant ramp, we noticed a man and his young son watching from the fence. Waves and smiles were exchanged as we walked into the modest restaurant with its endless rock-and-pine mountain vistas. Austin claimed a table overlooking the runway, while I went to wash up.

When I returned, I was surprised to find the man we'd seen at the fence, sitting with his child at the table next to ours and grilling my son.

"Was that you sitting in the pilot's seat?" I heard the man ask Austin.

"Yes," said Austin, "My Dad's a flight instructor and he lets me sit in the left seat."

---

[3] *Unicom* radio frequency is operated voluntarily by nonprofessional parties on the ground. At airports like Payson, without an operating control tower, unicom is commonly used to share landing information with inbound aircraft and also by pilots to announce their positions to others in the traffic pattern.

"From where we were standing, it almost looked as if you were actually piloting the plane."

"I was—I even made the landing."

"Really? Wow, that's neat! Do you do this sort of thing with your Dad very often?"

"Oh yeah, my Dad and I fly together a lot—it's really fun." At that point I introduced myself and sat down to join them.

"Nice meeting you," said the father, encouraging a shy handshake from his young son. "I'm Warren." He then explained that he and his family lived in Phoenix, but often made the two-hour drive to see his wife's parents in Payson. He peppered us with questions, like how long it takes to fly to Payson. "About half an hour, even in a small plane like the 152," I told him. It turned out that on visits to grandpa and grandma's house, Warren and his kids often ventured to Payson Airport to watch the planes land. Accordingly, he had many questions about procedures for flying a plane there and landing.

"Where else have you flown with your Dad?" he then asked Austin. Warren listened with rapt attention as my son recounted recent destinations through the Southwest and California. I rarely consider most places we fly exotic, but the expression on Warren's face reminded me that to most people piloting your own airplane from Phoenix to San Diego is heady stuff.

Throughout lunch, Austin and I answered eager questions about what it takes to become a pilot. Afterward, the four of us chuckled at the rock-on-a-rope "Payson Weather Station," then wandered the ramp together admiring airplanes parked there.

"Sounds like you might enjoy becoming a pilot yourself," I said to Warren, as Austin preflighted for the trip home.

"To tell the truth," said Warren, "I've been looking for a fun activity I can share with my own sons as they get older.

The Payson Weather Station.

Seems like all anyone does these days is work. I don't want to let my kids' teenage years pass without enjoying every moment together we can. Seeing you and your son fly in today makes me feel this could be the adventure we're looking for."

I'm a lucky guy, I was reminded at that moment—really lucky. Not only do I get to fly airplanes, but my son likes to do it too, and best of all, in my company. Like most teens, Austin generally avoids hanging around with "Dumb Dads Club" members like myself. But when it comes to flying, no one can keep us apart. In the cockpit we work as friends and equals to do the most professional job we can. Meeting that man at the fence gave me new appreciation of just how fortunate I was to share the special passion of flying with my son.

As for Austin, he stood about fourteen feet tall as he untied his wing under the admiring gaze of the younger boy, then climbed into the pilot's seat.

"Ready to roll, Dad," he said, showing thumbs up.

Two small figures could be seen back at the fence as Austin and I took the runway at Payson, so on climbout we "waggled" our wings goodbye.

"Think they could see us rocking the wings?" asked Austin.

"I'm sure they could," said I.

As we left the pattern and the land dropped precipitously into the Tonto Valley below, Austin turned to me with a smile and shared a high five with his free hand.

"Guess we're pretty lucky, getting to do this all the time," he beamed. "Hey! Want to fly down over Lake Roosevelt on the way home, and follow the Salt River through the pass? I like going that way."

"You bet!" I replied, hoping the intercom would mask the lump in my throat so I wouldn't have to rejoin the Dumb Dads Club any sooner than necessary.

"Awesome!" said Austin, banking left. "Oh, and Dad—think we could fly once more before vacation's over?"

GIFT OF FLIGHT

Our Own Flying Carpet

Austin preflights the *Flying Carpet.*

Rays of setting sun beamed apricot on the blackening landscape beneath us, then surrendered the Valley of the Sun to city lights. For a few more precious moments, we watched privately as the orb rounded the curvature of the Earth. It's a special privilege of pilots to view sunset after night falls for everyone else below. Stars appeared, and the small mountains scattered about Phoenix dematerialized to black voids in the fabric of illuminated streets.

"Time for some lights," said Austin, his face aglow in twilight. Fumbling, he searched the darkened instrument panel, flipping switches one at a time as he found them. "We'll have to get used to where everything is located in here."

This was to be just a short father-son flight, but a special one. Somehow the splendor of this particular sunset seemed appropriate for the mission at hand.

"How does it handle, Dad?"

"Great!" I replied. "Solid on the controls—plus I can't believe we'll have the luxury of an autopilot." Tonight, for a change, was my evening to fly, while Austin would copilot and handle the radios.

"Deer Valley Airport in sight, Dad. I'll radio for clearance. How many landings would you like to make?"

"Let's do two more, like we did at Scottsdale. It's official nighttime now, so I can get my night landing practice while checking out the plane." We touched down twice at Deer Valley, then set course around the McDowell Mountains toward Falcon Field.

"This is cool!" said Austin, taking a turn at the controls. "Trims out really nice. I just can't believe we now have *our own plane!* Think we'll get to fly it a lot?"

"I sure plan to, Austin. One reason Mom and I did this is to make more family trips before you and your brother head off to college. All those great times over the past few months—flying to Safford for the band competition, and even our little trip to Payson—made us realize we should invest in a plane now, before you guys move on to lives of your own."

"Not that I'm unhappy with this plane, Dad, but I was kind of hoping we'd get something with retractable landing gear. I love that sound of the wheels going up and down—plus those planes go faster."

"I know what you mean, but this plane will take us anywhere we want to go, and besides, what's our hurry?" I thought of Halliburton's biplane, and all the world to be seen when traveling low and slow. Like the adventurer's Stearman, this Cessna was simple and utilitarian. Other than being able

to carry four people in a closed cockpit, our flying would differ little from his.

"Where do you think we'll go, Dad?"

"Lots of places. We've never visited the Northwest. And I
want to make an East Coast trip, too."

"Now *those* sound like fun!" said Austin. "Seems like our
recent trips have mostly been short ones."

"That's a big benefit of having our own plane. We can fly
wherever we want, and stay as long as we like."

"I'd like to visit the Air Force Academy sometime—think
we could do that?"

"You bet! Put it on the list. Say, on a different topic, I'm
thinking of naming this airplane. What do you think of the
idea?"

"You mean besides the N-number painted on the side?"

"Yeah. How do you like the name, 'Flying Carpet'?"

"Not very exciting," replied Austin. "Let me think about it
awhile." He pointed ahead out the windshield. "Hey, look!
The fountain is going off at Fountain Hills." A white shaft of
light rose from darkness, the illuminated geyser being visible
from many miles away.

"I like it from this distance," I replied, smiling to myself.
"You can see Falcon Field, too, beyond the fountain and across
the reservation."

"I see it, Dad . . . already have tower frequency set in the
radio." He tuned in the recorded weather for our destination.

"Wonder how long it'll take for us to trust this airplane,"
I mused out loud.

"Are you worried that something might be wrong?"

"No, everything seems to be working fine. But it takes time
to bond with an airplane that's new to you—to learn its quirks,
trust its radios, and become friendly with the particular hum
of its engine. Until then there'll be little comfort flying over
water—or at night." Uneasily, we smiled at each other.

After landing, Austin and I walked a dozen times around that airplane, trying to convince ourselves that the prize was indeed ours and would fly upon our command and no one else's.

"I didn't like the color too much at first," said Austin, "but it's growing on me." It took a few more circuits, but finally we brought ourselves to get into the car and head for home.

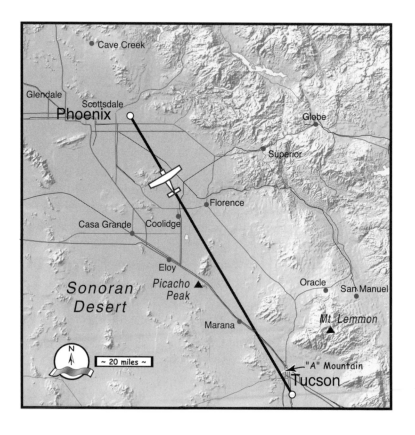

Just a few days later we were back at the airport. This was to be only our second flight in the new airplane, and our first real mission.

"Why would *anyone* want an airplane like *that?*" queried my son about the weathered Cessna 150 parked across from us. We peered through hazy windows into the aging two-seater; inside were cracked plastic and worn seats.

"Simple," I replied. "Have you ever met the owner?"

"Only once or twice. It's that older guy, right? Almost every time we come out here, he's already up flying."

"That's him," I said. "This plane cost less than many used cars, and even being retired the owner can afford to fly it any-time he wants. Suppose *you* could have this plane and fly all *you* wanted—would you take it?"

"My own airplane? Sure! I'd take it in a second!"

"Far better to fly a battered old 150, than to sit at home reading about jets."

"I see your point, Dad. Is that why we didn't get a retractable?"

"That's one reason."

We climbed into our own flying carpet, each a bit more respectful of the ancient Cessna's owner. Austin strapped for the first time into the pilot's seat, and worked his way carefully through the unfamiliar checklist. Then he turned the key.

"Starts right up!" he exclaimed. I thought of that father and son at the fence in Payson, and knew for the first time without a doubt that our family had made the right decision. An hour later we taxied up to Tucson's Executive Terminal. There, rampside, stood Conor Bailie and two of his college buddies.

"Mr. Brown!" Conor yelled to me as he motioned the little group in our direction, then broke into a trot. I was barely out of the aircraft when the beaming young man reached the plane.

"Dudes! Check this out!" he exclaimed to his comrades, gazing into the cockpit. You'd think he was examining an F-16, not a single-engine Cessna.

"I can't believe we're doing this!" said Conor, enthusiasti-cally cranking my hand. He watched with rapt attention as I preflighted, then absent-mindedly waved goodbye to his friends. Austin fielded endless questions while I picked up our taxi clearance.

Conor had been bugging me for a ride ever since I flew his brothers to summer music camp several years earlier. So when I learned he was coming home from college for the weekend, I'd emailed an offer. "Get yourself a ride to the Tucson airport Friday afternoon, and we'll pick you up there in the airplane."

If ever I'd doubted the young man's interest in flying, it was dispelled today. Conor, one of my older son Hannis's more colorful friends, was notorious for being chronically late, yet here he was waiting when Austin and I arrived. This was the first we knew of him ever being early to anything. I installed him in the front passenger seat.

"Wow!" exclaimed Conor as our nosewheel rotated skyward. "This is awesome!" burst forth as the main wheels broke free. The controller issued us the usual clearance to "overfly A Mountain, then climb on course to Phoenix." Our new passenger particularly enjoyed this instruction, because A Mountain commands Tucson's skyline with the University of Arizona's initial.

After recovering from the amazement of takeoff, Conor was next astonished by new perspectives of the familiar city below. "There's the U of A campus," he said, gesturing out the window, "and where we camp on weekends!" pointing out the foothills of Mt. Lemmon.

Flying home from Tucson, our young friend talked briefly of his roommate, of classes, and of a special girl he'd met. But each time conversation returned to what was out the window —sweeping views of mountains and deserts unlike any he'd seen before. Copper skies touched ribbons of city lights as we approached Phoenix, pierced by those same hulking mountain shadows Austin and I had observed a few days earlier. Conor stared, spellbound.

Sunlight spilled over the mountains, casting a crimson glow on the foothills.

"Did I ever tell you about my fascination with sunset, Mr. Brown?" he said, reverently. "Ever since I was a little kid, sunset has been my time of day. I often seek out some special vantage point to watch it go down." I'd never really considered before how much sunrise and sunset figure in the beauty of flying—but thinking back, it's a lot.

Runway lights punctuated blackness when we touched down, and after unloading, Conor tossed his bags into our car. Normally ebullient, he was meditative on the drive home —about life as a student, about that girl he'd met, and about flying.

"Mr. Brown," he said dead-seriously when I dropped him off, "this is like the most awesome experience of my entire life, and I can't thank you enough for giving me this opportunity." He paused for a moment while the trademark smile recaptured his face.

"And sunset! Never before have I witnessed a more physically beautiful phenomenon than an Arizona sunset as seen from the cockpit of an airplane. I was taken aback by the way the sunlight seemed to spill over the mountains, casting a crimson glow on the foothills."

"Pretty colorful," said Austin, closing the car door after Conor's departure.

"The sunset? Or Conor?" I asked.

"Both." He smiled.

Driving home I contemplated the gift we're blessed with as pilots, in conferring these special flights. In the short space of an hour I'd delivered Conor Bailie an experience he'll remember for a lifetime. What was for me routine will forever be branded in his mind as "the first time." To think that I have the power to deliver so much joy locked up in my head and hands, and a little scrap of paper in my wallet.

I looked to Austin. How many souls will thrill to that once-in-a-lifetime gift during our tenures as aviators? Of all the first flights I've bestowed, some recipients went on to become pilots and others did not. But each grasped a few moments of never-to-be-forgotten enchantment, all while flying with . . . *me!*

"Dad," said Austin as we pulled into the driveway. "Picking up Conor was pretty cool tonight. I can't believe how excited he was. And you know what else? For some reason, the name 'Flying Carpet' is growing on me."

A Watchful Eye
over the Shoulder

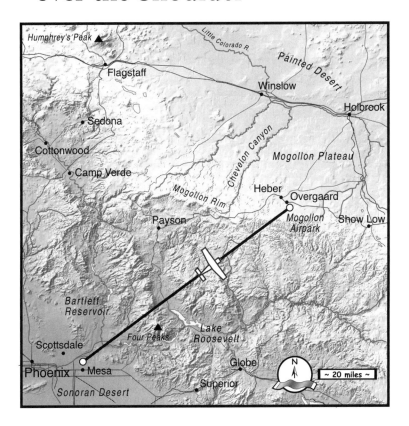

Fear. Nobody talks about it, but it's there—buried down deep in the heart of every pilot. Even after long periods of dormancy, it emerges occasionally to confront us. Fortunately, after it's over we're generally better pilots for having dealt with it.

It was one of those hot and lazy summer weekends when suffering desert denizens seek escape to cooler climes. Our salvation came in the form of a newspaper ad for an "open

161

house" at Mogollon Airpark, a remote private residential airstrip in Northern Arizona's wooded "rim country." Having often wondered what life might be like in such a place, I proposed visiting. "Too hot to do much around here anyway," said Jean. "Let's go."

At the airport, preflighting the *Flying Carpet* went quickly, especially with the neighboring airplane away so I didn't need to maneuver around it. Soon we taxied for takeoff, passing along the way a sad-looking Cessna minus the vertical fin of its tail. It looked like normal maintenance except for vehicles parked nearby. "Must have been damaged in the tiedowns," I observed to Jean. Soon we were rolling down the runway on takeoff.

My heart always swells with emotion during the climb from hot Phoenix desert to cool northern Arizona pines, especially when the 7,000-foot Mogollon Rim materializes ahead, stretching from horizon to horizon like the edge of the Earth. Despite having crossed it many times before, feelings of foreboding are unavoidable when approaching such a huge mass —even the chart's most earnest assurances can't quash feelings that this time we might not rise high enough to surmount it. Then follows the breathtaking squeeze of skimming suddenly low over the mammoth Mogollon Plateau, when at the same altitude only an instant earlier we'd been suspended many thousands of feet above lower terrain.

Peering ahead among tall pines for the airport, I twirled radio knobs and announced our intention to land. I didn't anticipate an answer, because this airport is unattended except for the residents.

"Mogollon Airport is closed," came an unexpected reply from a handheld radio, "Disabled aircraft landed wheels-up. Everyone's okay, but we need to clear the runway before anyone else can land."

We took advantage of our twenty minutes circling to ogle streets and homes nestled among the pines; best of all were the airplanes parked in almost every yard. When the runway cleared, we landed and visited the advertised home, a stereotypical A-frame in the woods, garnished with a climate-controlled hangar for pampering the lucky owner's airplane. Too rich for our blood, it turned out, but fitting for future dreams.

After wandering the airpark, Jean and I again rotated skyward in the *Flying Carpet*. With only two of us on board, fuel tanks at half, and no luggage, takeoff was brisk even given the 6,600-foot elevation. We sighed sad goodbyes to cool air upon departing the Rim, and shortly found ourselves descending into the hellacious heat of summertime Phoenix.

Nothing was stirring at the home field when we touched down—even the lizards were hiding beneath their rocks—and parking was a cinch with our neighbor's aircraft still gone. A friendly woman drove up in the fuel truck, armed with a cooler of cold drinks.

"Gettin' warm," I said in desert vernacular.

"That time of year," she replied, navigating the fuel nozzle up-ladder to the wing. "You hear what happened this morning?"

"Nope," I said, extracting an icy pop from the cooler, "what's that?"

"Midair collision in the traffic pattern." She gestured toward the empty tiedown beside us. "Your neighbor there was one of the planes involved."

Jean and I looked at one another in horror—years of safe flying and now two incidents encountered in the same day. I was almost afraid to ask . . .

"Are the pilots okay?"

"It was a miracle," replied the fueler, "two people aboard each plane and everyone walked away."

"What was the other airplane?" I asked.

"A high-wing Cessna, now parked over on the ramp."

"You don't mean . . . " I asked, disbelieving.

"Yep, the one without the tail."

"Mechanics removed the tail fin afterward?"

"Nope, the pilots landed without it."

It was beyond my comprehension that anyone could safely land an airplane minus its vertical stabilizer and rudder. Directional control would be largely impossible, and the aircraft's balance would be disturbed due to the lost weight of the missing structure.

"And the other plane?" I asked, glancing sidewise toward the empty tiedown.

"Ground the prop off, but otherwise it didn't look too bad."

Jean and I drove by the Cessna on our way home, again disbelieving. The stabilizer had been removed totally and cleanly as if by a mechanic. Another inch or two lower, and the other plane's prop would have severed the elevator cables controlling the Cessna's ability to climb and descend. That night and for many more afterward I dreamt of trying to land that 172, less a third of its tail.

More traumatic yet was learning afterward that I'd flown that very plane myself in the past, and knew its pilot. Eventually I got to ask him what was it like—landing a plane without its vertical stabilizer.

"I was teaching a student in the traffic pattern," he told me, "when we felt a 'thump.' Neither of us realized what had happened until hearing the other airplane report 'midair collision' to the tower. There was no time to think about it, once we realized what happened, so I just circled down to land. Didn't think we were gonna make it when I noticed on final that even minor power changes caused the plane to veer left and right."

They managed to touch down on the runway, but when the instructor reduced power, the plane veered diagonally off the pavement to the right. From there, they traversed grass, the parallel taxiway, more grass, and several hundred yards of paved ramp, before coming to a stop just short of a large hangar. Fortunately, the Cessna survived its wild landing roll with little damage beyond that suffered in flight, and the occupants emerged unscathed except for the emotional toll.

But for fate, the outcome might have been very different. Although midair collisions are statistically rare, the odds of all parties surviving one are slim. The fellow who lost his prop had a tough job getting down, but for the other to safely land his airplane minus the vertical stabilizer is incomprehensible. Literally an inch or two closer would have assured the loss of both planes and their occupants.

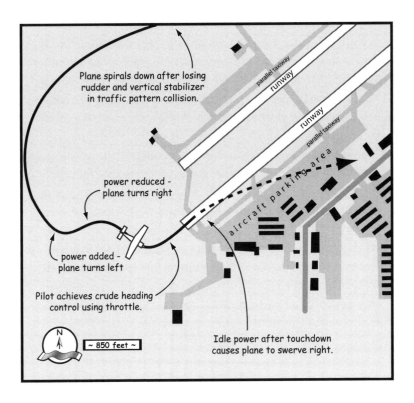

Plane spirals down after losing rudder and vertical stabilizer in traffic pattern collision.

parallel taxiway

runway

runway

parallel taxiway

aircraft parking area

power reduced - plane turns right

power added - plane turns left

Pilot achieves crude heading control using throttle.

N

~ 850 feet ~

Idle power after touchdown causes plane to swerve right.

How do pilots keep flying after something like this happens? Some don't—the Cessna's instructor hadn't recovered from the experience even months afterward, and I don't know if he ever got on with his planned piloting career. For most of us, however, the answer lies in comprehending how each accident might be prevented, and then taking aggressive action to avoid similar fates ourselves. "Don't make that mistake," we tell ourselves, "and I'll be okay." That approach works well in modern aircraft, which in themselves are pretty reliable.

It took a year, but gradually my own fear returned to its more comfortable position below the conscious horizon. I learned to keep it at bay by enthusiastically monitoring traffic around me when I fly, and by enlisting all eyes in my airplane to help. Always looking over my shoulder, you might say.

It's harder to imagine how pilots developed confidence to keep flying in the early days. Not long before Halliburton, it wasn't uncommon for airplanes to disintegrate spontaneously in the air. Engine failures were so frequent that in early North African airmail service, two planes were sent on every route— one full and one empty. That way if one went down the other could pick up the mail and continue on to the destination. Imagine flying every day in that environment.

When accidents do occur, however, the role of fate is far from gone. The ramp through which that damaged Cessna careened is normally blanketed with some 230 closely parked airplanes. But during the week of the collision those planes had been moved across the airport to accommodate repaving. Even after surviving the midair collision and successfully landing, on any other occasion the pilots would have plowed through thirty or forty parked airplanes during their uncontrolled rollout. Man, were those guys lucky.

Glad I Did the Preflight

We had now owned our *Flying Carpet* for four months, and we looked forward to its first long journey of exploration under our command. Neither Jean nor I had ever traveled the Pacific coast north of San Francisco. For our shakedown voyage, we decided to hopscotch northwest from Phoenix to Seattle, then linger on the way back along the northern California coast.

Even upon first glance at the chart, it was clear we couldn't fly straight-line to Sacramento, our initial stop, because of the Sierra Nevada mountain range of eastern California. This

167

300-mile wall of 14,000-foot peaks exceeds the climb capability of most light aircraft. The few passes through the range are often assaulted by strong winds and foul weather, plus much of the area is bracketed by restricted, military-use airspace. We decided that the path of least resistance would be to circumnavigate the High Sierra to the south.

With that in mind, our first leg after takeoff was westbound through Arizona and south central California. Beyond Twenty-Nine Palms, air traffic control cleared us directly over Edwards Air Force Base, where to our surprise we overflew the runway where space shuttles land. From there we navigated northwestward through the San Joaquin Valley, where the snowcapped Sierra consumed Jean's side window for the rest of the trip. Four-and-a-half hours after takeoff from Phoenix, we touched down at Sacramento. There was still time to hike the gold fields at Sutter's Mill before dining that evening with friends.

All hours in the air are not equal, though they might sometimes appear that way in a pilot logbook. Hours tinged by fear endure longest, followed by those touched by beauty. Our flight next day to Eugene, Oregon, was richly tinted by the latter; two short turns of the hour-hand offered visual impact to be remembered for a lifetime. Climbing out of the San Joaquin Valley, we passed within touching distance of 14,162-foot Mt. Shasta, only to surpass that thrill with the most spectacular from-the-air sight of our lives—Oregon's Crater Lake, formed when a volcano blew its top 7,000 years ago.

I had long dreamed of visiting Crater Lake. Having marked it on our chart ahead of time, we detoured east to look for it among high mountains. Adding to the lake's mystery, we soon learned, was the difficulty of getting there, even by *Flying Carpet*. With so much of Earth's water filling low places, climbing through 10,000 feet in search of a lake defies reason. Our minds dazed by altitude, it proved increasingly difficult to remain oriented between compass, charts, and featureless high terrain.

Uncertainly, we threaded our way between intermingled peaks, until beckoned by glints of sapphire, speckled by silver clouds. There we discovered the object of our quest, set gem-like in a sharp-edged ring of rock and green trees. Even in July, the crater's unspeakably blue waters mirrored crystalline snow on its 9,000-foot-elevation rim. Piercing the lake's surface like a beauty mark was the tiny peak of Wizard Island. Round and round we flew, futilely seeking that unattainable perspective promised by all perfect beauty. Not until Jean woke us from our trance did we finally tear ourselves away.

"Greg!" she said with surprise. "How's our fuel? We've been circling for forty-five minutes!" Now I knew how Homer's Odysseus felt, when bewitched by Circe to remain on her island. Always I'd been drawn to the air, but this was the first time my flying carpet had been seduced by an enchantress.

Adding to Crater Lake's mystery was the difficulty of getting there.

Near Eugene waited another surprise very different in character. Travel by flying carpet creates the expectation of magic in every destination. Rarely do you find it, of course—return to Earth often means disappointing descent back into reality. But there in a time warp at tiny Creswell airport, waited our good friend Dorothy, her curtained office sheltered under the eave of an ancient hangar. I wouldn't have been surprised had Toto rushed out to greet us, nor if Halliburton's black and crimson Stearman rested in the shadows of that aged hangar. Old airplanes peeked curiously at us from their doorless dwellings, and on the ramp surly linemen fueled our plane from a paralyzed truck of a bygone era.

Over the next few days we toured the Oregon Coast with Dorothy and her friend, Susan. Coming from sunny Arizona, Jean and I became increasingly astonished to find the world shrouded in fog, day after day. When time came to leave, we climbed through low ceilings from Eugene into blue skies above. There, snow-covered mountains guided us up the Willamette Valley toward Seattle, like rows of signposts piercing an endless sea of clouds.

Approaching our destination, we were vectored toward Paine Field. Towering mountains gave way to deep green islands and rich blue water glimpsed through holes in the clouds below. How lush it all seemed compared to the muted colors of the Arizona desert. An instrument approach to 200 feet seemed a worthy climax for pilot and machine, having successfully arrived at this far corner of the country.

There was business to do in Seattle, plus sightseeing and touring with friends. Among our hosts for the visit were Don and Kitty Darrow. Don, a longtime friend of my father's, had served as a Navy fighter pilot, then completed his career as a Boeing 747 check airman for American Airlines. Kitty flew extensively on business for the scientific instrument company she headed. The two of them might have retired from their professional careers, but they certainly hadn't withdrawn from flying.

The morning after we arrived, Don introduced us to his "other woman, Debbie," a lovingly polished Beech Debonair. In the corner of his hangar rested his project aircraft, a toy-like single-seat Mooney Mite he was restoring.

Then Kitty showed off her new Cessna 182. Her previous airplane was a Citation jet, which she often flew on business around the country. Smiling, Kitty told of her predictable reception when flying the bizjet. Invariably, a lineman would be waiting when she arrived to take the fuel order. After watching Kitty exit the airplane, the fueler would wait patiently for someone else to step out behind her. When no one did, the ramper would ask, "Where's the pilot?"

"*I'm* the pilot," Kitty delighted in replying, after appropriate pause for effect. No one expected a petite white-haired grandmother to be piloting a business jet.

Don and Kitty had each been flying for many years. Don flew Corsairs and Bearcats off carriers as World War II came to an end, and Kitty grew up in a flying family. While the four of us rode the ferry to Whidbey Island for brunch, Kitty told of one particularly memorable flight with her dad.

"When I was a little girl in the thirties," she said, "my father owned an Alexander Eaglerock." The Eaglerock was a contemporary of Halliburton's Stearman—my mind filled with images of a Shirley Temple-like little girl, bedecked in goggles and leather helmet while roaming bucolic countryside with her father in an open-cockpit biplane.

"We were flying one day," continued Kitty, "when the engine failed. Being only eight or nine years old, I had no idea of the danger involved, but it seemed like no big deal when my father landed the plane safely in a farm field.

"That evening, I'd just gotten upstairs on my way to bed when I heard my parents discussing the forced landing. My father being an extremely honest man, I remember being upset when I heard him tell my mother an untruth. After describing the engine failure and landing, he said to my mother, 'That was as close to a cemetery as I ever care to land.'"

Kitty paused to chuckle. "I knew that wasn't true, because I remembered clearly where we'd touched down—and there wasn't a gravestone to be seen anywhere around there."

Again I was touched by the brief history of aviation. In one short lifetime Don and Kitty had traveled the gamut from radial-engined biplanes to turbofan-powered jets, and were still active aviators today. I wondered what Kitty's father would think, had he seen his daughter piloting passengers around the country at 30,000 feet and 600 miles per hour.

Another highlight of our visit came after touring the Museum of Flight at Boeing Field. We were walking to the parking lot when in taxied the world's only flying Boeing 247. Before a backdrop of skyscrapers and landing jetliners, the seventy-year-old 247 shut down engines within yards of us. The door opened and out stepped a parade of local dignitaries, attended to by pilots and "stewardesses" in period dress.

Introduced in the early 1930s, the 247 was the world's first modern airliner, featuring all-metal construction, retractable landing gear, and then-revolutionary speed and comfort. At 160 miles per hour, it was twice as fast as its predecessor, the Ford Trimotor, far quieter, and featured a galley and lavatory. Given the fast pace of aircraft development at that time, the 247 was quickly superseded by Douglas's DC-2 and DC-3. Jean indulged me while we toured the historic vehicle and then watched it take off again. Never had I expected to see this rare model fly.

Soon it was time to depart for our most anticipated destination of the trip—a romantic bed and breakfast inn at Mendocino, north of San Francisco on California's rugged coast.

In taxied a Boeing 247, last flying example of the world's first modern airliner.

Climbing southward after takeoff, we broke free of clouds and traced the Washington and Oregon coasts to the remote northern California shore. Although the weather was clear a quarter-mile inland, maritime fog and stratus shrouded the low-lying coast almost the entire four-hour flight. The mysterious vapor only added to the fascination of the trip—from above, jagged rocks could be seen peeking through, along with bits of towns known previously only as dots on a map.

The low-lying stratus offered cause for concern, too. Our destination of Little River Airport had no instrument approach. If shrouded by clouds we'd need to detour across the coast mountain range to an inland alternate, then try to find transportation back. This being a sparsely populated area, the ability to find such ground transportation was an open question. Then there was the issue of fuel; no avgas was available at our destination. I had to ensure that enough remained when we landed to get us to another airport on our way out.

Not until arriving in the clear over Little River did I know for sure that we'd be able to land there.

When I say "arriving in the clear," that was actually only half true, relative to the airport. The runway, which lies more or less perpendicular to the coast atop a 500-foot bluff, was clear at one end and shrouded in low stratus on the other. We entered our landing pattern above the clouds, turned final and touched down in the clear, and then rolled under the overcast to a stop. It was like diving under bed-covers, headfirst.

After two days sampling seafood and hiking in fog through multicolored wildflowers along the shore, we were delivered back to the Skylane for our long flight home. There was a penetrating chill that morning, in wet mist—not the sort of weather I relish for climbing about an airplane on pre-flight inspection. What's more, low-lying clouds overhead meant we'd need to climb on instruments toward better weather inland.

As I prepared to load the bags, I noticed that although properly secured, the baggage compartment door handle seemed slightly askew. Older-style Cessna baggage compartment handles tend to protrude a bit over time, but this one showed a subtle twist I wasn't sure I remembered from before.

Carefully I checked cabin doors and contents, only to determine that no one had broken in. Maybe that slight twist was not new after all, I decided, or perhaps someone had tested the baggage door just to see if it was unlocked. After all, it would be easy enough for anyone to break into a Cessna if they really wanted to.

We removed the window sunscreens and loaded up our bags. Then, while Jean headed for the airport office to warm up, I climbed a portable step stool to visually inspect the fuel tanks located in the wings. The left tank was as I expected, but to my alarm the right fuel cap was ajar, as if someone had removed it and wasn't sure how to put it back.

That grabbed my attention, as I'd personally checked the fuel caps prior to departing Seattle, and was certain they'd been properly seated. In any case, the fuel cap couldn't have been loose en route—with fuel streaming overboard, we'd never have completed our four-hour flight nonstop. *Why would someone have opened this?* I wondered.

Differences in quantity between the two sides made me wonder if fuel had been siphoned out of the open tank. That would be the most benign reason for anyone to remove a cap, but I couldn't be sure if any had been taken, because fuel always seemed to draw a little faster from the right side in this particular airplane. Using a calibrated pipette, I carefully measured the amount of fuel remaining in each tank.

Finding plenty of gasoline to safely make our next stop, I now became concerned about the potential effects of several days' misting rain entering the fuel tank through the open cap. Water is heavier than gasoline; if enough had entered, it could accumulate at the fuel ports and silence the engine. Worse yet was the horrifying possibility of someone intentionally depositing contaminants.

When illuminated by flashlight, however, the bottoms of both tanks appeared perfectly clean. After extensively draining and testing the fuel, which proved consistently clear, I ran the engine for fifteen minutes in hopes that any not-so-obvious fuel problems would become apparent. Thankfully, the engine ran perfectly.

Having satisfied myself that the fuel was okay, I once again started my preflight from the beginning. Everything appeared in order as I made my way carefully around the airplane, until I came to the tail. There I found where the corner of the elevator trim tab had been forcibly bent 90° downward. Now it was certain—somebody had aggressively tampered with our airplane. The big question was, what else had they done?

After consulting with a mechanic and straightening the trim tab, I preflighted the airplane yet again—and this was as thorough an inspection as I've ever done. I examined the airplane inch-by-inch, from engine compartment to antennas, including scrutinizing the top of the airplane from a tall stepladder.

Happily I could find nothing else suspicious, other than where a soft shoe had disturbed dust at the base of the right wing strut; the vandal had obviously stepped there to remove the fuel cap. But with an overcast to penetrate and no way to return to this airport in case of problems, there was little comfort in applying takeoff power that morning. Rationally, Jean and I were satisfied that the plane was safe to fly, but even after the extensive preflight and a fanatically thorough engine run-up, the first few minutes of flight were mighty stressful. Not until reaching blue skies above the clouds could I even begin to relax.

It takes little imagination to consider what might have happened had I not so diligently preflighted on this particular day. What if we'd launched without noticing the fuel cap ajar? Assuming we didn't run out along the way, excessive drainage from the right tank would have hopefully become apparent in the fuel quantity gauges. Fuel gauges are notoriously inaccurate, however, and plenty of accidents have occurred because pilots didn't notice, or didn't believe their gauges when fuel seemed to be depleting more rapidly than usual. And what if someone had dumped contaminants in the fuel, unnoticed, and I had neglected to test it?

As for the bent trim tab, my mechanic told me it might have gone unnoticed in flight, or nearly so. But then again, he couldn't be sure. And what if the tab had been distorted to the point of interfering with another surface, perhaps binding the controls? Or if the hinges had been damaged so as to cause control flutter? What if, in missing relatively minor problems like these, we had not been alerted to more threatening damage?

Even following another examination by a mechanic at our first stop twenty minutes later, my anxiety was barely squelched. Not until some five flight hours afterward, as we navigated rose-colored barrens through western Arizona, did I begin welcoming back the warm trust that pilots put in their airplanes—most of the time, anyway. For the second time in only two months, I pondered the question that drives some pilots from their cockpits, while deterring would-be aviators from pursuing such dreams at all. First there'd been the midair collision to worry about, and now this.

Why is it, I wondered over sunset-tinted desert sliced by the silvery Colorado River, *that pilots can face exposure to serious risk, and still return to the cockpit?*

Again I was reminded that if the causes of aviation accidents couldn't be determined, and thereby anticipated and prevented by careful pilots, few of us would fly, because piloting would be little more than a life-or-death lottery. That's in fact how it was in the early days of aviation, which is why few sane people took to the air back then.

But these days we can continue to fly despite disasters, because we can usually learn what went wrong, and therefore how to prevent such exposure in our own flying. Fortunately, a century of powered flight has resulted in procedures that, if followed rigorously, can save our skins the vast majority of the time.

Preflight inspection is one of those procedures. In this case it worked as it's supposed to, and providing I keep preflighting diligently in the future, it should continue to protect me from certain kinds of problems. Like so many safety procedures, the challenge is to keep doing it thoroughly, time after time, on the 1-in-1,000 chance that something unexpected will turn up, from any number of possible causes, and the pilot will catch it. But beware of that 1,001st occasion, when you're preparing to fly and decide ("it won't matter just this one time") to skip the weather briefing or the weight and balance or the preflight inspection. Now *that* is Russian roulette.

Only once before could I remember finding something truly threatening on preflight, and it offered certain eerie parallels to this morning's experience. That time also involved testing fuel before flight. Although clear and free of water bubbles (gasoline and water do not mix), for some reason the fuel I'd collected in the strainer cup that day just didn't seem right to me. I smelled it and dribbled some on my hand—there was no odor or oiliness to suggest misfueling with kerosene (jet fuel).

Still, I was not satisfied, and after further agonizing, finally determined what was wrong. As it turned out, the strainer cup and several more after it contained *only* water, which had apparently entered through a leaky fuel cap during rain the night before. (Hence one concern about this morning's open cap.) So much water had entered the tanks that it had completely displaced the lighter gasoline from the bottom. We most certainly would have suffered engine failure had the problem not been detected ahead of time.

I then thought of that long-ago wintry day in Wisconsin, when Jean had defended my honor over the airport coffeepot. The water-in-the-fuel incident didn't occur until long after that. Another fifteen years had passed between then and this morning, with countless uneventful preflight inspections in the interim.

This morning, I calculated, was only the second time I'd been vindicated by examining the plane on a miserable morning, in almost thirty years of flying. Had I not, who knows what might have happened? But thanks to that preflight, the most memorable part of our flying vacation was nothing more and nothing less than circling pristine Crater Lake, Oregon, deep-blue and framed by the delicious icing of its snow-covered volcanic rim. And that's what any pilot would want to remember.

"Jean," I said. She put down her book and looked at me. "Do you remember that time back in Baraboo . . . "

"You mean when those guys at the airport made fun of you for preflighting in the snow?" she continued for me.

"Yes."

"I remember," she said, smiling. Then she leaned over and kissed me.

Just Meeting an Old Friend for Lunch

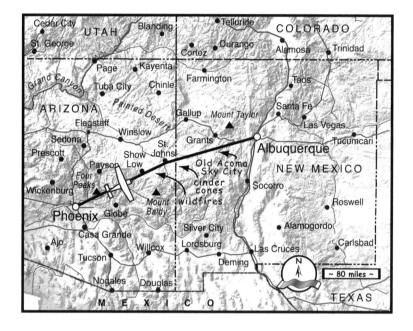

Albuquerque floated mirage-like before us on its sun-drenched plain, nestled against the hulking backdrop of Sandia Peak.

"Delta Nineteen-Sixty-Six checking in, runway in sight," interjected a radio call, among those vectoring us to final.

"That's him!" I said to Austin. "It's Mark!" I fought the urge to key the mic, to advise my old friend of once again sharing the same traffic pattern, but this time with him living his dream at the helm of a Boeing.

"How do you know it's Mark?" asked Austin. "He hardly said anything."

"By the flight number," I replied. "Mark told me that by coincidence he was piloting Flight 1966—the year of his birth." My throat filled with emotion as I thought back ten years to a young flight instructor student, warmly shaking my hand upon our first meeting. I knew from the first moment I met him that he would be one of my best students, and that likely we'd become friends. Even after earning his flight instructor certificate, Mark and I had flown often together. We'd worked side-by-side as both pilots and writers, then split to opposite ends of the country.

Only yesterday Mark had emailed me. "Don't suppose you'll be around Albuquerque tomorrow," he'd asked, only half serious, "I have a long layover there." He knew we lived 300 miles away—unrealistic to assume we'd come over on a Sunday, with no notice, just to share an afternoon.

I felt the same way at first; there were plenty of reasons not to go. "If only I'd known about this earlier," I told myself. But I hadn't seen Mark since he became a Delta pilot, nor since he and his wife Becky enlarged their family with twins. Then there was the flight across Arizona and New Mexico to consider, over enchanted terrain.

"Anyone want to fly to Albuquerque with me tomorrow?" I queried timidly.

"Not me," said my wife, "I'm playing tennis." Hannis was away at Flagstaff, having left for college there a few months before.

"How about you, Austin, wanna go?"

"I'd love to," my son replied, "but my plutonium poster is due Monday and I need to work on it tomorrow."

Only moments later he reentered the room. "Maybe if I work late tonight I could go after all," he said. "I hate to miss Saturday night hanging out with the guys, but . . . "

Here, I thought, is a kid who loves flying as much as his dad. "I'll help with the grunt work," I offered.

So after a late-night sojourn with computer and spray-mount, morning found us soaring over wooded eastern Arizona peaks, where wisps of smoke from isolated fires punctuated green trees and snow below. Suddenly, between flight duties I was struck by a thought.

"You won't believe this," I said to Austin, "but I've just remembered there's some sort of atomic museum on the field at Albuquerque. Wanna go?" We laughed, the plutonium connection being readily apparent.

Ski slopes at Mt. Baldy soon gave way to volcanic cinder cones on the New Mexico border, and piney peaks to juniper-dotted high plains. We were too far south this trip to view the jet-black "malpais" lava fields, their gigantic cracks visible from aloft like patterns on the sun-dried floor of a puddle after it's evaporated. But an equally anticipated treat still lay ahead, 1,000-year-old Acoma Pueblo, arguably the oldest continuously inhabited city in the United States.

It had been twenty years since I first gazed down from 12,000 feet en route from South Dakota and discovered that adobe city perched among red rock spires in an isolated canyon. Acoma's "Sky City" lies atop a 400-foot-tall mesa, I'd learned, and for centuries the only route to the top was by secret ladder carved in stone.

Obsessed with the place even after all this time, I'd been compelled ever since to seek it out whenever our flight path took us nearby. On this day Austin and I peered frustrated into the confusing maze of canyons. But just when we thought we'd missed it, Sky City granted us an enchanted glimpse, with the morning sun highlighting ancient geometry.

That wonder would be topped only by a radio call from Delta 1966, and the warm embrace of an old friend in Albuquerque. I conned Mark into a photo with me, his dapper uniform contrasting with my old blue jeans and tired tennies. Over lunch we talked friends and business and babies and flying, ogling airplanes while downing blue corn enchiladas smothered in cheese and green chiles.

Mark and I had spoken briefly on occasion over the previous few months, but this was the first time in years that we found ourselves with time to share inner feelings about flying, and how it fit into each of our lives. These topics were broached when Austin shared his dream of attending the Air Force Academy, a goal he aggressively pursued despite his young age.

I'd always admired Mark for similar reasons. He knew from childhood that he wanted to be an airline pilot and despite personal and professional obstacles never deviated until getting there.

"How's it going, Mark?" I asked, "Is flying for the majors all it's made out to be?"

"Absolutely," said Mark, "I work with a super bunch of people; the equipment is top-notch, and I love everything about it. Also, for the first time since getting out of college I have plenty of free time—to enjoy my family, to work around our house, and to appreciate life in general."

"You deserve it after those years of struggling through three regional airlines." I said, "Any regrets?" Of course I expected him to say no, or perhaps share minor complaints about trip schedules or parking difficulties at the airport.

"To tell the truth," said Mark, "I do have one regret." The words rang with gravity, like it was a good thing Austin and I were seated before pondering their meaning. "Greg, I feel like I've let the last ten years slip by me without having much fun. I love what I'm doing, but I now think I should have tried to enjoy the flying more along the way."

"What do you mean?" I asked.

"Well," said Mark, "I know you've always admired me for keeping my sights fixed on my professional goal, but sometimes I think I should have taken more time to savor life in the process. Remember those times you invited me to fly some-where in a 172 for lunch and I said no? At the time I felt that if I didn't need the flight hours, it would be wiser to invest the money in multiengine experience, or toward another pilot rat-ing. But now I realize that those years have passed and maybe I missed something." Mark paused for a moment, and his face brightened. "I plan to make up for it, though. One of these days I'll buy my own airplane to fly on days off—then I'll have the best of both worlds."

These words from a valued friend caused me to think seri-ously about my own flying career, both what I had missed, and what I'd gotten out of it. I, too, had once yearned to be an airline pilot—what young aviator doesn't? Yet despite not achieving that objective, I'd had great fun with flying, winging aerial adventures from New Orleans to Winnipeg, and from Nantucket Island, Massachusetts, to Mackinac Island, Michi-gan, to Catalina Island, California. I'd savored Fourth of July fireworks from the air and snow-covered fields at night; I'd lev-itated in balloons and soared in gliders. Perhaps best of all, I'd freed innumerable souls from the ground through the gift of a first flight.

"What sort of plane do you plan to buy, Mark?" I asked, returning to our conversation.

"I have an antique in mind," said Mark, "Ever heard of a Stearman? Ever since I was a little kid I've dreamed of having one of those big, radial-engine biplanes." I couldn't believe the coincidence.

"I know that model well, Mark. Ever heard of a guy named Richard Halliburton?"

"No," said my friend. "Who's that?" I told briefly of Hal-liburton's adventures some seventy years before; then Mark shared dreams of looping and rolling his own Stearman some-day. Time was running short, however, and with another mis-sion remaining to be accomplished we rose to leave.

A quick cab ride took us to the National Atomic Museum; although on the same airport, it was located across the field on a military base. There the three of us traced development of atomic power at nearby Los Alamos laboratories, including events leading up to the deployment of atomic weapons in World War II and beyond. It was both fascinating and horrifying to view beautiful missiles and airplanes designed for such deadly purposes. For Austin's poster, we photographed a twin of "Fat Man," the plutonium bomb that rained death on Nagasaki in 1945.

Escaping holocaust back to the New Mexico sun, we shared goodbyes with Mark and pointed our spinner westward toward home. By now the scattered fires of eastern Arizona had spread into conflagration—dense layers of white smoke flowed smoothly over mountains like water over rocks in a brook. What caused these fires in midwinter we could not imagine, but as with the atomic museum, we marveled at finding beauty and potential tragedy sharing the same setting.

Final rays of fire-red sunset silhouetted Four Peaks as we approached home, with silvery Lake Roosevelt floating in the foreground. Touchdown came in other-worldly darkness amid the sparkling lights of Phoenix. There was just time after dinner for Austin to update his poster with photos taken at the museum.

The following evening, when asked about the success of his plutonium presentation, Austin shared a small disappointment.

"I got an A," he said, "but if only I'd thought to be in the picture with the Fat Man bomb. The kids in class just didn't believe I really made a field trip yesterday to the National Atomic Museum in Albuquerque."

Maybe including him in the picture would have helped. But sometimes even a photograph can't convince people that you have done something extraordinary, like traveling on a whim across two states to meet an old friend for lunch, visiting

Final rays of sunset silhouette Four Peaks on the horizon. Beyond lies home.

wonders of the world along the way, and being home in time for dinner. Impossible, of course . . . except by flying carpet.

Ghost of
Christmas Flights Past

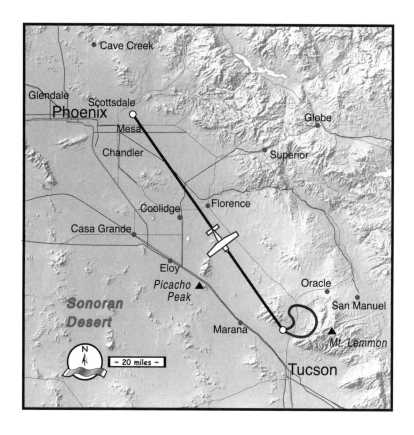

It just doesn't seem like Christmas, as we navigate our *Flying Carpet* southward over sun-drenched cacti of the Sonoran Desert. True, the baggage compartment brims with presents for distribution to nieces and nephews at my brother's Tucson vacation home. But even a dozen delightful years in Arizona

have not resolved snow-shrouded images of Santa and reindeer with the incongruous realities of parched desert and
wearing shorts in wintertime.

All the same, this yuletide flight brings back warm memories of holidays past, when annually we overflew white-
flecked fields and forests delivering gifts from Indiana to
relatives in Illinois and Wisconsin. The boys being small then,
holiday travel meant cramming four of us with bags and presents into the close confines of an aero club Cessna. It was easy
enough imagining Santa just as tightly packed into his sleigh
among towering piles of gold-and-red-wrapped gifts. Wonder
if *he* has to calculate weight and balance?

Often on those holiday rounds, temperatures dropped to
double digits below zero, so we swathed the kids like pigs in
blankets, wearing gloves and boots and sleeping bags for emergency backup. It never did get really warm in the plane, so Jean
and I peered out through frost-fringed windows to avoid errant
flying reindeer and identify our snow-camouflaged destinations.

We never doubted it was Christmas back then, thanks to
"Happy Holidays" clearances issued by friendly controllers.
Santa's sleigh and reindeer adorned Lafayette Tower every year,
and one of our destinations, Chicago's DuPage County Airport, offered a yuletide radio welcome. One year, the recorded
weather information was named to a seasonal phonetic
alphabet—"Information Christmas Tree, Information Reindeer, and Information Santa."[1] Another time, tower controllers recorded weather and landing information to the tune
of *Jingle Bells.*

For seasonal reinforcement, there was the abominable Midwest wintertime climate. Somehow we always made it to our

---

[1] Prerecorded weather and airport information is known as ATIS (auto-
matic terminal information service.) Normally it is coded to the standard
aviation phonetic alphabet: "alpha, bravo, charlie," etc.

holiday destinations, despite snow swirling about our propeller, slippery runways, and ice-filled clouds. Bad weather might mean arriving or departing a day late, but that just accentuated the warm reception of relatives in a bitter-cold world.

Shoveling snowy memories aside, I revel in today's mountain vistas and clear-blue skies. Perhaps there's a subtle rightness to this year's holiday travel, after all. It's the first time since moving to Arizona that we've had occasion to fly on Christmas Day to join with relatives. Traveling together as a family is all the more rare and special now that Hannis and Austin have grown to be young men.

Holiday traffic recedes below as in the past, though this time hardy souls drive convertibles with tops retracted instead of slithering through slush. Still, it's easy enough to imagine rowdy kids and colorful gifts inside those cars—and countless smiling white-haired grandmothers awaiting them at their destinations.

After skimming low over mountains, we turn final at private La Cholla airstrip, where prior permission has been granted to land. With its setting of rancho-style adobes among prickly pears and ocotillos, La Cholla plays the part of an old-time holiday ranch. Surely, Sky King's *Songbird* must be parked on the ramp. And if only Roy Rogers or Rex Allen would greet us on horseback, they could lead us in cowboy carols before a roaring fire and a Christmas tree in the aging airport clubhouse.

We taxi past the welcoming arms of a giant saguaro cactus on the slightly ragged ramp. No singing cowboys meet us, but there waits my sister-in-law Lesley with lovely teen-aged daughters Rachel and Jillian, and my young nephews Danny and Sean. Rachel ogles the cockpit but Danny and Sean are mostly interested in opening those little spring-loaded doors for accessing tire valves through our Cessna's wheel fairings. Peering inside with bottoms up and heads upside down, they seek whatever curiosities might be found there by little boys. The two scamper back and forth between one wheel and another, until distracted by the mountain of presents emerging from our baggage compartment.

Rachel wants to fly, so I look to my sister-in-law for approval. Despite her fear of flying, Lesley grants it with a "You *will* be careful . . . " smile and a nod of her head. Neither Jilly nor the boys want to go, so we install Rachel in the cockpit with headset and grin, and pirouette over her house nestled with its swimming pool against the nearby Santa Catalina Mountains.

"Would you like to fly?" I ask Rachel as we bank toward lower ground. She takes the controls, and I'm treated to the winning smile some lucky young man will fall for in the future. I know at this instant that Rachel's present is the best I'll give this holiday—yet one more ticket to a young person's latent dream of flying. She will never forget this moment, whether becoming a pilot or not. I suppose in this one regard I'm even luckier with my *Flying Carpet* than Santa is with his sleigh. After all, how often does he get to share his gift of flight?

Too soon for Rachel we touch down again on the narrow and rugged strip, and pile all together into a dusty van for the short ride to my brother's. More presents await us there, plus seductive aromas of turkey and pies and all the fixin's, undeniably of holiday origin.

"Put on your bathing suit," says my brother, after a warm embrace. "The margaritas are made, and the swimming pool is waiting."

Guess there are some good sides to this new holiday tradition, and I'll just have to get used to 'em. Eat your heart out, Santa.

Skimming Blue Waters

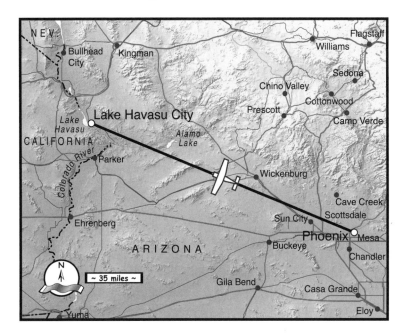

"Need help?" yelled the guy in the boat.

"No thanks," I replied, not daring to turn my head too far for fear of falling into the water. Our seaplane was adrift in the middle of the Colorado River. I was balanced precariously on one float, rear end against the fuselage and face down, pumping water out of the forward float compartment.

Great way to start a flight test, I thought. Twice we had tried to take off—both times unsuccessfully, given today's calm wind and glassy waters. "You must not have emptied all the water from the floats," said examiner Joe La Placa, finally. "Get out there and do it again."

The *Flying Carpet* had brought me to Lake Havasu City the night before, a routine flight except for the 100 miles of emptiness between Phoenix and the Colorado River. You can't help but ponder forced landings in the barren desert along the way. Then, no matter how many times you've done it, comes the surprise of finding the blue Colorado snaking through such arid terrain, with seemingly no impact on the surrounding desert except where humans have irrigated it.

I was here to earn my single-engine seaplane rating from La Placa Flying Service, well-known in these parts after some twenty-five years in the business. Joe and Jean La Placa train seaplane pilots from all over the world—this in a state with only one natural lake and four rivers that flow year-round.

My first hint that this flight would be different than usual came when I went to check out of my hotel room before training. "Mr. La Placa's students don't check out until after they're done," said the clerk, "He has nowhere to put their bags."

This woman sounds confused, I thought. But it made sense later when we bumped to a halt in Mr. La Placa's truck, on a barren lot overlooking the river. We hobbled down improvised stairs to a tiny cove, where a Cessna 150, orange weathered to ochre, sat lonely on floats atop a winch platform. There was no flight school and no ramp—nothing but the airplane itself and the welded tubing platform it sat upon. It was easy enough to imagine ourselves on some remote lake in the wilds of Canada.

As Mr. La Placa showed me around his airplane, I quickly learned it was unlike any other 150 I had ever seen. Cockpit bracing had been added to stiffen the windshield area. A supplementary electric fuel pump ensured gasoline flow to the engine during the high-pitch attitudes required for seaplane takeoffs. Between the seats was a lever like those used for flap extension in Piper Cherokees, but this one raises and lowers water rudders on the floats instead. Under the cowl lurked 150 horsepower, half again more than what originally came installed in this airplane. Floatplanes are no speed demons— the oversized engine is required to get the airplane off the water.

The floats themselves weighed only eighty-five pounds more than the landing gear they replaced, despite their large size. The reason, Mr. La Placa pointed out, is that except for heavier metal "decks" on top, and reinforcement underneath, the skins are "only one gauge thicker than beer cans."

Preflight was different, too. Like boat hulls, floats accumulate water inside, and therefore must be pumped out before every flight. I was to become expert at this task, using a hand pump carried onboard and one powered through the cigarette lighter receptacle.

"Drain the floats properly before leaving shore," Joe counseled me, "'cause it's a lot tougher to do in the middle of the lake." Those words would come back to haunt me on the flight test.

We next examined the propeller for water erosion and cracks caused by spray. Anyone who doubts the power of water to sculpt rock needs only to see how quickly it can erode a metal propeller blade. This problem is so serious that wilderness seaplane pilots carry hacksaws in their survival gear, for removing damaged prop tips if necessary to reach a place where proper repairs can be made. Water flying often requires improvising where help is not available.

I was also surprised, after the plane was winched into the water, to see two-foot lengths of tiedown rope still hanging from the wings. "Those show us which way the wind is blowing on the water," explained La Placa.

Unlike in landplanes where altitude is normally reckoned from sea level, we zeroed the altimeter to mark the lake's surface. Then I started the engine. "No need to test the brakes," observed Mr. La Placa with a smile. As soon as the engine started, we began moving—there's no ground resistance to hold you in place. With water rudders lowered from the floats into the water, this "idling taxi" proved surprisingly easy.

Next I learned high-speed taxi "on the step," which means hydroplaning like a speedboat at sixty to seventy miles per hour. From there it's a simple matter under most conditions to increase power and take off. Once in the air, flying was like a landplane, but more stable due to additional weight and lift from the floats.

Turns out the biggest seaplane kick was flying low—*really* low. In five hours aloft we rarely exceeded 500 feet above the lake, and mostly flew much lower. We flew landing patterns at 200 feet, with base leg prior to touchdown at 100 feet. Those are fractions of the altitudes flown in landplanes, so the feeling was more akin to driving a high-flying boat than a low-flying airplane.

Landing on water presents some interesting challenges. Determining your height above water can be difficult, especially under calm conditions. Therefore seaplane pilots stabilize descent early by establishing landing attitude and adjusting power; then they wait for the plane to land itself. (Similar technique is used by landplane pilots at night, when touching down without a landing light.) La Placa also taught me to skim the shoreline prior to touchdown, so as to better "feel" the level of the lake surface ahead. In any case, it's important to touch down softly, because there are no springs on seaplane floats and the water feels rock-hard upon landing.

For "short field" practice, we touched down in an isolated cove and beached the airplane for a break. More than anything else we did that day, stepping into surf at that secluded beach brought home how phenomenally different water flying is from what I was used to. Not only was I impressed with the freedom of landing anywhere wet, but also with the isolation should anything go wrong. Here again I pumped out the floats before takeoff.

With all going well I soon found myself on my final test preparation lesson, guided by one of Joe's instructors. My water takeoffs and landings were the best yet, but on return I landed past the docking area and inadvertently "plow taxied"

For "short field" landing practice, we touched down in an isolated cove and beached the airplane for a break.

back, meaning we slogged nose-high through the water carrying lots of power, without getting "on the step."

"You're not supposed to do that!" Joe chided me upon return to shore, "because it wastes fuel, erodes the prop, and [you guessed it] accumulates water in the floats."

Worse yet, I apparently didn't succeed in pumping all that water out for the checkride, leading to our takeoff debacle. If only that tour boat hadn't come by when it did. There I was, bent over the pump with my butt in the air—and all those people waving. Fortunately, my feverish mid-lake efforts paid off and we took to the air, hopefully vindicating me in the eyes of both examiner and watching boaters.

Once aloft, this flight test proved to be fun like none other I'd taken. Along with airwork and water maneuvers, we landed and step-taxied the rugged Colorado River between Lake Havasu and Needles, California, traversing wildlife-filled marshes and ancient Indian geoglyphs along the way.[2] Best of

---

[2] *Geoglyphs,* sometimes known as *intaglios,* are large native figures and symbols etched into the earth and visible from the air.

all was threading craggy Topock Gorge, its tumbled peaks cast aside as if by ancient gods playing like children in red clay.

When we returned to the 150's humble cove, Jean La Placa greeted us with completed paperwork, sweet home-grown tangerines, and a smile to match. A new warmth filled my heart for the tiny floatplane as we winched it out of the water. Then Joe handed me my replacement pilot certificate with seaplane rating, Mrs. La Placa took our picture, and suddenly it was over.

Ahead lay Topock Gorge, its tumbled peaks cast aside as if by ancient gods playing in red clay.

All too soon I was winging my way homeward aboard the *Flying Carpet*, low-flying images of sun and spray burned into my mind for now and forever. I guess that's what has kept me aloft for so many years. Whenever this piloting stuff seems conclusively figured out, some new challenge comes along to humble me.

Today's flying had been unlike any I'd ever encountered before. But even better than the learning experience had been the view out the windshield. Skimming blue waters at 200 feet . . . Wow! I still dream about it.

In Pursuit of a
Young Person's Dream

U.S. Air Force Academy Chapel.

"Big storm system coming in this morning," said the briefer. "It's already snowing in Denver."

I peered out the window in disbelief—skies were blue and temperatures hovered in the low 50s.

"When do you expect it to reach here?" I asked.

"Should be there within two hours," came the reply, "you'll certainly be staying the night."

A young man's dream had drawn our *Flying Carpet* here to Colorado Springs from Phoenix. Since age eleven when he invested three weeks' allowance to buy the application guide,

Austin had longed to attend the United States Air Force Academy. Now, some five years later, his former high school classmate, Cadet Adam Keith, had offered the tantalizing invitation to attend a day of classes there.

Three-and-a-half hours by Cessna 182 took us from Sonoran Desert over pine-covered plateaus and red-rock barrens, then through snow-clogged mountain passes at 12,000 feet to where Pike's Peak defines the westernmost edge of the Great Plains.

As if to reinforce the magic of flying from giant cacti to snow-covered mountains, there was the mystical setting of the Air Force Academy itself. Driving north that evening from Colorado Springs, we found it nestled against the very foothills of the Rockies. There, before the well-known Academy Chapel, squadrons of blue-uniformed cadets marched in formation among jet fighters.

But most inspiring was the boundless and hopeful future written on one young man's face, when next morning I dropped him at the Academy's Bring Me Men Ramp. There Austin shook hands with Cadet Keith, resplendent in knife-edged blue uniform and white dress gloves, and the two departed me for a day chasing dreams only a young person can appreciate. It was a sight I knew I wouldn't forget, regardless of what path Austin might ultimately follow through life.

Only then did I phone Flight Service to inquire about our planned trip home and learn of the approaching storm. I renewed our hotel room and then wandered the campus.

Even more imposing than the famous chapel was the Academy's endless parade ground. This vast surface incorporates malls and courtyards, passing even under the campus buildings themselves, which perch above ground on columns.

Also impressive were the hall and statue commemorating General Henry "Hap" Arnold, "father of the Air Force." This man in one amazing lifetime learned to fly in 1912 at the

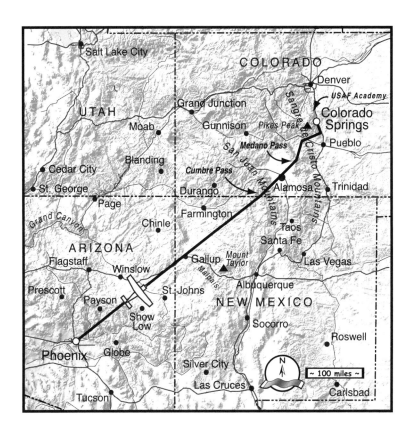

Wright Brothers' school, led our Army Air Forces to victory in World War II, and crowned his career molding the independent U.S. Air Force, which was established in 1948.

More sobering were exhibits honoring Academy grads who had lost their lives or been taken prisoner in service of our country. Perhaps most personally poignant was a photo of the bright-faced young woman who was the first female graduate to die in a combat zone. Reminded that the Academy is first and foremost an institution for training military officers, I struggled to ignore the darker risks associated with my son's glowing aspirations.

Before first snowflakes fell, there was just time to visit the Academy airfield, where cadets train in glider-flying and parachuting. Three runways and two control towers support hundreds of parachute jumps and glider flights on every nice day. Enthusiastic young people rushing about the ramp reminded me of how infectious is the dream of flight that drives us all.

By the time I returned to campus, wet snow blanketed the ground and burdened General Arnold's statue, tiring his great figure and aging him from his earlier sunlit demeanor. I collected Austin at the Bring Me Men Ramp, and on the wintry journey back to the hotel he regaled me with tales of his day at the Academy, along with hopes and plans fostered there.

He also queried me about our odds of getting home anytime soon, this being his first blizzard since moving to warm climates at age four. With the storm raging outside, we spent the evening watching TV and pondering the fate of our poor airplane huddled cold and forlorn on a snowswept ramp.

Next morning dawned gray but optimistic, so we slithered on icy roads to the airport, warmed and dried the *Flying Carpet* in the shelter of a friendly hangar, and took flight through haunting mist rising from the airport's freshly cleared pavement.

A few malingering clouds still hugged the peaks as we entered narrow Medano Pass where it pierces the 14,000-foot stockade of Sangre de Cristo Mountains. Snow-slathered towers of rock leaned menacingly from either side over our diminutive *Flying Carpet,* with only azure sky to resist the powerful summits from closing overhead. We barely had time to recover from the experience before reliving it again at Cumbre Pass through the San Juans beyond Alamosa. Never have I felt smaller, nor more dazzled or awestruck than when we escaped the jaws of those passes into the high desert of northern New Mexico.

Medano Pass, where it pierces the 14,000-foot stockade of Sangre de Cristo Mountains. The snow-covered San Juans are visible in the distance.

I was more than a little surprised, after such a majestic passage, to look Austin's way and discover him leaning dejectedly against his window.

"You okay?" I asked.

"It may sound funny," he replied, "but actually I'm a little depressed."

"Why's that?"

"Oh, it's just hard tasting life as an Air Force Academy cadet, and then returning to high school for two more years."

To break his funk we tapped some iced coffee from the cooler, ogled for one last time the wall of snow-covered peaks behind us, and then toasted Austin's future. (Just a very small toast, as we still had some 2–1/2 hours left to contain it.)

"Well, I guess it's not really a whole two years," Austin volunteered, perking up, "more like a year and four months." He sat silent for a moment. "I'm gonna work on that test study program when we get home, to help raise my score a few points on the college entrance exams next month—for my Academy application. Know what I mean?"

I knew.

Campfires on
Distant Shores

"Hello, Greg? It's your neighbor, Don, with a favor to ask."

"Sure Don, what's up?"

"Every summer our Boy Scout troop boats for a week at Lake Powell. Unfortunately, I had to work this year, and couldn't go. But I've just learned that I can join them on Wednesday—if I can find a ride, that is."

"You asking to fly there?" I replied, smiling into the phone.

"Well, yeah," said Don, "if it's not too much trouble. Not only would it save me a very long drive, but that way I could ride back with the boys. Is it feasible to fly all the way to Page after work on Wednesday?"

Don's son Erik had long been Austin's best friend, but until now Don had never expressed more than courteous interest in flying. There's nothing like a good mission to get a pilot's juices flowing, so I gladly accepted. We set 4:00 p.m. Wednesday for takeoff, late enough for afternoon turbulence to subside, but early enough for Don to make dinner with his troop. That schedule would also allow me time to escape northern Arizona's high terrain before darkness fell.

"Any problem if I'm a few minutes late?" asked Don.

"Not at this airline," I said, "I know the pilot."

Wednesday afternoon found us winging northward from Phoenix in the *Flying Carpet*. Temperatures were unseasonably warm and winds aloft moderate, meaning we'd endure a toasty cockpit and the potential for turbulence. But with clear skies and a nice tailwind, my passenger's first flight would be beautiful and comfortably short, under an hour and a half.

Overflying Don's house in first-flight tradition, we departed northbound over the Bradshaw Mountains, then crossed the expansive Verde Valley. Soon we found ourselves sailing an ocean of pines around 12,600-foot Humphreys Peak, tallest in Arizona and sacred mountain of the Navajo.

Nice as it was surfing a twenty-knot tailwind, I knew that shortly we'd pass to the lee of the giant peak. I shared my usual explanation with Don about how wind flows over mountains like water over stones in a brook, and how accordingly we should expect "a few bumps" on the downwind side. Over time pilots learn to see turbulence coming just as surely as bumps ahead on a gravel road. Not only is it fun sharing the knowledge, but when passengers anticipate turbulence it doesn't bother them as much.

Abeam Humphreys Peak we peered down into the exposed heart of knife-edged Sunset Crater, jet black amid its company of volcanic cinder cones. I felt like a real pro giving my new passenger this great ride, until I reached coolly into my flight bag and discovered that my Las Vegas Sectional aeronautical chart was not there. You never realize the comfort provided by a map until it's unexpectedly missing, especially in trackless country like this.

With measured nonchalance so as not to clue in my passenger, I retrieved radio navigation charts, normally used for instrument flying, and a bound airport guide. These would be poor substitutes for topographic information on the sectional chart, but given good visibilities, the charts at hand, and air traffic control following our progress on radar, I still felt comfortable in proceeding.

As if triggered by my error, turbulence began that instant in earnest, the *Flying Carpet* enduring slow cycles of alternating updrafts and downdrafts. These classic symptoms of mountain wave were undoubtedly caused by the sacred peak behind us, perhaps in anger at my ineptitude.[3] The bumps weren't bad, but maintaining altitude was impossible—fortunately there was no danger to us in this untraveled area, but it was attention-getting for a pilot nonetheless. Most battered was my ego for losing the chart.

"Doing okay?" I asked Don, as small items began jumping about the cockpit.

---

[3] When strong winds flow over mountain ridges, ripples form in the atmosphere for many miles downwind. This phenomenon is known as *mountain wave.*

"You bet," he replied, reading my mind, "I took some-thing for motion sickness before we took off, 'just in case.'"

Looking back at the instruments I then noted in astonish-ment the vertical speed indicator pegged at 2,000 feet per minute. Between the bumps and the needle hitting its hori-zontal stop on the right side of the instrument face, I couldn't tell whether we were going up or down. Gathering my wits, I examined the altimeter. Sure enough, we were earthbound in a hurry, though relatively smoothly.

Strange to consider that we could be descending vertically at twenty-five miles per hour and not notice it, though being so far from the ground with normal flight attitude, airspeed, and engine sounds, it made some sense. In any case, there was nothing I could do to arrest our descent, despite urging along all 230 of the engine's horses. Although the terrain is high here, it's relatively flat, so at least I wasn't worried about run-ning into anything. We continued plummeting for some thirty seconds until flying out of it. Unknowing, Don stared dreamily out his window.

"Just that one road down there," he noted, "Bet it's the one we'll drive home on Sunday."

Relieved that I could marvel privately at the granddaddy of all downdrafts, I continued descent toward as-yet-unseen Page and the Utah border.

Pilots flying the desert Southwest become accustomed to hours over featureless terrain, broken only by the occasional low mountain range. So there's no preparation for crossing yet another nondescript ridge, there to miraculously discover Oz —Lake Powell shimmering sapphire in an endless valley of nude golden rock. Thousand-foot scarlet buttes tower from the lake's surface, while their land-bound brethren pin the reservoir in place against a water-starved landscape.

Wind howled from the right as we turned onto final approach. I'd already warned Don that we'd touch down on one wheel, and after exercising long-dormant crosswind landing skills, we rolled up to the ramp.

"Unbelievable," exclaimed Don, checking his watch, "do you know how long it takes to drive here? At least six hours!" He thanked me warmly, and three times shook my hand. But I knew the magic was just beginning for him. Often, the glory of flight is not fully appreciated until later, when vivid memories capture the subconscious.

Armed with a new Las Vegas sectional chart, I soon departed against headwinds on the slow journey home. There were no further monster downdrafts, and the formerly aggressive turbulence settled to a burble as the setting sun met rock. I occupied myself by gazing at late-afternoon shadows delineating eight-sided Navajo hogans and fantastical towering rocks.

Night overtook me at the Verde River Canyon. There, even with the glow of Phoenix beckoning from ahead, I talked sweetly to my *Flying Carpet,* because this is no place for an emergency landing in the dark.

Approaching the welcoming lights of home, my mind surrendered to aerial images of glowing crimson columns piercing turquoise waters before sunset. Richer yet were visions of Don, describing that same scene at the same instant to Boy Scouts gathered 'round a campfire on now-distant shores.

JOURNEYS ACROSS TIME AND SKY

You'll Never Make It to Phoenix

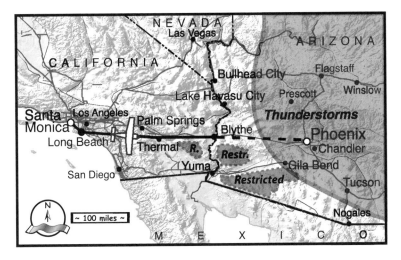

"The best part was when we flew through the storm!" exclaimed my eight-year-old nephew Ian to his mother, when asked about his favorite part of our trip to California.

"That's not quite accurate," I interjected, anticipating my sister's reaction to this news. "We didn't fly *through* any storm —we flew *around* some storms." Nobody's safety was put at risk on this trip, but certainly it was the sort of adventure that excites young children and pilots alike.

With a meeting to attend at Marina del Rey, Jean had suggested we journey to Los Angeles by *Flying Carpet,* accompanied by Austin and my visiting nephew from the East Coast. There, beaches and seafood promised welcome respite from summertime Phoenix heat.

I filed an instrument flight plan for the trip over, due to typical coastal stratus in the LA Basin. Following the usual vectors around such busy airspace, we shot an instrument approach into Santa Monica Airport. From there, a short cab ride took us to surf and sand at Venice Beach, where Ian demonstrated time-honored skills of sandcastle-building and excavating to ocean water.

Next morning while Jean attended her meeting, the boys and I cycled eighteen wind-and-sunswept miles to Manhattan Beach and back. My sister had alerted me to Ian's inquisitive nature, and during the ride I encountered it firsthand.

"What would happen if I rode off the pavement onto the sand?" asked Ian as we pedaled full speed along the beach side-walk known as "the strand."

"Oh, I wouldn't recommend that," I replied. "Your bike would stop suddenly and you'd fall down."

"How do you know that, Uncle Greg?"

"Trust me, Ian, that's not something you want to try."

Without another word my nephew drifted his bike off the edge of the sidewalk, stalled abruptly in soft sand and tumbled in front of me. My front wheel struck his fallen bike and I flipped over the top onto the pavement beyond him. Ian was unhurt, but I picked myself off the ground, bleeding. Austin got a good laugh out of it once he knew we were both okay.

"You were right, Uncle Greg," said Ian.

I restrained myself from answering, and concentrated instead on bending our respective bike wheels and fenders back into crude alignment. Later we made amends over ice cream at the Manhattan Beach Pier. Fortunately for both of us, Ian graciously accepted theoretical answers to his questions over the remainder of his visit, without the need for empirical testing.

We picked up Jean at the hotel, and shortly after lunch were back at Santa Monica Airport, checking weather for our flight home.

"Skies are clear through California," said the briefer, "but you'll never make it to Phoenix."

Ian examines the flight controls.

"Monsoon thunderstorms?"

"That's right. Severe thunderstorms run from central Arizona all the way into New Mexico."

Pilots may deal with such situations in one of two ways—either stay where they are or proceed as far as safely possible toward the destination. I chose the latter, on the premise that tomorrow's weather might obscure what was clear today. With all thunderstorm activity confined well inside Arizona, flight through California to the Colorado River appeared without risk. There were also plenty of airports along the way, should conditions deteriorate along our route.

Weather being notoriously fickle, the trick to flying safely on such days is to downplay the destination. My challenge would be to make sure that from any point where we flew, I could always achieve some safe haven for landing. The moment such options were threatened, it would be time to land. Sounds easy enough, but for it to work, pilot and passengers must be emotionally prepared to divert from the original destination. That's surprisingly tough, based on the number of pilots who commit to their destinations despite bad weather, and face the consequences. I'd been there myself, and didn't care to experience it again. Accordingly, I gathered my passengers for a bit of explanation.

"Just so you know," I said, upon briefing them, "we'll probably need to stay the night at Lake Havasu City, on the Arizona border." Then I went back to the fuel desk and ordered the fill-up I'd declined a few minutes earlier. Topped to the brim, our *Flying Carpet* could convey us all the way to Phoenix and back again. It was unlikely we'd ever need that much, but when the weather's bad, fuel in airplanes is life insurance—the more reserve you carry, the farther you can deviate and the more landing options are therefore available.

Our first hour after takeoff was smooth and clear, offering spectacular views of the Queen Mary in Long Beach Harbor. All too soon, however, tall cumulus clouds began billowing near Thermal, south of Palm Springs. There were other ominous signs, too.

"What are all those little dots?" queried Ian from the back seat. He pointed at the lightning detector on our instrument panel.

"Those are lightning strikes from thunderstorms up ahead," I explained. "Each new dot marks the location of a lightning bolt. By staying away from them we can avoid thunderstorms."

"How does it work, Uncle Greg?"

"Have you ever ridden in a car during a thunderstorm, Ian, and heard static on the radio when lightning strikes?"

"Yes."

"Well, the lightning detector plots those static discharges on this little map."

"And why do you keep pushing that little button?"

"The lightning detector isn't synchronized with our compass. Therefore I must clear the display every time we turn."

Clearly it was time for a thunderstorm update, so I excused myself from Los Angeles Center and contacted a weather briefer on another frequency. There we learned that the threatening weather had expanded dramatically westward—most of Arizona was now blanketed by a solid mass of thunderstorms.

"Echoes begin at Blythe, on the Colorado River, and continue east and north from there," said the briefer. "Every station in the Phoenix area is reporting thunderstorms right now." Clearly the issue was not when we'd get home, but rather how close we could safely approach before touching down for the night.

"That rules out landing at Lake Havasu or Bullhead City," I said, pondering the few western Arizona cities large enough to offer airports and hotel rooms. "How does it look south, toward Yuma?"

"Should be fine in that direction," said the briefer, "but you'll need to depart the airway before Blythe to get there."

Aided by radar vectors from Los Angeles Center, we maneuvered around restricted airspace toward Yuma. While preparing to land at that destination, I also evaluated the possibility of continuing eastward along the Mexican border.

"The thunderstorms have been moving south," said the Yuma Approach controller when we checked in, "but at this time the Victor-66 airway is still passable eastbound. That's where all the traffic's been going."

"How does it look beyond that weather? Could we safely turn toward Phoenix after passing it?"

"At this point, yes, based on my radar and reports from other aircraft. But keep in mind that the military restricted areas along Victor 66 are all 'hot,' so you won't be able to deviate far off the airway." Southwestern Arizona is consumed by a rat's maze of restricted airspace. Eastbound from Yuma we'd

Sand dunes near Yuma.

need to stay within a ten-mile-wide corridor to keep clear of
military bombing ranges and other unfriendly stuff.

"Fine," I said, "Victor 66 will be our route, with our alternate being return to Yuma if weather deteriorates."

The lightning detector shimmered with returns by the
time we reached Yuma, but fortunately all the activity corre-
sponded to ominous clouds north of our route.

"Don't forget to push the 'clear' button, Uncle Greg,"
reminded Ian as we turned onto Victor 66.

"Thanks, ol' buddy!"

Staying as far south as possible in the narrow corridor to
distance ourselves from the threatening weather, we proceeded
east. We remained in the clear, but increasingly I was mystified
by bizarre cloud formations materializing ahead. Again I
radioed for weather.

"How are conditions at Phoenix?" I asked, "and at Tucson?"

"All of the thunderstorms are now concentrated west of Phoenix," came the encouraging reply, "and Tucson is wide open." If we could just clear the nasty weather moving in from our left before it contacted restricted airspace on our right, we'd have a clean shot toward home with Tucson as an alternate. Yuma remained clear behind us, should that not prove feasible.

"Yuma Approach," radioed a Piper Saratoga as we returned to air traffic control frequency. "There's a giant dust storm here—lots of turbulence inside and we're unable to go around it while remaining clear of the restricted area. Requesting return to Yuma."

"Approved, as requested," replied Yuma.

"Is that aircraft ahead of us?" I asked.

"Affirmative," replied the controller, "he's unable to clear the weather and we cannot allow violation of the restricted area. You have about ten miles on your present heading before deciding whether to reverse course or accept vectors northbound to rejoin the airway."

Even as we spoke, the words of the Saratoga pilot congealed the confusing weather ahead into something I could comprehend. As far as the eye could see, a 6,000-foot-tall opaque tongue of rolling, boiling dust gushed ahead onto our path from under an encroaching overcast. These giant dust storms are called haboobs and occur only in the deserts of North Africa and those of the North American Southwest. What a strange coincidence—for a brief instant I was Halliburton, dodging dust storms en route to Timbuktu.

Ten miles doesn't take long in even the slowest flying carpet, so quickly I considered options. That dust cloud looked like a textbook thunderstorm gust front vacuuming up dirt, and certainly we did not want to enter it.[1] But the lightning

---

[1] *Gust fronts*, loosely defined, are bursts of wind driven before approaching thunderstorms.

A 6,000-foot-tall opaque tongue of rolling, boiling dust gushed ahead onto our path from under an encroaching overcast.

detector, to my surprise, indicated that the densely packed storms that had threatened us for so many miles now lay behind us to the left. I reconsidered the dust. Vicious as the haboob appeared, it was neatly and fully contained in its cloud, suggesting the limits of the turbulent air that carried it.

With permission from Yuma, I again radioed a weather briefer, who confirmed that all thunderstorm radar echoes now appeared behind our location. But although Phoenix weather continued to improve, the briefer had no pilot reports along our projected route. That was cause for alarm, given the ugly roll of dust filling our windshield. You can never have too much information when arm-wrestling difficult weather.

I radioed Yuma Approach, "My lightning detector shows the airway clear ahead from here all the way to Gila Bend. Are you talking to any other pilots along that route?"

"There are aircraft ahead at 7,000 and 8,000," came the reply, "neither with any complaints." Those altitudes would clear the dust storm by a healthy margin, yet still keep us below the overhanging cloud ceiling.

"Requesting instrument clearance at 7,000," I said, "and we'll take that vector northbound now." Topping the dust roll in visual conditions, we turned north under dark clouds.

"Don't forget to push the 'clear' button, Uncle Greg."

"Will do, Ian."

As so often happens after peering under clouds from sunlight, it wasn't nearly so bad there as expected. Distant lightning receded behind us to the left, and rain showers could be seen haphazardly scattered about the area. But the ride was smooth, the lightning detector clear ahead, and visibility excellent. I radioed the good news back to Yuma for the benefit of those who might follow.

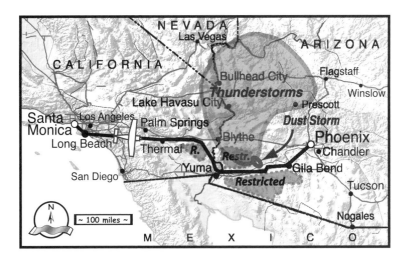

Before long the lights of Phoenix appeared. Behind them an orange sliver of sunset was trapped on the horizon by distant thunderstorms, their silhouetted rainstorms salted with frequent dashes of lightning. Our awestruck stares were interrupted by a radio call requesting that we monitor air-to-air frequency.[2]

"Hi there," said a friendly but unfamiliar voice, once I'd switched over. "We're en route to Chandler, and I just wanted to call and say 'thank you.'"

We in the *Flying Carpet* looked at each other, surprised.

"We've been listening to you all the way from Blythe," said the pilot, "and knew by your radio calls that we could follow your lead. You asked all the right questions, and the answers gave us confidence to continue."

"Well, thanks!" I answered, feeling mighty good about receiving such kudos in front of my family. "Are you flying the Saratoga that turned back to Yuma?"

"That's me," came the reply. "but thanks to your pilot report we reversed course again, overflew the dust storm, and will now make it home." Of course I complimented him right back for having the guts to abort his mission with the plan of returning to Yuma. In the absence of weather avoidance equipment or pilot reports it was the only smart thing to do. But the bottom line was that we had unknowingly aided this pilot in getting home for the evening, and he was mighty happy about it.

"I helped, phoo!" announced Ian from the back seat, his words garbled by celebratory cookies. We rewarded him with high fives, said our goodbyes to the folks in the Saratoga, and shortly were handed over to Phoenix Approach. With nobody much flying due to the weather, the controller cleared us direct through Phoenix airspace to our home airport.

There's nothing like a familiar voice from the control tower to warm your heart after a tough flight, or the small

---

[2] Air-to-air frequencies are set aside for communication between airplanes in flight.

pleasure of tucking your plane into its berth when you never expected to make it home. So despite everyone watching, I patted the *Flying Carpet* on her spinner before driving away.

Certainly Ian understood my soppy behavior, even if no one else did. Coupled with the wind and waves of sunny Southern California, this was the sort of flight never to be forgotten by an inquisitive eight-year-old watching from the back seat, nor for that matter, by the much older kid lucky enough to be at the controls.

Convergence
Friends from Separate Worlds

They come from separate worlds, Chris, Penny, and Austin. How strange that an Alaskan teenager and a southern Arizona ranch wife should converge with my son at the same time and place, and on such an important day.

"Cleared to land on Runway One-One-Right," said the Tucson tower controller, interrupting my thoughts. "Use caution for military A-10 traffic landing on the left runway." From over my shoulder two jets approached rapidly in formation, overtook me, and landed on the parallel runway. All the while my *Flying Carpet* hovered as if standing still on final approach.

Refocusing on my own landing, I noted a lone red 172 holding short of my runway for takeoff. *I wonder if Austin is flying this morning,* I thought. Austin was here in Tucson to complete his private pilot's license. We had chipped away at it together for a year, but other factors had now urged the process along. Besides, I was still mindful of the difficulties in teaching family members to fly; Austin and I had agreed that the viewpoint of another instructor might benefit his training.

"Hi Dad," broadcast a familiar voice through my headset.

"Hi Austin!" I replied instinctively. After so many hours flying together, it was the first time I'd heard my son's professional radio voice emanating from another aircraft. I bit my tongue—despite pride overflowing from a father's veins, this was no place to talk. Although I couldn't see him, my son floated like a spirit somewhere in the traffic pattern. Realizing that he might be watching with his instructor, I concentrated on greasing the landing—but bounced twice anyway. Hoping no one noticed, I taxied in.

Nearing the tiedown, I observed a slim, dark-haired young man walking out to greet me. Until now I'd seen Christopher Sis only in pictures. I'd first met Chris in a pilot forum I hosted on the Internet. He showed up week after week, asking smart aviation questions and sharing knowledge beyond that of most participants. Over time I'd concluded he was a commercial pilot. But then one day Chris surprised me by asking about college admission requirements.

"Are you returning to school?" I'd emailed.

"Oh no," he replied, "I'm only fifteen. I haven't even taken any flying lessons yet."

When Chris began training—first in San Diego and then after moving with his family to Juneau, Alaska—he regaled me with tales of learning to fly. Quickly I discovered that this young man was not only an astute pilot and aviation buff, but also a talented writer. Joy filled his stories, along with celebration of the small experiences that enrich the learning of every pilot. Soon I waited eagerly to read of each lesson.

Through his keyboard, Chris told of practicing flight maneuvers over water. There's no flat land around Juneau for such purposes, only mountains. He wrote of using hair dryers to thaw fuel drains frozen by the Alaskan winter. He shared laughter about forgetting with his instructor to untie the tail of their airplane—then trying to taxi away.

Chris made his first solo cross-country flight at age sixteen, traversing eighty wintertime miles from Juneau to Haines. After landing he searched with cold-numbed fingers for change to call his worried mother, then on the return trip circled humpbacked whales cavorting in frigid waters.

By now I had completed my checklist and shut down the engine.

"Chris!" I said, climbing out the door.

"Hi Greg." We shook hands, and while making small talk, tied down the airplane. Despite the richness of his written

After landing, Chris searched with cold-numbed fingers for change to call his worried mother. (Photo by Christopher Sis.)

communications, it was refreshing to find a shy teenager in the real person.

Following two years of writing me those wonderful stories, Chris had earned his pilot's license at age seventeen. Now, just nine months later, he was here in Tucson to earn his instrument rating. When I'd learned Chris was coming, I'd arranged for him to room with Austin, who was within days of his own seventeenth birthday. While Chris earned his instrument rating, Austin would complete his private pilot certificate.

"How's your instrument training going, Chris?" I asked.

"The actual flying doesn't start until tomorrow," he replied. "But already I'm enjoying the knowledge part. It feels like a privilege, getting to use the approach charts. Until now they seemed so mysterious, filled with all those little symbols and numbers." It was exactly the sort of reflection that so intrigued me about the young man. I imagined King Arthur's sorcerer, poring by candlelight over massive leather volumes filled with procedure turns and other hieroglyphics.

"Like opening Merlin's Book?" I asked.

"You could say that," he laughed. "Like opening Merlin's Book and suddenly finding you understand it."

With Austin still flying on his lesson, Chris and I walked inside.

"Where can we meet a friend for brunch?" I asked the girl behind the counter. "Preferably someplace interesting and nearby. We need to be back by 1:00 p.m."

"There's a funky place in an old railroad dining car," she replied. "I'll drop you there on my way to lunch." Soon Chris and I sweltered on a dusty highway corner, squinting under searing Arizona sun for a tall redhead driving a pickup truck. Trying to ignore the unfamiliar heat, Chris told of his first flight with passengers.

"I flew my Dad and my little brother from Juneau to Sitka," he said. "The flight over went great, but when time came to leave, I couldn't start the engine."

"What did you do?"

"Luckily, I found a mechanic there to help me start it. The hard part was trying to convince Dad and my brother not to be nervous after that happened. The flight is mostly over water, you know."

"Did they do okay on the return flight?"

"Yes, except for one funny thing. On the way home, I was watching for sights to show my passengers so they'd forget about the starting problem. I spotted another whale, like on my solo cross-country, and descended to circle it."

"Were they impressed?"

"Not after we got closer. Here were the two of them staring excitedly out the window, and it turned out to be nothing but a big rock." He laughed again, then wiped his brow with an already-damp sleeve.

Even stories of wintertime Alaska couldn't temper mid-July desert temperatures in the 100s. I reflected on the TV

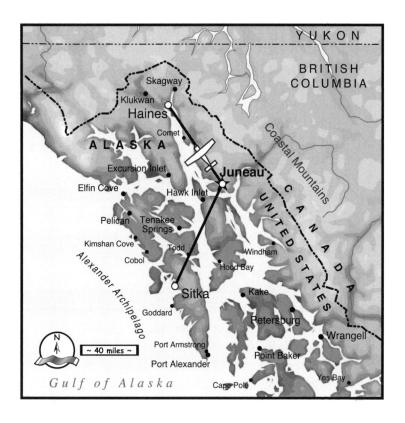

Westerns of my youth, with their swirling music and soft-focus sun into which cowboys always stared before dying of thirst. These were truer than seemed possible, as I'd learned after moving here.

"I know we're early," said my young Alaskan friend, red-faced and wiping his brow, "but I hope Penny gets here soon."

Moments later a truck pulled up to the diner car, and out stepped Penny Porter. Six feet tall with flaming red bouffant hair, Penny was likely pushing seventy, yet freely shared the giggle of a twelve-year-old upon seeing us. Slim and beaming through sparkling brown eyes, she wore a cowboy print blouse and squash-blossom necklace.

Just as those early flight instructors guided my piloting, Penny had molded my pen. She taught me to look deep for the inner emotions that make people squirm, then reveal them on paper. "Everyone has those feelings, Greg," she once told me, "but few dare reveal them. The stories most personally hard to tell are the ones readers best relate to."

Penny and her husband, Bill, had long worked a southern Arizona ranch, raising a large family there. Only later did she begin writing professionally. Joyfully interpreting her children's interactions with the surrounding menagerie of animals, she'd achieved success in books and popular magazines. Although fearing the airplanes that so inspired Chris and me, Penny imparted her wisdom through advice and example.

Over time I'd learned that every note from Penny, every email, and every short conversation carried within it gems of humor, beauty, and advice. In Chris's writing I had discovered similar jewels, though still rough-cut. My favorite of his stories I shared with Penny, while in turn mailing my mentor's books and stories to Chris for inspiration. No wonder it seemed important to me that they should meet.

I introduced these disparate friends—the mature teenager and the youthful senior—then took a quick photo of the diner. Together, we stepped inside. The place proved uncomfortably dark and dingy, the only other occupants being a large man reading the paper and a waitress studiously ignoring us.

After much feigned busy-ness, the waitress acknowledged our presence with coffee and orange juice. "I've already eaten," said Penny, examining her dubiously clean cup. Chris and I were too hungry to be picky. We had just ordered huevos rancheros with hash-browns and refried beans, when the big man approached our table.

"I saw you photographing my restaurant," he said, sternly.

"This is a special meeting we wanted to remember," I said, surprised that anyone owning a railroad-car diner might not want it photographed. I introduced Chris and Penny. "These are my friends from Alaska and Tucson," I explained. "The three of us have never met together before. And your diner car seemed like the perfect place to do it."

"In that case," he said, suddenly brightening, "let me show you around." Shrugging silently at one another, the three of us stood. Proudly and deliberately the owner guided us through his rail car, leaving no secrets unturned and no doors unopened. He lived here, it turned out, and was especially proud of the furnishings and paneling made from discarded giant cable spools. The three of us "oohed" and "aahed" appropriately at all we saw, including dingy bathroom, overflowing closets, and dirty laundry heaped on the bed. Following an extended tour of the smallish place, we were relieved to see the waitress setting out breakfast.

Returning to our table, Chris and I doused our spicy meals with glass after glass of water, while Penny looked on, amused. I couldn't decide if my feverish sweating was due more to the stuffy train car on such a hot day, or the incendiary salsa verde topping my breakfast. Between quenchings, we talked of writing and flying and life on a ranch. Despite the warmth of our conversation, there was an awkwardness, too. So many personal details had been exchanged through our pens that it would take awhile for the physical presence to catch up.

Chris and I had an appointment to meet, so too soon, it was time to go. Before dropping us at the airport, Penny observed that the surrealistic railroad-car meeting had somehow been appropriate for writers like ourselves.

"We couldn't have written a more bizarre setting had we tried," she giggled, "nor could we have invented better characters to frighten the visitors."

Arriving back at the flight line, Chris and I looked for Austin. "Dad!" came words flying after us. *"Dad!* Did you see me solo? I just flew the airplane around the traffic pattern—by myself!"

"I thought you weren't soloing until after lunch," I said, hiding slight disappointment at having missed the event. I shook Austin's hand and patted him on the back.

"Well, my instructor said I was ready, so I did it! Just now!"

Proudly Austin marched Chris and me out to his airplane. Sure enough, it was the weathered red 172 I'd seen earlier holding short of the runway. As the three of us posed smiling for pictures, I thought back to my many flying adventures with Austin over the years. Most vivid was that flight to Payson, when the admiring father at the fence with his young son observed the richness of me piloting with my own.

"Time to fly again, Dad." said Austin, with justifiable bravado. "Thanks for coming down." I resisted the urge to embarrass him with a hug, and instead we again shook hands all around. "Hope it was okay saying 'hi' on the radio when you landed this morning," he added as I walked away. "It was pretty cool, watching the *Flying Carpet* touch down from another cockpit." He turned to preflight the plane for his next lesson.

Pride in my son's accomplishment engulfed me when flying home later that afternoon, yet at the same time burdened me with new-felt age. Young pilots Austin and Chris were overtaking me like those speeding jets on final to land this morning. Yet Penny proved the potential for youth to last far into the future.

Long-separate parts of my life had come together today in a wonderful way, but I'd also suddenly realized that the halcyon days of young children in my family were over. With Hannis pursuing a musician's career and Austin that of a pilot, both my little boys were now accomplished young men.

Bouncing warm and uncomfortable through summer turbulence, I looked down upon craggy Picacho Peak, then back at Tucson, and ahead toward home on the horizon. Although only some hundred miles each way in physical distance, today's *Flying Carpet* ride had in some ways carried me the greatest emotional distance of my life.

Following Railroad Tracks to the Horizon

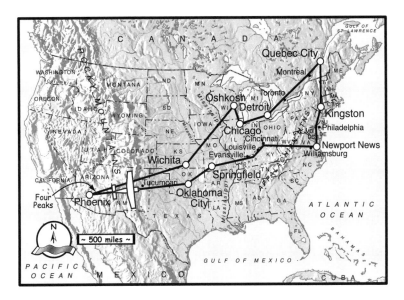

Sweat burns my eyes as the *Flying Carpet* claws skyward, heavily loaded for such a hot day, but aloft at last after a discouragingly late start. Tempers flared this morning during last-minute preparations for our long-awaited journey. But now, upon reaching cooler air at 7,500 feet and saluting Four Peaks as equals, smiles spread through our cabin, and problems begin slipping away as they always do upon setting course for some distant destination.

I begin to relax, and looking ahead find to my surprise that although we're not yet thirty miles out of Phoenix, I can visualize quite clearly our entire route lying before us—over Arizona's rugged Sierra Anchas and the White Mountains, past New Mexico's red and yellow high country, and then, beyond Albuquerque's Sandia Peak, the long, downhill cruise to the Atlantic Ocean. It's all there, just outside our windshield.

You know the journey's a long one when charts cost almost as much as fuel to complete it. But great as the distance appeared when we conceived this trip on paper, from our new vantage aloft it seems cast of little more than the short cross-countries I make every week. How often on one-hour flights have I turned to passengers and said, "Wouldn't it be cool if we could just keep on going?" Well today I'm doing it, living the young person's dream of following railroad tracks to the horizon.

Entering the Great Plains we'll cross Texas and Oklahoma flatlands pocked by irrigation circles, then overfly verdant Ozark hills in Missouri. Next comes the Mississippi, a veritable flowing ocean compared to the meager trickles that pass for rivers here in Arizona. That fluid ribbon which seems so logically to divide the country in half won't appear until we're two thirds of our way to the Atlantic.

From the Mississippi we'll travel as partners with the Ohio River over places where flatboats once docked, like Evansville and Louisville and Cincinnati. And then, just short of our destination will rise the deceptively curvaceous Appalachian Mountains, shrouded as always in jagged flying weather.

"But those mountains are so low, Dad," says Austin, newly rated as a pilot and sneaking peeks at a chart near the bottom of the stack, "What are they—maybe 4,000 feet high? I just don't see how the weather could be so bad there." Having recently flown with him through the 14,000-foot jaws of the Rockies, I understand his skepticism.

"They're like Mom," I say, "more petite than you or I, but a lot tougher." A groan emanates from our third pilot in the back seat.

"You'd better be nice if you want lunch," says Jean. "Don't forget, I have the cooler back here." Weak humor notwithstanding, Austin will have to personally experience the Appalachians to appreciate their very different character and the moods that pervade them.

Not so easy to anticipate through this crystal ball of a windshield are cards held by the weather, which tomorrow will demand hours of instrument flight and drive us by the skin of our teeth around thunderstorms from Lexington to Richmond. We'll barely be granted our destination of Newport News. ("*Those* are the Appalachians, Austin!") Yet despite the challenges, we'll make the East Coast from Arizona in only two days and two stops.

And although our route lies so clearly before me, even the most vivid imagination cannot predict the fun we'll have at stops along the way. We'll watch Colonial officers drill young spectators to fight for Virginia at Williamsburg, ponder glide distance to the shores of massive Chesapeake Bay, and sample the game of cricket at Wilmington, Delaware. Then we'll dine Philadelphia-style before tracing cracks in the Liberty Bell, and visit the desk where the Declaration of Independence was signed. Until now Austin has known these places only through history books. Removed as they are from the Spanish and Native American roots of our own Southwest, he'll be surprised at the emotions budding even within a teenager upon visiting such historic sites.

Among other gems we cannot foresee is Pennsylvania's bucolic New Garden Airport, where gliders and classic airplanes hide from the present under an army of tall trees—pilots must fly back fifty years on downwind to land there.

We'll marvel at the flight of ancient airplanes over the Hudson Valley, walk historic ramparts in Quebec City, and ogle Oshkosh aerobatics amid the Wisconsin dairylands where first I became a pilot. And at every stop, we'll be greeted by the words, "You flew all the way from Arizona?"

But that's all in the future. For now, as we cross Lake Roosevelt barely forty miles after leaving home, only red rock fills our windshield, eventually to be replaced by green grass and then blue waters, all warmed friendly by the accompaniment of my family.

Sure, there's the paper target of Tucumcari, but that's just a dart tossed randomly along a freewheeling line sketched across a dozen maps. (We'll dine in Oklahoma City, it turns out, and sleep in Springfield, Missouri.) With cares dissolving behind us, the way east is clear and the horizon our only destination.

Hardest of all for me to imagine, as we commence our journey this hot but beautiful morning, is how in a mere two weeks we will actually return from this trip to the horizon, three tired souls touching down in our *Flying Carpet,* permeated with wonder from twice traversing diverse landscapes of earth and sky, over an entire continent.

Funny how each individual leg of such a trip seems no more difficult than a short flight from home, yet after so many hours of watching the land change chameleon-like beneath our wings, we are forever seasoned as adventurers.

Skies of Our Ancestors
Pilgrimage to Old Rhinebeck

New Standard biplane on final to land at Old Rhinebeck Aerodrome.

"Rat-tat-tat-brrrrrrrmmm, rat-tat-tat-brrrrrrrmmm!" I could scarcely believe my ears. Dogfighting over my head, were World War I fighters—SPAD, Fokker Triplane, Camel, Albatros, and Nieuport—marques I had read and dreamt about, and even seen in a few museums. But never had I guessed that one day I'd actually hear them fly.

Most aviators would agree that Oshkosh is the Mecca of the skies, to which true believers must eventually trek by slow aeroplane and camp under a wing, there to be drenched by a cacophony of aircraft engines, a downburst of sweat, and perhaps some rain.

237

But if Oshkosh is Mecca, Rhinebeck Aerodrome is Medina. So when I was drawn to Oshkosh after fifteen years away, 1,300 extra miles seemed like nothing to visit Rhinebeck and make my pilgrimage complete.

Old Rhinebeck Aerodrome is an ethereal grass strip carved from dense woods along the Hudson River, where World War I aeroplanes and their predecessors still fly. Ever since succumbing to Sir Walter Raleigh's 1922 classic, *The War in the Air,* I've been captivated by early aeroplanes and the men and women who flew them. Structurally limited, powered by primitive engines, and barely able to lift their own weight, these planes duked it out over Europe only a dozen years after the dawn of powered flight.

Rhinebeck's oldest flying aircraft is an original 1909 Blériot, like the one its designer flew across the English Channel that same year to global acclaim; Blériot was the Lindbergh of his day after conquering twenty-six miles of unbroken water.

But it was the World War I aircraft that especially drew me to Rhinebeck. Some are original airframes and others faithful reproductions, but all are true to their heritage and powered by original engines. I sought in particular the mystical sound of rotary engines that powered so many of them, primitive devices with radially mounted cylinders that spun with their propellers around fixed crankshafts bolted to the airframe. That's right—the whole engine turned, improving cooling at the slow airspeeds of the day and saving weight through mechanical simplicity, but aggravating handling due to gyroscopic effects.

In rotary engines, fuel was distributed by centrifugal force to the cylinders—no carburetors or throttles were installed. The engines ran wide open all the time, so to reduce power, pilots pressed a kill switch, suspending ignition to the spark plugs. "Brrrp . . . , brrrp . . . ," was the music on final as pilots blipped engines on and off for landing.

Rotary engines powered early aircraft like this 1913 French Caudron. The open lower cowl directs expelled castor oil downward from the spinning powerplant.

Castor oil was the lubricant of choice for these spinning engines, and it was distributed centrifugally along with the fuel. There were no return lines, so the lubricant migrated out to the exposed valves and then streamed back over the fuselage, rendering laxative and emetic effects on the pilot. That's one reason early aviators wore scarves—to wipe castor oil from their faces in futile attempts to stave off its effects on the bowels and stomach.

The difference between maximum structural speed and stall speed on early aircraft was as little as ten miles per hour, with death lurking at either margin. Stalls and spins were considered unrecoverable in the early days, while shedding of fabric and structural failures were common at higher airspeeds still far below cruise of a modern Cessna. Strange to think that in many respects our modest *Flying Carpet* could outperform almost every aeroplane in World War I.

Perhaps most incredible of all, pilots at the height of the war in 1916 received as little as eight hours of training in unstable aircraft far more difficult to fly than ours today—no wonder their lives were measured in only weeks upon arriving at the front.

An Albatros D.Va joins the evil forces of Rhinebeck's tongue-in-cheek "Black Baron." Germany's real Red Baron, Manfred von Richthofen, actually scored more victories in the Albatros than in his famous red Fokker Triplanes.

Imagine doing battle aloft after just a few hours of lessons, in an aircraft having only a ten-mile-per-hour speed range, questionable structural integrity, and an unreliable engine that hampers turns in one direction and makes you sick—then surely you'll understand why I had to see such aeroplanes fly.

Finally the long-anticipated day arrived. We shoehorned our *Flying Carpet* between tall trees and the Hudson River bridge at Kingston-Ulster Airport, then journeyed by taxi at inflated fares over the bridge to Rhinebeck Aerodrome.

We toured primitive hangars filled with ancient aeroplanes while a 1929 New Standard biplane delivered open-cockpit rides to the faithful. Then we watched two Rhinebeck "pioneers" take flight: a bird-like 1910 Hanriot reproduction, and a marvelously crude 1913 French Caudron.

But the main course was Rhinebeck's famous Sunday show, conceived by the Aerodrome's founder, Cole Palen. Complete with good guy, villainous Black Baron, and kidnapped heroine, it's a silent movie melodrama perverted with enough noise to keep everyone holding their ears throughout the show.

Ancient autos scrambled, early aeroplanes battled an original World War I Renault tank, dogfighting took place, bombs "fell," bad jokes by the announcer proliferated, and all was encompassed by an outrageous story line that could hardly have fooled the most gullible spectator. Add some clever tricks pulled on the audience, hot dogs, and a sunburn for full effect, and we were altogether transported back to our distant origins as pilots.

Rhinebeck Aerodrome is crude, hammy, and yet a wonderful diamond in the rough. Every enthusiast having the slightest tinge of aviation romance should visit this rare place where World War I aeroplanes still fly. Some day it will end and missing it would be a sin for any real aviator, like pilgrims missing Mecca or Medina.

As we cleared the Hudson River bridge outbound that afternoon, the smooth rumble of our *Flying Carpet* was displaced in my ears by uneven music from ancient aeroplanes. Peering over my shoulder to foil attack from the sun by the Black Baron, I was overtaken by words from Walter Raleigh.

"The engine is the heart of an aeroplane," he wrote in 1922, "but the pilot is its soul."

Rhinebeck's famous Sunday melodrama, complete with good guy, villainous Black Baron, and kidnapped heroine.

Turning north toward Canada, I then gazed down upon the beautiful Hudson River, and realized that eighty years of progress haven't dulled the miracle of flight one bit.

L'Aventure au Québec

Try as we might, we could not see it out the window—that razor-sharp line proclaimed by our chart to slash Vermont's soft Green Mountains in two. Frustrated, I switched frequencies from Boston Center.

"Bonjour, Montréal," tumbled words from our radio before I could say anything, *"Twin Comanche Golf-November-Victor-Lima, on prendrait la descente pour Québec."*

There's something about borders . . . here we'd been staring out the window for that all-important invisible line, but it took a radio call to see it.

"Bonjour, November-Victor-Lima, Montréal," came the reply, *"autorisé à 3000 pieds, la 24 en usage à Québec, l'altimètre 29.26."*

Radio communications delineate this part of the Canadian border far more eloquently than any line on a map. In Quebec province, air traffic control is bilingual, in French and English.

Cool northern light touched green hills below us, in stark contrast to the sun-seared orange cragginess of our own far-away Arizona. Moreover, even now at 8 p.m., sunset was still over an hour away. By our summertime clock at home it would have set more than an hour ago. But not until hearing those words of French did we fully appreciate our true distance from home, nearly a continent away.

This would not be our first visit to Quebec, but rather the latest chapter in a longstanding friendship that began thirty years before. Following high school that year, I traveled from Chicago with two friends on a post-graduation road trip.

My steed at the time was a '39 Chevy two-door—even then very old. My Dad had cleverly encouraged me to buy it, knowing that I'd need to fix it aplenty and thereby learn the mysteries of mechanical things. He was right. Only a few hundred miles from home, the car's water pump began leaking.

After a discouraging day in Detroit pursuing replacement parts for the aging vehicle, we limped across the international bridge to a waterfront parking lot in Windsor, Ontario. There we put youthful heads together and over a period of hours, replaced the pump. To the joy of three kids just out of high school, no calls home were required and our repair job worked.

Cruising town the next night in *Trois-Rivières, Québec,* we picked up a young French Canadian hitchhiker. The guy spoke no English and we spoke no French, but eventually we determined where he was headed, and delivered him home. His name was Marcel, and through a bilingual friend he invited us to sleep that night in a cottage behind his parents' house.

While my travelmates slept, Marcel and I conversed late into the night about everything from my road travels to his passion for duck hunting, all via French-English dictionary and scratch pad. Next morning a sleep-shattering horn awakened me to a monstrous oceangoing freighter just outside the window. I'd gathered that the St. Lawrence Seaway was nearby, but never guessed that a false step in the dark would have toppled me in.

I later hitchhiked from Wisconsin to visit Marcel during college, then returned by car several years later with Jean, when we were dating. Flying ourselves to Quebec for the first time ten years later, we met Marcel's ebullient new wife Lise, and introduced our respective firstborn infant sons. The Browns and Duvals had remained close ever since, swapping kids over summer vacations, hiking, rafting, and whale-watching together.

Such memories flooded my mind as we approached Quebec City, cloaked in ancient walls above the St. Lawrence and guarded by a solitary thunderhead. Evening sun tinted the towering cumulus orange against purple sky, while glinting silver off the city's tin-roofed steeples.[3]

We touched down in this otherworldly setting, and by the time I'd phoned Customs and secured the airplane, Marcel appeared grinning at the gate. He rushed to embrace me, then twirled Jean off her feet. The long dark hair from our first meeting was now mostly gray, but the mischief in his eyes sparked stronger than ever.

Lise enraptured us that evening with homemade culinary delights worthy of the finest French restaurant. Next day we hoofed cobblestones through historic *Vieux-Québec,* which dates from the city's founding in 1608. Wandering ramparts

---

[3] Every little town along the St. Lawrence has at least one stone church crowned in silver, proclaiming like an exclamation point, "This *is* Quebec!"

that unsuccessfully defended the city against British capture in 1759, we noted a particular cannon carriage carved many years ago with the initials of young lovers—Marcel and Lise when they were dating.

Marcel guides us through historic *Vieux-Quebéc.*

French is Quebec's native language, and my guess is that there are fewer English-speakers here than in Paris. I am still thrilled upon every visit to rediscover foreign tongues and narrow European streets so close to our northern border.

Next day we traveled by ferry to *Île-aux-Coudres* in the St. Lawrence, circumnavigating that idyllic island by bicycle. Soft breezes and sparkling waters were complemented along the way by purple wildflowers and good-natured ribbing among friends. Especially captivating was Marcel's young niece, Virginia, a magical little girl who kept us all in stitches despite lack of a common tongue. Then came a swim in the Duval pool overlooking the omnipresent St. Lawrence, followed by champagne toasts and homemade coquilles St-Jacques. But sadly our visit was ending and it was time to fly back to Earth.

Photos, hugs, and tears marked our departure next morning—only the irresistible lure of flight could coax the *Flying Carpet* to depart our charming hosts and their enchanted city. Even then we emotionally hugged the mighty St. Lawrence as long as possible, savoring every last syllable of air traffic control French until handed off by Montreal to the gentlemanly voices of Toronto Center.

"Au revoir, beau Québec," we cried upon parting, with likely despicable pronunciation. "We *will* return!"

Having escaped the sirens of French Canada, we passed Toronto and soon found ourselves over Windsor, Ontario, across Lake St. Clair from Detroit.

There, peering down through thirty years of haze, I thought I saw an old green Chevy in a waterfront parking lot, hood open, and surrounded by three long-haired kids. I couldn't be certain, murky as it was and quickly as we passed, but tears filled my eyes all the same. Exactly thirty years had passed since completing that roadside repair and picking up a young French Canadian hitchhiker up the road.

"Just a bit of dirt in my eye," I said to Jean, noting the surprise on her face. Quickly I shifted thoughts to our next destination. Thankfully, flying always offers new adventures to soothe fond memories of previous ones. Onward, *Flying Carpet!*

On Dark Nights,
Follow the Freeway Home

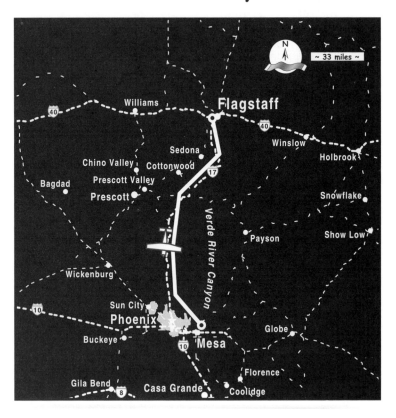

"Your oil change is all done," said the mechanic. "Help me button up the cowling, would you?"

"Sure," I replied. I looked to see that the filler cap and dip-stick had been replaced, then held the top cowl in place while he tightened fasteners near the windshield. I glanced at my watch. Austin and I were on our way to pick up his older brother from school, and we were running late.

"We'd better get in touch with Hannis," I said, "so he won't be waiting at the Flagstaff Airport and wondering what happened to us." To speed things along, Austin offered to pre-flight the plane while I phoned his brother. "That would be great," I said.

"Excuse me," said the mechanic as I turned for the phone. "I've just remembered that we didn't include any additive with the oil. Did you want me to put some in?"

"The chief mechanic has been encouraging me to use it," I replied. "Sure, go ahead and add some. And thanks for reminding me."

By the time I'd reached Hannis and laid out our plans, Austin was finished preflighting the airplane.

"Find any problems?" I asked. It's always important to pre-flight carefully after maintenance has been done, more so since we'd now be flying home at night.

"Everything's fine, Dad. We're all set to go. Can I fly the leg up?"

"You bet." I replied. The young man being a rated pilot and meticulous, it seemed inappropriate to recheck behind him unless he had concerns. No sooner were we airborne, than the sun settled colorfully behind the Bradshaw Mountains.

"Something educational . . . " I observed to Austin in twi-light, aiming my flashlight just above the instrument panel. "See that smattering of fluid at the base of the windshield? The same thing happened after the last oil change. Turns out it's solvent from cleaning the engine."

"That's good to know," said Austin. "I might have thought it was an oil leak."

We landed at Flagstaff just after nightfall. The ramp was so dark that had Hannis not met us at the tiedown, we would have been hard-pressed to find him.

"You guys are really late," he said, agitated.

"Sorry," I replied. "We got off to a late start and then the oil change wasn't finished when we got to the airport. I guess the mechanics got busy during the afternoon."

"I understand, Dad, but let's get going. I'm supposed to go out with friends back at home, and they won't wait for me."

We loaded Hannis's bags and I did a quick walkaround. Soon we were airborne and climbing in blackness to 9,500 feet.

"Should we go direct?" I asked Austin, "Or follow the freeway home?"

"Take the shortest way back," interjected Hannis with urgency from the back seat. "I don't want to get stuck home alone on a Friday night."

"Mom and I will be there," I said.

"Seriously, Dad, let's go the fastest way."

"What do you think, Austin? It looks mighty dark up there, on the straight line route over the Verde River Canyon."

"I agree, Dad. But on the other hand we've been flying the plane for an hour and a half and everything's working fine. Have you ever had a problem going home that way?"

"No," I replied. "But if the engine quit over there on a dark night like this, we'd have no idea what we were landing on."

"How much time would it add, following the freeway?"

"Not much—maybe ten minutes. Landing on the freeway at night would be no fun, but it would sure beat descending blindly in darkness along the Verde. We could be heading straight into a mountainside and never know it. We might not be found there for days, either."

"It's up to you, Dad." said Austin, deflecting my usual admonishment to him back my way. "You're flying this leg."

"Tell Albuquerque Center we'll follow Interstate 17 to Phoenix," I said. A groan came from the back seat. "Sorry about that, Hannis. I promise it won't cost us more than a few minutes." There was no reply.

Before long the distant glow of Phoenix gave way to bright lights. While Hannis snoozed in back, Austin negotiated our descent with Phoenix Approach. Clearing higher terrain to the north, I cut corners across the Bradshaw foothills toward home.

Shutting down in darkness after landing, I stowed headsets and flight cases while Austin opened the hangar and pulled out the car. "I must admit that this beats driving," said Hannis as I unloaded his bags. He looked at his watch. "I should still make it home before the guys head out." Each young man pushed a wing strut while I guided the *Flying Carpet* into her lighted stall.

Then, at the same instant, all three of us saw it—engine oil coating the lower cowling and fuselage. We looked at one another in horror.

"I'm surprised we didn't notice any oil leaking at Flagstaff," said Austin.

"Me, too," I said. "It was so dark there that I must have seen only what I specifically looked for with the flashlight. The oil being new and relatively colorless probably wouldn't help, either. Seems like there are some mistakes to learn from this evening."

"What do you think happened?" he asked.

"I have a pretty strong idea. Did you check the oil filler cap on your preflight?" I reached for a small access door atop the engine cowl.

"No," replied Austin, "just the oil level on the dipstick. I've never opened that other door on top." On this airplane, the oil filler neck is mounted on top of the engine, and the dipstick resides under a separate door forward of the pilot's window. I'd always added any oil through the filler door myself, never considering that as a result Austin might not think to check it. (The 172 he trained in incorporates dipstick and filler neck in a single unit.)

I motioned him over and opened the filler door. Inside lay the oil filler cap atop the engine, never replaced by the mechanic after installing the additive.

"Wow, Dad, I can't believe I didn't check that. Is the engine ruined?"

"I hope not, Austin, but that's definitely a possibility. We'll see what the mechanics say about this tomorrow." I reached for the dipstick.

"I am *so* sorry."

"It was my mistake too, Austin. I should have double-checked it after the additive was put in." Encouragingly, the engine oil level still showed above minimum.

Next day our mechanics would examine the engine and pronounce it in good health, but not before a good deal of soul searching took place between Austin, the mechanic who did the oil change, and me. Each of us had learned a valuable lesson, and there would be general agreement that no one present would make that particular mistake again. But as we closed the hangar door that evening after returning from Flagstaff, even the threat of engine damage was not the most pressing thing on my mind.

"You know, guys," I said, increasingly shaken the more I thought about it. "What matters most is how fortunate we are tonight. We just flew two hours over mountains—more than half of it at night—all while our engine oil blew slowly overboard. Had the crankcase emptied, our powerplant would have seized."

Consumed by images of engine failure over the rugged and uninhabited Verde River Canyon, I said no more about what might have been. Austin was likely visualizing the same thing, though I didn't dare ask him. As for Hannis, he'd never been one to dwell on such hypothetical concerns. After that dark night, however, he never again complained about investing an extra few minutes to follow the freeway home.

Rock Art Ranch
Flight across the Centuries

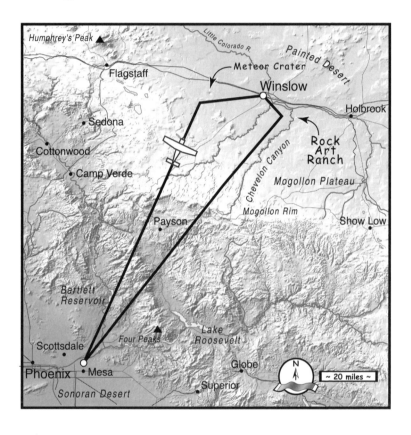

"Never did I imagine ever finding myself in a place like this!" said Purna, as we lurched along the rutted cattle track, like characters from a Navajo detective novel. "Always I have lived in the city, and this is unlike *anything* I've ever imagined."

Only a few hours earlier Jean and I had plucked the young native of India and her fellow graduate student, LeeAnne, from plush Scottsdale. There the two visitors from Chicago were working with my wife to complete requirements for their doctoral degrees.

In just an hour's flight we'd transported them from urban landscape to northern Arizona's high-desert plateau. This stark land is notable from the air not so much for its own featureless surface, but rather for the buttes and mountains to which it leads your eyes in the distance.

Parched and treeless below us, high plains rolled like soft flesh to the horizon, slashed here and there by deep incisions cut by water zigzagging through the land. *What's down there,* I wondered, *in those crevices rendered bottomless by harsh desert shadows?*

The only other deformity marring the smooth softness of the terrain was famous Meteor Crater, scarring Earth's cleanshaven face like a misplaced lunar feature. We circled the crater in awe, then landed at Winslow's Lindbergh Airport, laid out by the adventurer shortly after his transatlantic flight.

Winslow is a quiet place, sustained by traffic on Interstate 40 and the adjacent transcontinental rail line. We passed a pleasant few hours there, touring its restored railroad hotel and eyeing Route 66 souvenirs. Then we shot photos at Standing on the Corner Park, where a bronze young man waits eternally with his guitar for the "girl, my Lord, in a flatbed Ford" immortalized in the Eagles song.

But none of this was why we came. Soon we found ourselves treading gravel toward Holbrook on historic Territorial Road. Our plume of dust was the only feature piercing grassy barrens except for occasional cattle laying claim to the road. Purna and LeeAnne expressed astonishment at the unbroken horizon, encompassing pink Painted Desert ahead, distant Navajo Nation mesas to our left, and Humphreys Peak sixty miles behind.

After driving for miles through featureless terrain and passing a particularly ominous black bull, we were directed down dirt wheel ruts by a hand-lettered sign. Immediately we were

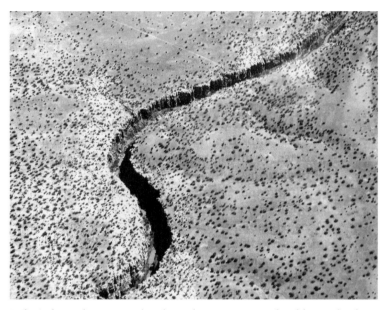

What's down there, I wondered, *in those canyons rendered bottomless by harsh desert shadows?*

impressed by the roughness of the narrow track, especially with no place to turn around, and the convincing appearance of leading to nowhere but oblivion.

"We can see so far," blurted Purna with alarm from the back seat, "and not a house in sight. I do hope we are not lost!" But then suddenly, from land that had appeared flat and empty only a moment before, arose a motley collection of broken-down buildings and decrepit farm equipment straight out of a dust bowl photo.

"Rock Art Ranch," said the traditional sign crowning the entry, and there to greet us was Brantley Baird, owner and resident since his father bought the place "back in '45."

Baird's blue eyes reached out from under his battered felt hat like those of a favorite uncle, and immediately it was clear that this man was the genuine article from a vanishing breed.

I squinted through blistering sunlight at our urban visitors, trying to gauge their thoughts as they shook hands with a *real cowboy.*

Baird showed us an old blacksmith forge and hired hands' cabins from the original Hashknife Ranch that once covered this territory "from over by Flagstaff all the way to the New Mexico border." When he got to Native pottery and arrowheads, I knew we were nearing our journey's goal.

He then led us over sand-and-rock-choked terrain, past metates[4] and stone fireboxes left by ancient residents, to the brink of one of those incisive canyons that had so intrigued me from the air. So often, pilots peer down into nooks and crannies of the world, wondering what secrets might lie there if only we could reach them. One of those mysteries was now revealed, and it was more delicious even than my imagination.

There, hidden in the shaded bottom of this narrow channel through such parched and desolate terrain, was an oasis of wild walnut trees, desert rose, and cattails. Strung like pearls along Chevelon Creek, they were garnished with red, white, and yellow wildflowers.

Reaching the crystalline lifeline at the canyon's bottom, Baird paused reverently to drink.

"Go ahead, have some," offered the old cowboy, noting our hesitation. "It's cold, and clean as can be!"

He then led us to the first of many giant blackened panels in the sandstone walls of the canyon, each decorated by ancient visitors with unmistakable outlines of people, animals, and hands.

Countless human figures populated those canyon walls, alone and in groups. Hunters stalked herds of deer, and the god Kokopelli played his flute. There were geometric symbols,

---

[4] *Metates* are stones used for grinding corn.

too, along with images of bears, snakes, scorpions, and other creatures we couldn't recognize.

Most wondrous of all was the image of a woman. Wearing Hopi-style sideknots in her hair, she could be seen unmistakably giving birth to a child. Remembering the deliveries of our own children, Jean and I momentarily shared a bond with that woman, across the centuries.

While the rest of us wandered this sheltered Eden, Baird relaxed in cool shade, absorbing our wonder as only the latest beings over thousands of years to seek solace here from the sun. Only the lengthening of shadows induced us to move on.

Countless human figures populated those walls. Most wondrous of all was the image of a woman, unmistakably giving birth to a child.

Upon departing windswept Lindbergh Airport that evening, we peered intently at the high desert below. Mellowed by its descending position low in the sky, the formerly vicious sun now caressed Earth's soft skin, accentuating the mysterious scars engraved so raggedly by Chevelon Creek and its siblings. It was easy enough to imagine ancient inhabitants looking up from those dark shadows of Chevelon Canyon. What would they think of us, removed as we are from them by time, culture, and the miracle of flight?

Yet we too had sought shelter in their canyon, and shared emotions common to all human beings through their artwork. Perhaps it wasn't so strange to feel a connection with those ancient peoples, each of us exploring life in our own ways—they through the miracle of a hidden, water-sparked oasis in their desert, and we attaining that same destination through the time machine of a flying carpet.

Best Flying Ever

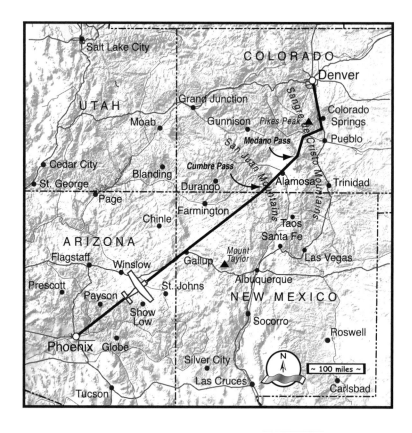

I was on the ramp at Denver Centennial Airport, pre-flighting the *Flying Carpet* for our long flight home to Phoenix, when the young fueler arrived at the airplane.

Bryan was his name, and as he neatly topped the tanks without spilling a drop, I asked if he was a pilot.

"Workin' on my commercial," he said with justifiable pride. "One day I'm going to be an airline pilot." Then, while servicing the tires we talked about his flying, his studies, and his plans for the future.

"Ever do any pleasure flying?" I asked, rolling the plane fore and aft so he could chase the tire valve inside the left wheel fairing.

"Yeah," he answered, "there's a girl I know in Ames, Iowa. Just got back from visiting her there last weekend."

"That's quite a trip," I said, "What did you fly?"

"A Cessna 172—took just over fourteen hours round trip."

He then told me about this special girl, how they'd met at a concert, and how she's in Denver every summer but he tries to fly out and see her once a month during the school year.

"Lots of instrument flying on that trip," I observed.

"That's for sure. I've learned plenty!"

I in turn told him about my own long-ago flying romance, shuttling a much shorter trip back and forth between Champaign and Indianapolis. "It was great fun," I reminisced, "and in the course of it I tapped every friend I ever had and then some, to ride along and share the cost."

As we moved to the other main wheel, Bryan began telling me of his own pilot friend, who shares expenses and flying on those lengthy Iowa trips. But my own thoughts had rolled back twenty-five years, to flights in the Flying Illini Piper Cherokee and Cessna 172. It was only an hour each way to visit my girlfriend, but often in challenging weather.

I remembered flying the landing pattern for Eagle Creek Airport, over a blue reservoir brimming with sailboats. And sneaking into dorms after hours at Butler University to visit a bubbly dark-haired girl with sparkling eyes and a knack for wisecracks.

On my first flight to Indianapolis I couldn't find Shank Airport, where the two of us had planned to meet—turned out that although still on the chart, it had closed several months earlier. Somehow we found each other anyway.

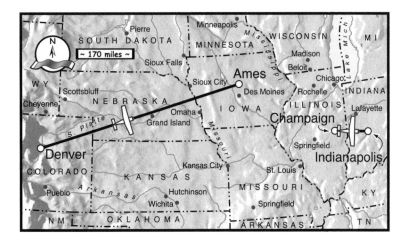

Another time we departed Champaign to take her home, but returned after takeoff due to snowy weather. Conditions were too slick for my old Chrysler convertible, so we drove her back in my roommate's drafty VW bug with the hole in the floor.

We made other special flights together, to faraway places such as Rochelle, Illinois, for her brother's wedding, and Madison, Wisconsin. Then there was my embarrassing emergency bathroom landing, on the long trip from Champaign to Beloit in a Cessna 150—not so cool for a young man trying to impress his girlfriend.

"Hey," interrupted Bryan. "Can you push the plane back a hair? I can't reach the tire valve inside the nosewheel fairing."

I pushed.

"Ever fly faster airplanes on that long trip to Ames?" I asked, seeking to continue the conversation and the memories.

"I did check out in a retractable landing gear model—you know, in preparation for my commercial," he replied, "but after all, one objective is to get flight hours so there's no point in taking a faster plane." He paused for a moment. "Besides, I

don't plan to be flying this little stuff for long anyway; *I'll* be
flying *jets*!"

By now Bryan had almost finished cleaning the windshield. He asked a polite question or two about the *Flying
Carpet,* and how long it would take to get to Phoenix. Then he
walked to the truck, stopping just before he got there to throw
the windshield cleaner inside. But before getting in, he turned
back in my direction.

"Say," he said, brow furrowed as I hadn't seen it during our
brief conversation. "Hope you don't mind me asking. But
what ever happened to that girl?"

"Huh?"

"That girl you flew over to see, you know, in Indianapolis."

"She married me."

"Great!" he said, suddenly beaming, "because I'm hoping
this girl will marry me, too!"

With that he shook my hand warmly, climbed into the
cab, revved up the engine, and drove away.

There wasn't time to tell Bryan what was going through
my mind at that moment. Probably it's just as well, because
he'll have to travel that airway himself to believe it.

But one day—I desperately wanted to tell him—twenty
years from now when he's commanding a Boeing, he's going to
ease back in his seat, having completed the cruise checklist, and
say to his young first officer, "You know, this airline flying is a
blast, but did I ever tell you about the *best* flying I ever did?"

"No," his young first officer will answer. "Was it one of
those old Learjets you flew on your way up the ladder?"

"Nope," Bryan will reply, "the best flying of my life was a
fourteen-hour round trip I made every month during college,
in a Cessna 172, all the way from Denver to Ames, Iowa, to
see a very special girl there. And you know what?"

"What?"

"She married me!"

Filled with those thoughts I walked to the parking lot, from there to drive to a nearby hotel and pick up a dark-haired, sparkly eyed girl, who by now would be done with her meeting and ready for the long flight home.

Best flying I've ever done, I thought.

*FULL
CIRCLE*

Raise the *Flying Carpet*
Shipwrecks over Arizona

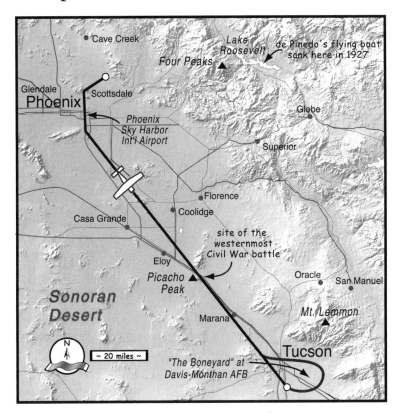

"Important message," said Jean, as I walked in the door. "You need to call Penny Porter right away . . . Something about the conference next week."

Surprised, I doffed my biking helmet and headed for the phone. I knew Penny was directing the annual writers conference in Tucson—in fact, we'd first met at one in the past—but I couldn't imagine why she'd be calling me on the topic.

"Greg, you're such a dear to call me right back," said Penny, upon answering. (All grandmothers speak that way, even six-foot-tall redheads.)

"We're in a real bind with the conference, and desperately need your help."

"Me?" I replied.

"That's right," said Penny, "Our keynote speaker had to cancel at the last moment, and the conference is only a week away. The good news is that I've found someone terrific to replace him. Can you believe that Clive Cussler has agreed to speak on such short notice? And what's more, he insists on donating his fee to charity."

"Clive Cussler!" I said, "He writes the Dirk Pitt novels, like *Raise the Titanic* and *Inca Gold.* And he discovered the Confederate submarine, *Hunley.*"

"That's right," said Penny. "You're still coming, right?"

"Wouldn't miss it," I said, "And I can't wait to hear Clive Cussler speak. But how do I fit into all this?"

"I haven't told you the whole story," said Penny. "Clive has agreed to present at Saturday's luncheon and sign books afterward. The problem is that we must get him home by 5 o'clock for another engagement. You're still planning to fly to the conference, right?"

"Yes."

"You'd be back well before five, right? The conference is near Tucson International, and Clive lives only a few miles from Scottsdale Airport. Is there any way he could ride down with you in the *Flying Carpet?*"

"Spend the day with a famous author?" I replied. "You bet!" Even Jean was excited. Upon hearing the news, she changed her tune from "boring writers conference," to "you're not going without me."

With umpteen *New York Times* bestsellers under his belt and 120 million books in print, Clive Cussler lives adventures exciting as those of his fictional hero, Dirk Pitt. He also chases lost shipwrecks. Among some sixty he has found are the Civil War *Hunley,* first submarine to sink a ship in battle; *Carpathia,* rescuer of *Titanic's* survivors; and *L'Aimable,* lost by seventeenth century explorer Robert LaSalle.

When I phoned to make arrangements, I learned that Cussler has aviation blood, too, having served as a C-97 crew chief and flight engineer during the Korean War. (C-97s were Boeing Stratocruisers in military livery.) My excitement grew as he shared stories about fifteen-hour round-engine cargo flights from Hawaii to Japan.[1] What's more, his shipwreck-hunting partner and *Sea Hunters* co-author, Craig Dirgo, would be joining us for the flight to Tucson.

Cussler is a tall man—we discovered when meeting at Scottsdale Airport—with graying hair and a warm handshake. Although I'd described our single-engine Cessna in advance, he appeared surprised to find the *Flying Carpet* nestled uncomfortably between corporate jets, like a gnat among eagles. But any concerns were forgotten after takeoff, when he and Dirgo watched jets land beneath us at Phoenix Sky Harbor Airport.

Sky Harbor! With these passengers on board the name brought to mind ships—and shipwrecks! Not until departing congested airspace did serious conversation begin. Clive is a casual man, with a not-surprising knack for story telling. We learned of his past as an advertising writer, and how while carousing with friends one night after work he helped conceive the award-winning but outrageous Ajax White Knight and its slogan, "Stronger than dirt."

Of course the real fascination was in learning how Cussler and Dirgo hunt for shipwrecks. I had assumed that navies of

---

[1] *Round engine* refers to radial piston engines, so named due to cylinders configured radially around a crankshaft.

experts would be required to find lost ships, but in fact the two rarely assemble more than a few people for these adventures, and work doggedly from a rented boat. Months of research are required before taking to the water, and once there it takes a lucky combination of skill and persistence to find ships missing for decades or even centuries.

The search for a lost Confederate blockade runner, for example, was fruitless until Cussler determined that methods for reckoning latitude and longitude had changed slightly following the Civil War. After applying that correction to 150-year-old charts, he found the wreck. (Cussler and Dirgo leave salvage to others—their thrill comes from locating the remains.) It seemed odd for a moment, discussing Confederate shipwrecks over the Arizona desert, but then our windshield filled with Picacho Peak, site of the westernmost battle of the Civil War. Funny how history ties things together.

Cussler's next tale turned from ships to the search for a mysterious locomotive—lost in a Colorado river, it simply couldn't be found. How, the men wondered, could a locomotive disappear from beneath the bridge where it fell? Clever sleuthing revealed a 100-year-old insurance scam. It turned out that after collecting payment the owners had secretly salvaged the wrecked locomotive for use under a different name.

I almost dropped my chart when the team brought up their latest project, an aerial mystery. Having in the past located the lost 1930s Navy airship, *Akron,* Cussler and Dirgo were now pursuing a famous airplane. Only days before his May 1927 transatlantic flight, Charles Lindbergh learned that two World War I flying heroes, Charles Nungesser and François Coli, had departed Paris for New York in their Levasseur biplane, *L'Oiseau Blanc.*

Lindbergh thought he'd lost the race, but as it turned out, Nungesser and Coli disappeared without a trace, and the rest is history. Many historians think *L'Oiseau Blanc* went down off the coast of France, but Cussler believes it successfully crossed the Atlantic and crashed in the United States. Finding it would rewrite history.

I took the opportunity to share a related story having a local connection. "Did you know that one of Lindbergh's would-be competitors lost his plane here in Arizona?" I asked. Italy's Marquis Francesco de Pinedo had already completed a South Atlantic crossing from Europe to South America via Africa in February 1927, in a twin engine Savoia-Marchetti flying boat named the *Santa Maria.*

Months ahead of any potential competitor, de Pinedo decided to complete a goodwill tour of the United States before proceeding to New York for a return crossing over the North Atlantic. Flying via Central America with a crew of three, de Pinedo proceeded toward California.

Early in April, the *Santa Maria* landed in Arizona's Lake Roosevelt, one of few Southwest lakes substantial enough to accommodate a large seaplane at the time. There, the plane was ignited during refueling by a stray cigarette thrown into the water, and sank. By the time de Pinedo received a replacement from Italy and completed his tour, Lindbergh was on his way.

"Wonder if they've found the remains of that plane," said Cussler, always looking for a new mystery.

By now we were approaching Tucson, and Craig Dirgo asked if we might circle "the boneyard," that monstrous grave-yard at Davis-Monthan Air Force Base where old military air-planes go to die. "It's in one of my books," said Dirgo, "and I want to see that I've described it properly."

"Circle as long as you like," offered Tucson Approach when asked, so from low altitude the four of us ogled neat rows of fighters, bombers, and transports. Try as we might, however, we couldn't locate a single C-97 from Cussler's Air Force days. "Too old even for the junkyard," he said as we banked toward Tucson International.

Dirgo asked if we might circle "the boneyard," that monstrous grave-yard where old military airplanes go to die.

Soon the famous author was enthralling writers at the con-ference, while Penny beamed from the sidelines. But for Jean and me, the adventure was only half over; on the flight home we would learn more about how a master conceives fiction, and even where Dirk Pitt got his name (after the author's young son). We circled Cussler's house before landing, and afterward he even honored me with a compliment on my piloting.

But on this trip I was in a sense just a lucky passenger—on a captivating journey through history piloted by a master sto-ryteller. Jean and I did agree on the way home never to become the subject of one of his books, however. Although we enjoyed participating in a very minor Clive Cussler adventure, we just didn't like the sound of *Raise the Flying Carpet*.

Friends in High Places
Flight over Lonely Lands

Bold brush strokes splashed orange beneath us, on the gray-green mountains of northwest Arizona. Anyone who doubts the power of numbers need only witness the magic of tiny California poppies from 10,000 feet.

We were bound from Phoenix to a meeting in distant Reno. Others might logically go by airline, but there was new terrain to explore along the way. So often, traveling by airline is like passing though a closet—walking in one side and then

273

stepping out on the other with little sense of time and space to your destination. We were only an hour from home, and already the poppies had justified travel by *Flying Carpet*. Better yet, an unexpected invitation now steered us toward lovely Lake Tahoe, in the crook of California's elbow.

"How well do you know these people we're visiting?" asked Jean.

"Not well," I replied. We'd met at a cocktail party—Tom, Laurel, and I—and airplanes were the glue that held that brief conversation together. Connecting us was passion for aerial adventure, we by *Flying Carpet* and they in their tiny Cessna 140, *Putt-Putt*. Only two short emails had followed that five-minute conversation: "Nice meeting you," and then just a few days ago, "Come stay with us!"

Tom and Laurel live only thirty-five miles from Reno, but a world away in the heart of the Sierra Nevada. Gleefully I'd canceled that smoky Reno hotel ringing with slot machines, and instead plotted course for Truckee, just north of Lake Tahoe in the high mountains of eastern California. Somehow the magic of flying works strongest when traveling to places away from hotels and meetings.

Beyond the poppies and Las Vegas, Jean and I found ourselves over lonely lands. Endless droning over featureless desert strangely jumbled our feelings—conflicting senses argued whether we were conquering great distances, or getting nowhere at all.

To occupy ourselves, we matched exotic names from our chart with barren landmarks below: Pahrump Valley, Funeral Mountain, Furnace Creek in Death Valley, and Jackass airport. Always in the background loomed the impenetrable white wall of the Sierra Nevada, crowned by tiny clouds and as inescapable as the backs of our minds.

Flying for hours above 12,000 feet lends euphoria to such a trip—and a headache. Anxiety played its role, too. Jean and

I could not escape visions of landing powerless on these barrens that stretch 100 empty miles to the horizon. It seemed impossible that anyone would ever find us if we went down here, or even that other airplanes might pass this way again. Were we not the first to cross this desolate frontier? Perhaps time would somehow warp during this endless droning, abandoning us over a primeval world with no airports or civilization to be found at our destination. Precautionary canteens and hiking boots offered little comfort from the back seat.

These small concerns were replaced by others as lowering clouds cloaked the Sierras in vapor, squeezing us downward among lesser mountains and silencing the scratchy radio voices of Oakland Center. Thunderheads peeked through distant holes in the overcast, and airliners could be heard requesting deviations from far above. I found myself gripping the control wheel—and sweating.

Thankfully, Mono Lake appeared mirage-like between misty mountains, granting us renewed confidence to continue. At Minden, we discovered Spooner Pass exactly where Laurel had promised, with silvery temptress Lake Tahoe beckoning from her ring of mountains on the other side. Ducking heads we scooted beneath clouds through that passage, then turned north over the lake. "Keep the ski slopes to your left," reminded Laurel from the email I'd printed. Beyond the ridge waited Truckee Airport between parted rain showers, like a friendly bed with blankets turned back to greet us.

It seemed so appropriate, finding Laurel and Tom at this mystical airport surrounded by snow-covered mountains. They fly 1,000-mile cross-countries from this 6,000-foot valley, drawn aloft by only 100 horsepower.

"We tour Truckee's neighborhoods to gain altitude after takeoff," joked Tom over lunch that afternoon, "and carry only twenty pounds of personal baggage—five for me, and fifteen for Laurel."

Mono Lake appeared mirage-like between misty mountains, granting us confidence to continue.

Laurel is a writer and flight instructor; Tom, a ski instructor and professional photographer, is a 400-hour student pilot. "Why rush to finish my certificate?" he said. "With Laurel I fly all I want." Traveling sixty miles per hour slower than even our leisurely *Flying Carpet, Putt-Putt* delivers worthy magazine adventures for the couple to capture through writing and photographs.

Jean and I reveled in high-mountain hospitality, at our hosts' Victorian cottage by the railroad tracks. Laurel served homemade carrot soufflé with dinner, and Tom treated us next day to oatmeal garnished with dried fruit and brown sugar. To remind us of home there was only a stuffed javelina in a Truckee boutique; clerks there suffered our tales of the wild pigs munching prickly pear in our Arizona front yard, spines and all.

Next evening, after the meeting in Reno, we surrounded ourselves with Boeing flying boats at a theme restaurant and dined with friends old and new. Dorothy was there from Oregon, and Laura brought friends from Louisville. ("She always travels with an entourage," observed Laurel.) Elizabeth came from Maryland, as did Julie, who craves a Cessna 140 like that flown by Tom and Laurel. A dozen gesturing pilots made that one raucous dinner noisier than all our eight hours behind a spinning propeller.

Climbing through mist the following morning from Truckee Airport, we skimmed that ridge near the ski slope, only to find Lake Tahoe more tantalizing than ever. This time she wore cobalt, with bits of fog dancing on her surface among reflected clouds and snowy peaks.

Homeward bound we were haunted and lonely, as on the trip up. Only two other airplanes showed themselves in four hours—strangely, they converged simultaneously under the watchful eyes of Las Vegas Approach. A jetliner banked regally 500 feet below us, while a Cessna flitted the same distance overhead, their contrasting plumage eerily fluorescent against gray landscape and pale blue sky.

This time during long desert lulls, Jean and I forgot emergency landings and talked instead of old railroad Truckee, of snowy mountains ringing blue Lake Tahoe, and of golden poppies. How different our conversation might be had we traveled by airline—just a smoky hotel to remember and that one enjoyable dinner.

Most of all we thought of Laurel and Tom, their warmth and interests, their humor, and their travels cross-country in *Putt-Putt*. We'd found in our hosts so much more than shared interest in flying. Rich conversation had seasoned our visit, perhaps best conveyed by the contents of their bookshelves. There, alongside ski manuals and cookbooks and mysteries, we discovered romantic flying stories such as Beryl Markham's *West with the Night*, and an original edition of Longfellow's *Evangeline*.

Tom and Laurel overfly Mount Rushmore in *Putt-Putt*. (Photo by George Kounis, *Pilot Getaways* magazine.)

Only once on that long flight home did those gracious hosts fully escape our minds, and that was over Jackass airport. There it seemed appropriate to think of someone else.

Big Boots to Fill

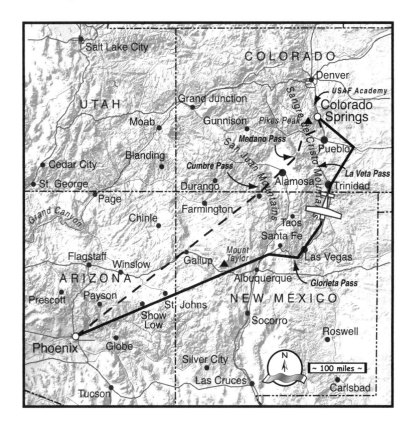

At long last we're headed home. Austin snoozes peacefully against his window, the snow finally melted from his new boots, while Jean stretches sleeping across the back seat. For the second time in as many visits, we're returning from the Air Force Academy after being stranded by a spring blizzard.

Flying from Phoenix to Colorado Springs can be breathtaking when weather allows straight-line travel through the Rocky Mountain passes framing Alamosa. But this particular trip has been grueling from the moment we left home three days ago. That morning we awoke to low ceilings and strong winds battering our route.

"We can depart safely," I told my wife and son, "but it'll be a rough ride and we could get stranded going either way. We might not make it home on schedule, either." This last I shared because both Jean and Austin had plans for our projected day of return, plus we were expecting visitors at our house. "Should we consider going by airline?"

"No way!" said Austin. "You promised we'd make this trip by *Flying Carpet.*"

"That's right," said Jean. "What do you think we are, wimps?"

Foolish of me to ask, I suppose, when for years my family has calmly endured whatever the weather dished out. Jean has even been known to claim that "turbulence is fun."

A direct route was out of the question under such conditions, so I filed a flight plan the long way to Colorado Springs, dogleg over Las Vegas, New Mexico, and then north along the front range of the Rockies. Although it added an hour to our flight, that would be far safer than tackling high mountain passes in such weather.

An hour later, Austin climbed us on instruments through damp clouds from Phoenix, planting us on course with a memorable tailwind. (Speeds approaching 200 miles per hour earn bragging rights for a straight-leg Skylane.) The ride wasn't bad at first, but when bumps arose over western New Mexico, Austin reclaimed control from the autopilot.

The true carnival ride began in Glorieta Pass near Santa Fe. With belts cinched tight, we battled the elements at maneuvering speed for two brutal hours to our destination.[2]

---

[2] *Maneuvering speed* is a reduced airspeed used to prevent structural damage or loss of control in turbulence.

Never before has Austin begged and then ordered me to take the controls so he could rest. Exhausted, we landed in thirty-five knot winds at Colorado Springs.

Like our visit last year, we were here pursuing Austin's long-time dream of attending the Academy. After a day of briefings he sampled dorm life overnight, then attended morning classes with a cadet host. That afternoon we were to leave. But as it had the year before, snow began around noon and quickly accelerated into a blizzard. Austin and I couldn't believe we were two for two at getting stranded in Colorado Springs.

Next morning we awoke to news that the airport was closed even to airliners. Although the snow was gradually tapering off, surface winds still gusted over forty knots. Some stations along our route reported errant blasts approaching sixty. With little else to do, Austin donned the new boots he'd purchased on campus, and the two of us trudged irrationally for miles through stinging snow. Jean chose instead to read in the warmth of the hotel lobby.

Wishfully, perhaps, we checked out at 3 o'clock and drove to the reopened airport in hopes that improving weather would allow us to leave. But there we were greeted by an even greater shock. To our horror, the *Flying Carpet* and surrounding airplanes had been shifted some thirty degrees in their tiedowns by the strong winds. Frantically we examined the airplane for damage, but fortunately found none.

By now surface winds along our route were gusting merely to thirty knots, with winds aloft forecast at thirty-five from the west. Mountain-flying wisdom says "don't go" when ridgetop winds exceed thirty knots, and time was running out for our departure. This is not a trip to make at night, and only a few hours of daylight remained. Worse yet, flight service warned of another storm approaching tomorrow. Just as we plunged into cumulative oh-no-not-another-motel-night funk, our savior taxied in.

It was a Mooney pilot, and encouraged by the first moving lightplane we'd seen, I interrogated him eagerly at the coffeepot. He had just come from Santa Fe—directly along our route—and shared the valuable advice that comes only from an experienced local flier.

"The ride's not bad," he said, "providing you know the tricks. With strong westerly winds like these, the worst turbulence forms downwind of La Veta Pass. Distance yourself by flying east of Pueblo to a point fifty miles south, then via Trinidad to Las Vegas. It also helps to stay low; 8,500 feet will keep you beneath most turbulence that extends out that far."

Armed with that wise counsel, we secured our belongings and launched into a howling crosswind. The ride was bumpy, but nothing like what we'd experienced on the way up. Through our mentor's guidance, we slipped smoothly beneath cloud streamers trailing twenty miles from the passes. After skimming green foothills near Trinidad we turned westward over Las Vegas. It was then, with headwinds slowing us to a crawl and the first promise of reaching home beyond the horizon, that new enthusiasm warmed our cockpit and my companions dropped off to sleep.

"Hey Dad," says Austin, awakening suddenly. "Remember talking last year, on the flight home?"

"Sure do," I reply. "It was just beyond Cumbre Pass through the San Juan Mountains. You said that your next trip to the Air Force Academy would be as a new cadet, and made me promise we'd travel there together by *Flying Carpet*."

"That's right, and we've accomplished both those things." says Austin. "I'll never forget Mom yelling '*Yippee!*' into the congressman's ear when he called to say I was accepted to the Academy." Jean chuckles sleepily from the back seat.

"And wait'll my friends see these combat boots!" he continues. "That snow has already started breaking 'em in." Recent travails melt away, as the three of us proudly retrace one young man's journey in achieving his first career goal. There will be more special Colorado flights in our future, and hopefully at least a few of them will be completed according to plan.

Austin shows off his new boots to cousin Ian.

"Mom . . . Dad . . . " says Austin more seriously, "thank you both *so much* for coming with me to new cadet orientation."

Those special words sustain me another hour until at last we cross into Arizona. Finally, we know with certainty that we'll sleep in our own beds tonight. The mere thought of it drops Austin and Jean back into happy slumber.

As mountain lakes near Show Low silver with sunset, I revel in keeping my promise to our son. After all, it was small cockpit adventures like these that stimulated his dream in the first place. And whatever Austin's future exploits in the service of his country, I know he'll never forget his first official report to the United States Air Force Academy, piloting his mom and dad through challenging weather by *Flying Carpet*.

"Why Are You Up Here?"

Friday night jazz in Flagstaff.

"No way I'd work at an airport," says Hannis with irritation, as we get into the car. "It'd be totally boring."

"Really?" says Austin, "I think it would be awesome, watching all those planes take off and land."

Austin and I have just deplaned at Flagstaff to attend Hannis's weekly jazz performance, and conversation has opened with summer jobs.

"All that noise," says Hannis. "I wouldn't be able to stand it."

"Louder than playing bar gigs?" I ask.

"That's different," he replies. "That's music, and people . . . not like listening to airplane engines all day long. Besides, I hate the smell of gasoline."

Funny how people learn to appreciate even the mundane things associated with their passions. "I always recognize the *Flying Carpet* when you fly over," Jean often tells me. "Skylanes have the most distinctive sound of any airplane." Probably true for us, anyway, after all the hours we've spent listening to one from the inside. While the sweet rumble of a radial engine draws me irresistibly outside to look, my neighbors likely grumble and grit their teeth. I doubt they appreciate the distinctive whines of jets and turboprops either, nor the drumming of helicopters.

"Hannis," I ask, "as a musician, do you actually learn to like the smells of old cigarette smoke and stale alcohol?"

"It's part of the atmosphere," he dryly replies.

"How about you, Austin? Being a runner, do you enjoy breathing sweat in the cross-country team locker room?"

"Don't know if I'd use the word *enjoy,*" he laughs. "But you do get used to it after awhile. Kinda goes with the sport, I guess."

My nostrils fill for a moment with the remembered aroma of warm oil on a dipstick, followed by the acrid smell when a few drops splash on the hot engine. What pilot doesn't savor the fragrance of cockpit leather warmed by the sun? Even aging plastic and mildewing seats have their appeal in an old airplane; but like the scents of beloved pets, only people with longtime familiarity can appreciate them.

Soon we arrive at a campus coffeehouse where colorful strains of Ellington, Coltrane, and Mingus sail from the instruments of young musicians. Tight and powerful melodies fly from this rough-and-tumble bunch, and I find myself intrigued by the way unkempt strings poking from Hannis's guitar contrast with his rich mastery of chords. The same might be said of the broken latch marring his guitar case and the missing amplifier caster replaced by a cardboard box—somehow they add color to the music rather than detracting from it. Parallels come to mind in the stop-drilled cracks and sheet metal patches found on old airplanes—their crudeness renders flight all the more miraculous.

We fly here often to hear Hannis's Friday-evening gig, cruising home to a different sort of music late at night. Usually I plan my concert-going around the lunar calendar, the full moon being such a precious wingman over remote terrain at night. This evening, however, the moon has abandoned us, so again we'll follow freeway lights.

Taxiing out in darkness, we're soothed by friendly tunes from the creaking windshield and rattling control cables so familiar to Cessna pilots. The tower is closed at this late hour, so I click the microphone button five times to activate the runway lights.

"Did you check the oil filler cap?" I ask Austin before applying power.

"Heh. You know I did."

"So did I."

The engine's warm rumble on takeoff sings reassuringly of an uneventful flight. In an instant, we are severed from Earth. Stars mingle with lights from the ground, and together they jumble into space. No ups or downs here, just embers glimmering randomly in a void. We settle into cruise, and the abstract world outside gradually becomes familiar and comfortable. Some pilots like to brighten their cockpit lights at night, to defend themselves from nothingness beyond their windows. Others prefer to revel in the blackness. Either way, with the weather good and the engine humming baritone, night cruise is nirvana.

I turn down the instrument lights, adjusting them ever lower as our eyes acclimate to each level of darkness. Eventually, this dimming renders the cockpit below the level of starlight (except for some errant instrument that's always brighter than the rest), thereby directing our consciousness outside. We hurtle in our capsule through space, and comprehend no reality beyond it. The cockpit is, after all, the head, eyes, and brain of an airplane. Just as we rarely think of our feet or arms while walking, the cockpit is the total universe of consciousness at night. The wings, the engine, the tail, and even people riding in the back seat cease to exist.

I contact Albuquerque Center for radar flight following on the way home. "We'll be following Interstate 17," I tell the controller, when asked about our southwesterly heading. "It's a little out of our way, but at least we'd have the freeway as an option if we needed to land."

"Roger that," replies the friendly controller. Unexpectedly, another voice chimes in.

"Why are you up here?" It was one of those deep voices that comes only from God or an airline pilot.

Surprised, Austin and I look at each other.

What does he mean? We ponder the same question though no words pass between us. The query had been issued without inflection. *Is this guy really questioning why we'd sail skies bursting with stars on a crystal clear night? Or does he just wonder where we're going?*

Troubled, I babble some nonsense about attending a concert in Flagstaff. But what I truly want to say is, "Do you really not understand why we're up here? Have you lost the magic?"

It's true that night flying is contradictory stuff. On one hand it can be dangerous, especially in the presence of unforgiving terrain, weather, or mechanical problems. I know that, both from accident statistics and personal experiences such as the one with the displaced oil cap. In the early years of aviation, night flying was actually believed to be impossible, due to the number of fatal crashes by those who attempted it. Not until World War I, when the British were faced with defending themselves from night Zeppelin attacks, did night flying techniques and lighting begin aggressive development. Now pilots do it all the time.

Safety in flying—in anything, for that matter—boils down to risk management. Hazards are greater in light planes at night and must be managed accordingly. For me, the rewards are worth those greater risks, though for others they might not be. *Why are you up here?* Perhaps the pilot who asked that question falls in the latter group. Or maybe he just wondered where we were going.

My mind rambles through other late-night odysseys, like a particular journey years ago from Lafayette to Indianapolis. The sky was so black that night that only a smattering of stars proved its existence at all. Below us, flat land glowed blue-white to the horizon under a flawless blanket of snow. How the light of a few stars could reflect so brightly I will never know, but the effect was as though the heavens had been flipped topsy-turvy with Earth. Yet there was a rightness to it at 2:00 a.m., like the distortion in one's mind of late night radio. These things just don't happen in daytime. What if I had missed it?

"Traffic ahead, Dad."

Austin rouses me to flashing lights on the horizon. It's another Earth-origin projectile, bound in the opposite direction 1,000 feet below us. Red and green navigation lights soon materialize among the strobes, signifying other souls approaching at a combined speed of 300 miles per hour. Kindred spirits, perhaps, so we flash our landing light—a friendly wave at 9,500 feet.

Like kids plunging our arms at a passing truck, craving a toot from the air horn, we wait. Maybe the occupants of that other craft haven't seen us. Perhaps they're busy setting radios or reading charts. Or maybe that cockpit is occupied by the other kind of pilot—the sort who doesn't hear the music or see the colors.

Two bright lights suddenly wink, one after the other. A most elementary communication, yet surpassing in richness all but the most intimate conversation. Other ships flash by as we approach home, bound for exotic places like Las Vegas, Cheyenne, and Newark. Some are distant worlds I've never visited, and therefore hardly less curiosity-inspiring than Mars or Saturn.

From blackness, the lights of Phoenix soon spill out before us, like the Milky Way in the manner children always hope for when called outside to see it. Buildings, roadways, and taillights shimmer under bottomless skies, oscillating with patterns and color.

It's late when we land. The airport glows blue in starlight as we taxi in, and parked airplanes loom silhouetted around us like hulking animals deep in sleep. Exhausted, Austin and I pause for a moment while securing our plane, savoring the warm-oil smells and percussive creaking of the hot engine. Plaintive scales sound softly in the background from instrument gyros winding down. If only Hannis were here to sample the music played by airplanes.

Why are you up here? Still the question haunts me, but now I choose to feel sorry for the guy who raised it. If he needed to ask, certainly no mortal like me could satisfactorily answer. We pat the *Flying Carpet* on her spinner, breathe in the cool night air, and turn silently to drive home.

Eight Long Minutes
over the Grand Canyon

I knew even before opening my chart that flying from Phoenix to St. George would be great adventure. After all, how many other trips involve crossing the Grand Canyon? Then there was the mission. Jean would rendezvous with our sister-in-law, Lesley, in the remote southern Utah town to attend tennis camp. Somehow flying is always more meaningful when others benefit.

Originally Lesley had agreed to join us for the flight from Phoenix, but when the time came her chronic fear of flying drove her to make other arrangements—she'd fly airlines to Las Vegas and then book a two-hour van ride to St. George. No matter. Either way, I'd have the pleasure of flying Jean to her destination on Sunday, then returning to pick her up on Wednesday. There would even be time to lounge poolside for a few hours after delivering her to the resort.

Sunday morning we climbed northbound into blue Arizona skies. Soon we found ourselves gazing down upon Embry-Riddle University's west campus at Prescott, then at old Highway 66 passing through tiny Seligman. But the best was yet to come—crossing the "big ditch."

Navigation over the Grand Canyon can be challenging, because the government has topped it with complex airspace restrictions to protect the environment from intrusive noise. Overflights below 14,500 feet must follow visual corridors between irregularly shaped "flight-free zones." These corridors do not align with radials from navigational stations, nor are they easily identified using physical landmarks pictured on the Grand Canyon Aeronautical Chart.

I knew from past experience not to wait until getting there to figure these things out; Jean flew the plane while I entered GPS navigation points for the crossing well in advance. Traffic is an issue, too. Remote as the canyon's location may be, air tour planes and helicopters crisscross the area. By planning ahead we'd remain clear of the flight-free zones upon reaching there, while keeping our gaze outside the cockpit to scan for traffic and ogle scenery. With preparations complete, Jean and I began peering ahead for the main event.

Fortunately, it takes more than bureaucratic doodling on a paper chart to tarnish one of nature's great wonders, especially when viewed from an airplane. Those who have not been to the Grand Canyon would likely be surprised to find it cutting through a more-or-less flat plain, as it does. Having skimmed low for miles across treeless plateau, we suddenly found ourselves over a pine forest, then rocketed without warning beyond the edge of the Earth. Surely I'm not the only pilot to suffer a twinge of fear, watching flat land so suddenly cascade a mile downward from beneath our wheels.

Once over the void, striated jumbles of pink, orange, and green stretched as far as our eyes could see, camouflaging the canyon's true shape and dimensions from human understanding. Only after the Colorado River revealed itself far below, could we comprehend the bottom. Then orange rock climbed quickly back up to meet us on the other side. Eight minutes may sound short on a two-hour flight, but when crossing this place it seems like eternity.

Just forty miles later we came upon St. George, nestled green like an emerald among buttes and spires of red and yellow rock. A single north-south runway perches on a mesa overlooking town. It reminds me of an aircraft carrier, except that unlike the seagoing version, designers couldn't direct the mesa into prevailing winds. As a result, westerly crosswinds assail the runway much of the time, plunging as they do across desolate terrain unbroken for many miles in any direction.

After landing, we spent a leisurely few hours sunning among flowers and ripening strawberries at the resort pool; then I waved goodbye to the girls and braved a stiff crosswind departing for home. The Canyon offered all-new vistas southbound, with an added tinge of crimson as sunset approached.

How lucky I am, I thought on the way home, *getting to do this again on Wednesday!* Just the prospect kept me fired up for the next two days. In anticipation, I prepared my camera for some serious shooting over the Grand Canyon, and scheduled

Surely I'm not the only pilot to suffer a twinge of fear, watching flat land so suddenly cascade a mile downward from beneath our wheels.

a business visit to the Dixie State College flight department at St. George.

The weather was so obviously wonderful on Tuesday, that I foolishly called flight service that evening just to savor the great flying weather I anticipated on Wednesday. That was a mistake. A powerful cold front was expected to straddle the Utah-Arizona border next day, accompanied by very strong winds—not the sort of thing a pilot likes to hear when planning a trip over one of the world's deepest canyons.

One can legitimately argue that watching the weather for a few days before a trip is a good idea, in order to see trends develop. But on the other hand, knowing ahead of time that the weather might be bad is of little value except for interrupting sleep. For that reason I rarely check weather the night before a trip unless significant planning is required.

After a restless night, I awoke in the morning to the most difficult kind of decision. The weather sounded like it could get nasty, but was not quite bad enough to be a definite no-go.

Although generally light at the time of my early morning call, surface winds along my route were forecast by afternoon to gust from the northwest at twenty-eight knots—potentially challenging, but not beyond my capability. However, just a few more knots or a shift in wind direction could make landing at St. George impossible, given the north-south runway.

A similar dilemma applied to winds aloft. If correctly forecast at twenty-five knots, they would make for a rough but manageable ride, given the mountainous terrain along my route. But winds much stronger than that could mean severe turbulence—downright dangerous.

Also concerning me was the slight possibility of low clouds and precipitation. Although St. George was expected to remain clear, forecasters called for occasional mountain obscuration by ceilings and rain only fifty miles north—not far away, in meteorological terms. Out East one might file instruments if that happened, but here that would be impossible due to minimum flight altitudes above the freezing level.[3]

On the positive side, at this time of morning everywhere within 100 miles of my route was reporting clear skies and light winds. Clearly there was no risk in taking off along that route, so long as I was prepared to land or turn around if

[3] Little instrument flying is done by light planes over the high mountains of the West, partly because at the altitudes required to top them, temperatures nearly always fall below freezing and therefore present icing hazards in clouds.

weather deteriorated. The bigger issue was how bad it might become later on, and how quickly. Jean would not be ready to leave St. George until 4 o'clock.

One other yellow flag arose when I queried the briefer about weather beyond my immediate route. It turned out that surface winds at Las Vegas, 110 miles west of St. George, were forecast to exceed forty knots by afternoon. Worse yet, at this time of morning they were already gusting to thirty-seven.

"Why do you think Las Vegas winds are so much worse than everywhere else?" I asked the briefer.

"Probably due to local terrain," he replied. That answer was only marginally fulfilling. Since most area airports have only automated weather reporting equipment, I decided to cover my bases by phoning the flight department at Dixie State College. Sometimes additional insights can be had from a real human observer looking out the window.

"Winds are currently light and variable here at St. George," said the dispatcher. "Just keep in mind that we sometimes get very strong crosswinds here, due to the north-south runway. Winds of thirty-five knots off the wing are not uncommon. We've had five or six aircraft run off the runway in just the past year, including a Learjet. So don't take any chances. If winds pick up, I recommend you land thirty miles away at Colorado City—more runways there."

Armed with that cautionary information I telephoned Jean, who was distinctly not enthused about the possibility of riding a ground shuttle two hours to Las Vegas for an airline flight home.

"But it's beautiful here!" she said. Given that the weather appeared flyable this morning, but could go either way in the afternoon, we agreed I should make the trip up. We could always stay overnight if conditions deteriorated. So I packed my overnight bag, filled my emergency canteens, and drove to the airport.

Even then, I debated whether to phone for one last weather update. Should I hurry on my way before conditions deteriorated? Or call again to identify any developing trends?

Among the challenges of flying in this part of the country are the great distances between airports. Not only are there few landing options in case of weather or mechanical difficulties, but weather reporting is severely limited. On this trip I would fly some 270 miles each way, but cross only two paved airports, Prescott and Seligman, of which only Prescott reports weather.

Can't hurt to get a quick update, I decided. But some guy was using the pay phone on the ramp. I tossed my gear into the airplane, then upon further reflection drove to the airport office and called flight service from there. The forecast was unchanged; there were no new alerts for threatening weather, and St. George winds remained relatively light.

There were no pilot reports from other aircraft either, but that could mean anything. Either everyone was experiencing a smooth ride, or no one was flying at all. In short, there was nothing new in the standard flight service briefing.

Desperately seeking comfort with my departure decision, I requested surface winds for airports within the surrounding three-state region. Although winds had picked up some at Cedar City, fifty miles northeast of St. George, they were still within reason. Las Vegas, however, was even worse than before, with winds now gusting over forty knots and turbulence reported by airliners.

"How about Grand Canyon Airport?" I asked. Sixty miles east of my route, the control tower there had earlier reported winds light and variable.

"Whoa!" said the briefer, "Grand Canyon Airport now reports winds from the northwest, gusting to thirty-seven." That certainly got my attention; powerful morning winds were not localized at Las Vegas, after all.

"What's more," he added, with a further note of surprise, "they report standing lenticular clouds to the northwest." Mountain fliers know that "lennies" form in the lee of high terrain as a result of very strong winds aloft. Such clouds indicate the likelihood of severe turbulence, along with possible downdrafts exceeding the climb capability of light aircraft. And "northwest of Grand Canyon Airport," suggested the "big ditch," not far from where I'd be crossing.

I now had the answer I needed, even if it wasn't the one I wanted to hear. Some days you're simply not destined to fly.

I returned my carefully prepared camera to its case and canceled my appointment at Dixie State College. Then I phoned Jean at St. George with flight information so she could reserve an airline seat home to Phoenix; I'd be waiting at Phoenix Sky Harbor to pick her up.

"What will you tell Lesley?" I asked, thinking that this would only cement my sister-in-law's fear of flying with us in the future.

"I'll tell her that this is exactly why flying with us is so safe," said Jean. "When the weather's bad we don't take any chances."

Finding myself back at the airplane with bags packed and nowhere to go, I polished bugs listlessly from the wing. Running through my mind as I scrubbed, were images of myself negotiating severe turbulence over the Grand Canyon in a Cessna 182. Those might truly have been the longest eight or ten minutes of my life. Realistically, I'd have checked weather along the way, would have learned of the situation and likely returned home. Yet at the same time, all risk had been averted when I made that additional phone call, then probed and probed until I had the information I needed to make a proper decision. ("You wouldn't believe the rough ride we had coming home on the airliner," Jean would later tell me. "You did the right thing.")

This was a day to be proud, rather than discouraged, I soon realized. Flying could easily wait until a better day. But some sort of extravagant consolation treat seemed in order. Suddenly, I had a brainstorm.

I'm gonna finish polishing off these bugs, I told myself, *then stop on the way home to indulge in an iced caramel cappucino.* Not quite as delicious as flying across the Grand Canyon, I know, but on this particular day it seemed like a darned good alternative.

Sky City

Old Acoma pueblo. (Photo by Tom Till.)

We stood atop a lonely New Mexico mesa, in a 1,000-year-old mud-brick city. Sun-warmed spires of crimson rock pierced the surrounding canyon and touched the silhouette of distant Mt. Taylor. Overhead, squadrons of bubbling cumulus sailed a cobalt sky, commanded from the horizon by darker clouds that might soon deliver lightning. Jean and I looked to our guests. Like us, they were awestruck—from here, their home in French Canada must seem a galaxy away. The four of us clasped hands.

301

"Where can we take Marcel and Lise, that they'll never forget?" Jean had asked just two weeks before. "They'll be visiting for a only few days." We'd struggled with the question ever
since learning that our friends would be visiting from Quebec
City. All we knew for sure was the need to escape soul-sizzling
summer temperatures in Phoenix.

"That's a tough one," I'd replied. "Every time we visit
Quebec the Duvals take us somewhere incredible. How do
you match whale-watching in the St. Lawrence River? Or
white-water rafting in the Laurentian Mountains?"

"How about the beaches of California?"

"That would be fun, but Marcel and Lise often winter in
Florida. No, there must be some other interesting destination
that would be totally foreign to them."

Finally the answer came to us. We would fly to Santa Fe.
Marcel and Lise had visited the Southwest only once before.
Like me, Marcel was a history buff. He, too, would enjoy the
contrasts between Quebec City and Santa Fe, founded only a
few years apart by France and Spain under vastly different circumstances. Not only would our guests enjoy seeing the second oldest city in the United States, but the Spanish and
Native American influences would be unlike any place they'd
previously visited.

The two had flown with us only once, a short flight many
years before during a previous visit. En route to Santa Fe, the
Flying Carpet would reveal wooded mountain vistas, volcanic
cinder cones, and the desolate malpais, those prehistoric lava
fields that look from the air as if they just hardened yesterday.
Only from an airplane could such sights be fully appreciated.

"We'll even overfly Old Acoma Pueblo," I observed to Jean
when proposing this grand plan. The words had barely left my
mouth when I realized that she'd never visited the ancient
Native American community; nor could a more exotic destination be imagined for Lise and Marcel.

"Could we land anywhere near there?" Jean asked. Examining my chart, I spotted a nearby airport for the tiny communities of Grants and Milan, New Mexico. One call later I was hooked.

"We'd love to have you!" welcomed the warm voice answering the telephone. "We've just extended the runway length to 7,100 feet, and you can rent a car from the auto upholstery shop here in Grants." Wes was the proprietor's name, and he made me feel that flying into his special airport would be like visiting boyhood at a small-town strip during the golden age of flying.

"Lots to do around here in addition to Acoma," he said. "Ever been to the ice cave, down in the malpais? Stays frozen all year around, even when it's 100° outside." Soon I had my road atlas out, planning visits to Acoma and Malpais National Monument, along with the associated ice cave.

Also nearby is El Morro Monument, a watering hole where travelers have left graffiti since ancient times; there we could view marks of Native Americans, Spaniards, and westbound settlers from over the centuries. Just beyond, beckoned historic Zuni pueblo, with its delicate needlepoint jewelry. All these being remote places that few people visit, I became increasingly excited about this stop on our trip.

Our initial plan called for visiting Acoma on the way to Santa Fe, but that soon changed. By an odd twist we could fly nonstop from Phoenix to Santa Fe, but not the other way. The reason was differences in airport elevation. Our home airport near Phoenix lies at only 1,400 feet above sea level. From there we could depart fully loaded with four adults, light baggage, and enough fuel to reach Santa Fe 2-1/2 hours away.

Most of New Mexico lies atop high plateau, however, with both Grants and Santa Fe near 6,500-foot elevation. (I've always wondered whether hypoxia explains my fascination with the state.) Thin air at those altitudes, further diminished by summertime heat, meant our *Flying Carpet* could not take off safely from such places fully loaded. Fuel would have to be left behind so we could get off the ground.

The solution was to visit Acoma on the return trip instead. We'd fly nonstop to Santa Fe first, take off from there light on fuel, and refuel at Grants on the way home. These sorts of tricks add safety and utility to flying light airplanes.

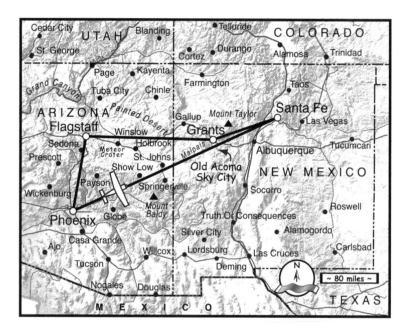

A week later the four of us touched down in colorful Santa Fe. I've always been intrigued that one of the earliest European settlements in our country should be landlocked in such remote terrain. The reason, of course, is that the Spaniards founded it as their northern territorial capital of New Spain (including the present country of Mexico), which existed long before settlement of the Northeast Seaboard.

The town is also historically important as the terminus of the Santa Fe Trail, and has long served as a center for arts and Native American culture. That afternoon we munched chile rellenos in the shadow of the Governor's Palace—built in 1610, it's the oldest continuously used public building in the United States. But even as we wandered through art galleries and historic sites, I found myself preoccupied with tomorrow's destination.

Old Acoma had haunted me ever since I first spotted it from the air those many years ago. Since then I'd ogled it often from aloft but visited on the ground only once, with Hannis and Austin ten years earlier. Finally I was to return with my wife and closest friends. They didn't know it yet, but Sky City would offer them sights never to be forgotten. Try as I might, I just couldn't get my mind off of it.

Next morning we departed early from Santa Fe, clutching complimentary sunflower-seed salsa collected with our fuel purchase. Within an hour we were skimming the wooded flank of Mt. Taylor. I chopped engine power and we plummeted down to the 7,800-foot traffic pattern for Grants-Milan Airport.

"Welcome Greg," offered unicom when I radioed for winds and active runway. I could tell from the voice it was Wes. He was waiting outside when we taxied in—tall, white-haired and dressed comfortably in overalls. At the airport office a few minutes later, he phoned the upholstery shop for our car, then offered a map and driving instructions.

"What time do you close?" I asked, suddenly realizing that avgas was offered only at a fixed pump down the field, and that we'd need to move the airplane to get it. "We'll need fuel, but we've already tied down the airplane and I don't want to inconvenience you if we depart late."

"I'll be here until after six," said Wes. "But if you miss me, don't worry about it. Just leave cash for the fuel and I'll pick it up in the morning." Such an offer indeed harks back to simpler times—I was reminded of how Halliburton once borrowed keys from an oil company to refuel at a remote desert storage tank. Wes lived on the field, it turned out, offering his services as aircraft mechanic and flight instructor. Based on his hospitality, the man must have many loyal customers.

Once in the car, we found Old Acoma's isolation emphasized by a lack of road signs. In the course of many wrong turns we literally drove from one end of the reservation to the other looking for it. Whether by luck or magic, we finally found the place, perched regally on its mesa 400 feet above us. Until recently, the only way to the top was via secret stone ladder carved in the folds of the mesa, but nowadays a road provides access to the top.

Despite its idyllic location, Sky City has suffered a turbulent history. Claiming status as the oldest continuously occupied community in the United States, Acoma was already over 500 years old when occupied by Spanish conquistadors in the 1500s.

After reaching the top of the mesa, our first stop was the early Spanish mission church with its cemetery—at merely hundreds of years old, it's the most modern building in Old Acoma. Our guide described how, during construction, pueblo residents were forced as slaves to carry the church's giant roof timbers by foot from distant Mt. Taylor. "If they dropped a timber along the way," he told us, "they were beaten and forced to return to the mountain for another."

Acoma rebelled against its conquerors during the Pueblo Revolt of 1680, but that ended in tragedy. To assert their mastery, the Spaniards amputated the right foot of every Native male upon reconquering the area ten years later.

Fortunately, the rest of our tour reflected happier times, hospitable people, and unearthly beauty. The name Sky City well describes both the location of the place and its urban character. Yet the multistory attached dwellings seem strangely juxtaposed against the surrounding barren canyons, red rock pinnacles, and distant mesas. If it weren't for mud-brick mortar tying the buildings visually to the land, you might think the community had been magically transported to the middle of nowhere from somewhere else. I imagined for a moment a medieval European neighborhood brought by sorcery to the desert. *Might Timbuktu look anything like this?* I wondered.

With adobe tenements and fifty-mile vistas as their backdrop, Acoma artists sell their wares directly to the public. Before descending the ancient stone ladder down hidden folds in the mesa, Jean and I invested in one of the coil-wound red, black, and white pots for which the pueblo is famous.

By now Old Acoma had consumed our interest for the bulk of the day, and there was barely time for rushed visits to Malpais Monument and the ice cave. Zuni and El Morro would have to wait until another day. Urging us along was a line of evil thunderclouds, fast approaching from the east and spurting lightning against black shafts of rain. Fortunately for us, when time came to leave, fair skies still beckoned westward toward Arizona. Not so lucky was the Bonanza pilot waiting forlornly on the ramp—he was bound east for Abilene.

Even after such a fulfilling day, one more adventure yet awaited us. Flagstaff lay only an hour west; there, Hannis's jazz combo would season our dinner at Macy's Coffeehouse. Rotating skyward, we climbed red rock canyons toward Gallup, destined to enjoy a kaleidoscopic sunset over the Painted Desert and last rays of twilight caressing Meteor Crater.

"Traveling the Southwest by airplane . . . " said Marcel to Lise out of nowhere, as if continuing a conversation started earlier in his head. "Even with all the pictures we've taken, our friends back home will never comprehend what we've seen."

Best Landing Anyone
Ever Made

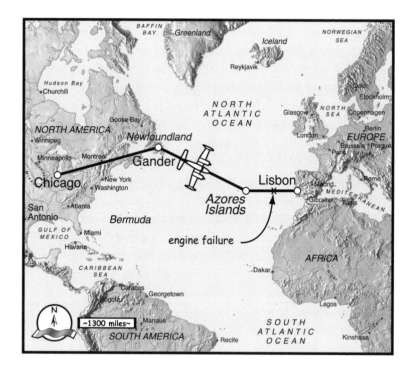

"We're out of control!" yelled my father, grabbing the wheel.

"No we're not," I replied, grabbing it back.

Overriding my father wasn't easy—he'd been a pilot since before I was born. After training in a Piper Cub, he bought his first airplane in 1949, a tiny fabric-covered Aeronca Chief. Soon afterward he traded for an all-metal Ercoupe, which he landed in a Missouri farm field to wait out thunderstorms. Pilots don't do that sort of thing anymore.

"We're in trouble! I'm taking over the plane!"

"Dad! Please believe me. We'll be okay."

Next had come a triple-tailed Bellanca Cruisaire. "Most efficient airplane I ever owned," Dad used to tell me. "It flew 150 miles per hour on 150 horsepower." He earned his instrument rating in that Bellanca, using just a headset, compass, and turn-and-bank indicator. Back then pilots flew "aural range" airways defined by Morse code. The sound of the letter "a" indicated one side of course ("dot-dash"), while "n" denoted the other ("dash-dot"). On-course aviators were treated to a steady tone. No frilly GPS or moving maps in those days.

My dad's one metal-bender occurred in that treasured Bellanca, which had retractable landing gear manually extended by many turns of a crank. Approaching New Orleans one day on instruments, he was interrupted by radio calls and forgot to finish lowering the wheels. Fortunately, damage was slight and his bird soon flew again.

"We're icing up!" shouted my father, jolting me back to the present.

"Dad," I replied. "We'll be home in twenty minutes. Please relax!"

Serving in the Air Force during the Korean conflict, my father tried the controls of early jets, such as the T-33 and B-47. But he was proudest of authorization to land his Bellanca on base in San Antonio, often flying it home on leave to see my mom in Chicago.

After his tour in the service, my dad moved up to V-tailed Bonanzas—three in a row. Then, in 1960, he bought the hottest personal airplane of its day, a twin-engine Cessna 310. We kids knew it was a big deal, because Sky King flew one on his popular TV Western.[4] It was easy enough to imagine ourselves chasing those bad guys in our own airplane. Heck, Sky's *Songbird* was even painted like ours, though we couldn't be

---

[4] In earlier episodes, Sky King's *Songbird* was a Cessna Bobcat, a.k.a. "Bamboo Bomber."

sure it was the same two-tone green from our black-and-white television set.

It took more than TV adventures to satisfy my dad, however. With my mother, he flew frequently to Canada, Mexico, and islands of the Caribbean. My mom, although afraid of water, even accompanied him 650 miles offshore to Bermuda, though she declined his biggest aviation adventure.

That occurred in 1962, when my father swapped the 310's back seat for a 140-gallon gas tank and flew with a buddy to Europe. They didn't take the northern route commonly flown by light airplanes, but instead navigated via Newfoundland and the Azores Islands to Portugal. The longest overwater leg exceeded ten hours.

On the way home after touring Europe, the aviators experienced engine roughness between Lisbon and the Azores. With instruments reading normal, the two pilots debated on which engine was acting up, not wanting to kill the good one 300 miles from land. Eventually they shut down the left engine, which proved to be the correct decision. Relaying their position through a nearby airliner, they proceeded to the Azores.

It turned out that one cylinder of the failed engine had cracked almost all the way around, and was within half an inch of blowing off altogether. The two pilots dined that evening with the crew of the airliner that had relayed the message. Several days later a new cylinder arrived, allowing completion of the trip. I still have the photo of my dad kissing the good right engine after landing, and the broken cylinder, which he made into a lamp.

"We're going down!" yelled my father, again grabbing for the wheel.

"Harold!" replied my mom from the back seat, "Leave him alone or you'll kill us all!"

We loved that green 310 bearing flag decals from so many countries, but the time came when our family of six could no

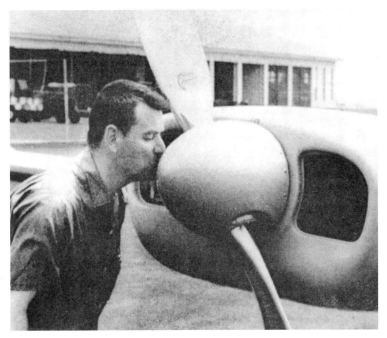

I still have the photo of my dad kissing the good right engine, and the broken cylinder that he made into a lamp.

longer fit in a five-place airplane. For awhile one sister rode belted on a cushion in the baggage compartment (field-approved by the FAA, in those simpler days), but finally my dad bought a newer six-place model. In it, one special evening, he flew Jean and me across Lake Michigan, along with my mother and future in-laws, to celebrate our engagement. We dined at Win Schuler's famous restaurant in Marshall, Michigan, then flew back to Chicago. It was the first time our parents had met, and Jean's folks were suitably impressed.

Often my parents traveled with other pilot friends, flying multiple airplanes on group vacations. My dad became notorious among that group for his unorthodox sense of humor. At one of their destinations, for example, he observed a workman dragging assembled plumbing into a church. Noting that the pipes were configured in the form of a giant "X," he quipped, "Is that who I think it is?"

That same observant humor made him a captivating storyteller, and incidents he described from those trips remain with me today as richly as my own flying experiences.

For example, one time a couple was returning in smooth air from the Bahamas to Chicago. During level flight, their twin engine Beechcraft Travel Air suddenly ballooned upward several thousand feet. Startled, the pilot reclaimed control from the autopilot and wrestled the airplane back to level flight. After discovering that the plane would now fly at only a fraction of its normal cruising speed, he set course for the nearest airport. Not until approaching to land did the pilot discover the source of their problem—the wing flaps were already fully extended. It turned out that while reaching for her purse, his wife had unknowingly caught the flap lever with her sleeve, activating landing flaps while the plane flew at cruise speed.

Another pilot, returning from a group trip to Florida, discovered that his Cessna would not fly straight after takeoff. "The plane seemed to operate normally in other respects," he explained to my father after landing, "but I had to hold full rudder all the way home." Not only was the pilot exhausted from forcefully pushing the rudder pedal for so many hours, but due to concerns about the possible cause, he flew at reduced speed for the entire flight. At this point in the pilot's explanation, his first-time passenger chimed in.

"I was suspicious that we might have such a problem even before we left Florida," announced the non-pilot to everyone else's astonishment. "I did my best to fix it."

"What did you do?" asked my dad.

"I saw that little metal thing on the tail was bent," said the passenger, "so I straightened it before we took off." The object in question was the rudder trim tab, which on this model is adjusted on the ground by maintenance personnel to make the plane fly straight. Funny as Dad thought this was, he was equally intrigued that neither pilot nor passenger had brought this up during the eight-hour flight.

It was a sad day when my father sold his final airplane. Struck down by degenerative disease, he slowly deteriorated, physically and mentally. My dad and I never flew much together over the years, because he was the kind of guy who mostly put his kids in the back seat. But following in his footsteps as a flight instructor, I had the pleasure of delivering him one last joyful flight at the controls. One afternoon when he was lucid, I offered the left seat of a Cessna to fly from Phoenix to Sedona. He did a credible job of taking off and getting us there, though I made the landing. It was a special flight for both of us, at least until he lost the ability to remember.

But by now, several years later, my Dad could no longer separate real events from imagined ones. While the rest of my family watched in horror, he continued grabbing for the controls, convinced that we were flying through the storm of a lifetime.

In reality, we were struggling for the steering wheel of a minivan, under clear skies on Interstate 10 between Tucson and Phoenix. After the most trying auto journey of my life, I pulled into our driveway and shut off the engine. With that, my Dad sighed relief like a man snatched from death. Beaming respect, he shook my hand.

"Gregory," he said, "that was the best landing anyone's ever made."

I wasn't sure whether to laugh or cry. Like many fathers of his day, my dad was spare with praise. In his mind, I had just saved all our lives, and these were admiring words from a forty-year aviator. Suddenly, I knew what to do. I put my arms around him and hugged him. From one pilot to another, I knew I'd never receive a better compliment.

New Beginnings

There have been two first flights in my life. These weren't first flights in the sense of first solo, first time soaring, or first balloon ascension, though such milestones were memorable each in their own way. Rather, they were moments when I discovered, fresh and new, the pure joy and freedom of flight.

The first of those experiences occurred in a banking turn, flying a Cessna 150 over the cracked ice and windblown snow of Lake Mendota in wintertime, at Madison, Wisconsin. I don't remember if it was as a solo student or new private pilot —it doesn't matter. At that instant, I escaped for the first time the nagging traumas of becoming a pilot, and the consuming minutia of doing what pilots must do to remain aloft.

I found myself seeing through the eyes of a bird, soaring with other birds over a landscape I'd never before experienced in quite the same way. Instead of fearing the terrain below as a threat to be avoided, I noted with fascination sailing ice boats and ice-fishing tents among which I'd skated between college classes in wintertime. While skating I'd experienced the fast-moving ice boats only as flashes of color passing me by. From the air, however, I could see their forward progress across the lake, and the paths left by their runners for miles behind.

The pressure ridges that blocked my progress when ice skating could now be seen in their entirety. Cracked and buckling they formed huge rational patterns stretching for miles like spider webs across the lake. I soared and gazed, soared and gazed, and knew that day for the first time that I'd achieved the ranks of birdmen and would never be cured.

My second "first flight" occurred on a summery autumn day just short of thirty years later—three weeks and two days after twisted souls hurled peaceful airplanes against skyscrap-

314

ers. At first the grounding of all things flying seemed appropriate, in homage to those who had died and revulsion to the dark turn taken during the normally beautiful act of flight.

For days afterward I walked our quiet street, gazing up in wonder at a tranquil sky never before seen devoid of airplanes. I'll admit to enjoying the peace of it for a time, and finding myself content with the quiet and solitude afforded by empty skies. But when airliners were again released to fly, my mood changed and I was soon overwhelmed with jealously. Overhead, airplanes traversed skies I was no longer allowed to tread.

As days passed, sadness turned to depression. Then hopelessness took over as I realized that such a part of me might be gone forever. There had been other disruptions in my flying over the years—the Arab oil embargo and the air traffic controllers strike among them. Although challenging, none had ever been like this, threatening the very freedom of flight.

The *Flying Carpet,* between whose wings I had spent so many happy hours, was now no more than a throw rug. What if she were destined to rot amid cracking Royalite and flattening tires like other poor derelicts I'd seen fading in airport corners over the years? To me, neglected airplanes seem as melancholy as down-and-out people; these lingering visions of decay saddened me to a degree I wouldn't fully recognize until later.

On this particular sunny October day, however, I found myself unexpectedly released from my cage. Only instrument flying was to be allowed for the time being, but that was still flying. Tears filled my throat as I turned toward the hangar. Like other pilots, I suspect, I'd been unable to face my *Flying Carpet* since those unfathomable events occurred. There was a shame in being part of humankind that an airplane would never understand, her mission of flight being so simple and pure.

The *Flying Carpet* was covered in dust when I opened the hangar, her cockpit stale as I'd never smelled it before. Instead of the usual rich welcoming fragrance upon releasing the cabin door, only the slightest hint of drying leather was traceable in air tainted by mustiness.

Compassionately, I pulled the neglected craft into sunshine, recharged her tires and cleansed her windshield. Were those tear streaks marking the dust of her acrylic? Or just bug trails from flight in a long-ago life? As the engine croaked, then stuttered and rumbled to life, my heart warmed at saving this bird from the clutches of death.

Rarely do we fly instruments in the sunny Southwest, and as I collected my flight clearance I sensed the strangeness of it all. I'd lived here thirteen years, and it was my first instrument flight outbound from this airport.

I was headed for Flagstaff to see Hannis—that destination to which I'd flown so many times before. This time, however, I would not fly direct as in the past. Rather, I'd be routed northwest over Phoenix, then follow a circuitous series of airways via Prescott. I taxied for takeoff.

"My favorite part of flying is when we taxi out onto the runway and line up with the centerline."

How appropriate that Austin's words should greet me at this particular time. The young man had departed only a few months earlier to follow his calling at the Air Force Academy. While filled with pride at both boys' accomplishments, I deeply missed their company. Nowhere was the void greater than in the adjacent empty pilot seat. I relived Austin's words after savoring the engine run-up. Even the usual noisy gyro threatening failure didn't bother me this time. I urged the *Flying Carpet* down that centerline . . . and she flew!

That's when I experienced my second "first flight." Climbing over familiar terrain after weeks believing I'd never fly again, I felt anew the grace and privilege of soaring with hawks. Compounding the sensation was knowledge that tomorrow it could all be taken away again.

How we've been betrayed, I thought. In the backlash of terror I'd been chained interminably to Earth, constrained by people to walk around uncomfortable, like a bowlegged cowboy off his horse. Fortunately what might have been a life sentence was now for the moment commuted.

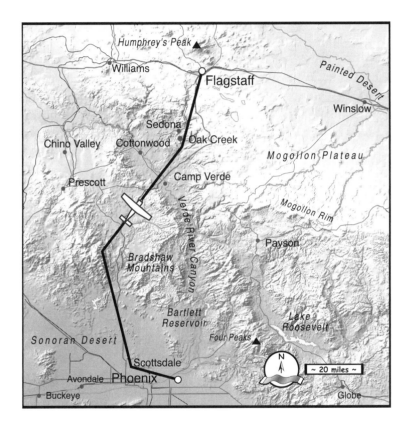

Welcomed by blue skies as I ascended toward the Bradshaw Mountains, I again felt all that was flight. There is comfort and beauty in flying over familiar terrain. Those rooted to the ground imagine aviators fluttering lost from one teetering branch to another, closing their eyes and setting out like messages in bottles for points unknown.

We pilots know that's not how it is. Every town, every mountain, every lake and river is connected to another in continuum. Flying familiar country is like tracing the body of a lover. Aviators over time grasp the true shape of every pond, the course of every railroad track, and where each road and gravel lane may go. Ranches lie hidden in mountain valleys far off the highway—but no matter how secret, we've been there. Yet also like a sweetheart, even the most well-known hills and valleys never become so familiar as to preclude a new adventure on every trip. Each unique palette of clouds, time, and light paints a fresh perspective.

Looking down, I noted progress over the village of Oak Creek. I'd never set foot in the place, yet in some respects knew it better than its residents—how the town emerges from vermilion buttes when approached from the south, the pattern formed by its streets, and the true meandering of its namesake creek (not just the view from occasional road crossings). Moreover, I knew the community's true location—how and where it really lies relative to its red rock surroundings and the human fabric connected with it.

Flagstaff's position I soon recognized from long familiarity, well before seeing the city itself. Slowly it materialized as expected, in the great shadow of snow-covered Humphreys Peak. Hannis was waiting to greet me at the airport. We drove downtown as so many times before, and dined al fresco at our favorite sidewalk cafe.

It was there, sipping fruit smoothies in the shade and talking music with Hannis, that I finally felt whole again. Behind me in my logbook was the equivalent of 180 work-weeks in the air. I'd believed it was over. Now, in the rich company of my son, I knew there was at least one more glorious flying hour to look forward to—the journey home. What more could I ask? Always I had envied the boundless joy of new pilots; now I'd be one again.

About the Author

GREG BROWN has long wandered the skies of North America with family and friends. His love of flying is apparent to anyone who reads his *Flying Carpet* column in *AOPA Flight Training* magazine, or his stories in *AOPA Pilot* and other publications. An aviator since 1972, Greg was 2000 National Flight Instructor of the Year, winner of the 1999 NATA Excellence in Pilot Training award, and the first NAFI Master Flight Instructor. He holds an airline transport pilot certificate with Boeing 737 type rating, and flight instructor certificate with all fixed-wing aircraft ratings. Despite such accomplishments, Greg has never lost touch with his roots as a new pilot flying light airplanes. To this day, every takeoff is as exciting for him as the first one. Of course he's not alone; all pilots feel that way.

Other books by Greg Brown include *The Turbine Pilot's Flight Manual*, *The Savvy Flight Instructor*, *You Can Fly!*, and *Job Hunting for Pilots*.